Fun Foods of America

of

America

Outrageous Delights,
Celebrated Brands,
and Iconic Recipes

SUSAN BENJAMIN

Essex, Connecticut

*To the staff at True Treats, who bring fun foods
and their stories to the world every day.*

Globe
Pequot

An imprint of Globe Pequot, the trade division of
The Rowman & Littlefield Publishing Group, Inc.
4501 Forbes Blvd., Ste. 200
Lanham, MD 20706
www.rowman.com

Distributed by NATIONAL BOOK NETWORK

British Library Cataloguing in Publication Information available

Library of Congress Cataloging-in-Publication Data available
ISBN 978-1-4930-7467-9 (cloth : alk. paper)
ISBN 978-1-4930-7468-6 (electronic)

∞™ The paper used in this publication meets the minimum requirements
of American National Standard for Information Sciences—Permanence of
Paper for Printed Library Materials, ANSI/NISO Z39.48-1992.

Contents

Brought to You by . . .
Six Women and a Movement

No food is useful unless people eat it. And no eating is possible without preparation, be it cooking, picking, or selecting the good from the bad from the deadly. That's where food history comes in: it tells us the complex and often outrageous stories of how everything from green beans to chocolate cake got on our plates. That being said, the story of fun foods is especially poignant. Those foods are no mere blips in the food chain—they're benchmarks for how we live and love. So, what are fun foods exactly? Here's a definition:

Food we eat because we love it. Fun food can be healthy and nutritious or not, as the case may be. Fun foods are neutral on the subject. It's the experience of eating it that matters.

Food we eat as a community. Enjoy cake at a wedding full of relatives or popcorn at a movie theater full of strangers? No matter. We do it together. Who eats a wedding cake alone?

Food that usually has symbolic or ritualistic value. Think pumpkin pie at Thanksgiving, cotton candy at fairgrounds, or time-honored recipes reawakened at family reunions or gatherings of friends.

With that in mind, fun foods didn't appear ready to go like fresh berries. They were *created*, assigned purpose, and passed on as a legacy for generations. Modern fun foods especially were passed on by food lovers equipped with cookbooks, advice columns, advertisements, and demonstrations. Some were real, some surreal, all amazing. Here are six of them.

Eliza Leslie
Pioneer, Snob, and Absolutely Appropriate

Eliza Leslie, aka Miss Leslie, is no footnote in the cooking world. She was outspoken and unafraid—a pioneer and a snob. Her many cookbooks weren't the first to be published in the United States—that was Amelia Simmons's *American Cookery*, circa 1796. But Miss Leslie's cookbooks were a riot of information. These were supported by her other books about appropriateness and flawless manners, a critical component, in her view, of what it meant to eat well. Her audience was the well-to-do in general, and well-to-do women in particular. These women didn't actually do the cooking. They wouldn't dare. That simply wasn't their station in life, and they stuck to it. Regardless of who was cooking and why, Miss Leslie provided insight and instruction that eventually shaped the American palate.

ABOUT MISS LESLIE: A VERY-BRIEF BIO

Eliza Leslie was born in Philadelphia in 1787. Her father was a watchmaker, inventor, intellectual, and friend of such people as Benjamin Franklin and Thomas Jefferson. When her father

Miss Leslie, 1846, *Godey's Lady's Book, Wikimedia*

died unexpectedly in 1803, Eliza and her mother had to turn their home into a genteel boarding-house to make ends meet. Among Eliza's duties was supervising the chef. Only problem: she knew nothing about cooking.

So, in her early thirties, Miss Leslie signed up for classes at the nation's first cooking school, run by the much-esteemed Mrs. Goodfellow. The school's mission was to give the daughters of the very wealthy navigational tools to uphold their status in life. Food, made by the hired, indentured, or enslaved helpers they would manage, was at the apex of their success.

Miss Leslie took copious notes during the instruction, which were reborn as her first cook-book, *Seventy-Five Receipts for Pastry, Cakes, and Sweetmeats, by a Lady of Philadelphia.*[1] *Receipt*, in this case, was an early form of the word "recipe." Regardless, the book, published in 1827 or 1828 (the year is unclear), was an immediate hit. The entries consisted of cakes, puddings, preserves, custards, and fried delights such as dough nuts [*sic*], too delicious (and difficult to make) for the modern mind to grasp.[2] A later book, *Lady's Receipt Book* (1847), contained the first American chocolate cake recipe.

Of Miss Leslie's many books, nothing was quite the smash hit as *Directions for Cookery: Being a System of the Art, in Its Various Branches.* First published in 1837, it became the most popular American cookbook of the 1800s, reprinted over sixty times between 1837 and 1870. By 1840, 40,000 copies of the book had been sold, and in 1851, its forty-first edition appeared. No edition was less than a thousand copies.[3, 4]

But fine foods cannot excel by recipes alone, and Miss Leslie had a razor-sharp focus on decorum, whether the intricacies of table settings or the appropriate greeting for guests at the door. She also provided priceless strategies for managing the disastrous lower class. Butter, for example, was no mere spread at a

Want to Read Miss Leslie's Cookbooks?

You'll find plenty of paperback editions online at Google, Internet Archives, and the Library of Congress. You'll get the full text, including yellowed paper and age marks, for free. Well worth a trip online!

tea table, but a sign of affluence and good taste, which but one negligent servant could sabotage in an instant. Here is what she said:

"We have heard of tea-tables (even in splendid establishments) being left entirely to the mismanagement of incompetent or negligent servants; so that when the company sat down, there was found a deficiency in some of the indispensable appendages; such as spoons, and even forks, and napkins—butter-knives forgotten, and (worse than all) cooking-butter served in mistake for the better sort..."[5]

Regardless, Miss Leslie did establish a foundation for other women, and even men, to build on even without hired help.

Fannie Farmer
The Antidote to Highbrow Cooking

Fannie Farmer, born in 1857, came from an educated, affluent family. Like Miss Leslie, she suffered a pivotal downturn in young adulthood—in this case, an enduring illness likely related to polio. Also, like Miss Leslie, she turned her home into a well-heeled boardinghouse. Then, at the age of thirty, she too enrolled in a cooking school; this time, the Boston Cooking School. Again like Miss Leslie, she never had children, never married, and became an authority for women who did both.

Boston Cooking-School Magazine, Wikimedia

At the time Fannie Farmer started taking classes at the Boston Cooking School, lessons generally focused on Miss Leslie's approach to the kitchen: teaching well-to-do women how to manage household help and teaching would-be servants how to serve the well-to-do. Entertaining food, thoughtfully composed and presented, was the call to action.

But the Boston Cooking School was different. Its mission was to transform women from cooks to authorities on cooking, knowledgeable in everything from the economics of food to the correct diet for the sick as well as healthy. To achieve this, the school taught groundbreaking classes, gave talks to the public as well as students, and published widely, including its own pamphlets and a magazine, *The Boston Cooking-School Magazine*.

It was here that Fannie Farmer thrived, going from student to assistant principal to principal in a matter of years. In 1896, she achieved one of her great accomplishments: writing the *Boston Cooking-School Cook Book*. Miss Farmer's book was intelligent, clearly written, and, unlike her predecessors' efforts, targeted a large popular audience.[6]

At the time of Miss Farmer's ascension in the food world, a seismic shift was occurring. A movement first called "domestic science" and later known as "home economics" was forming to address a problem: men in the workforce were trained in the tenets of math and science critical to their success—but not women. There was no training. No examples. No help. Even the cookbooks were woefully inadequate, providing only general weights and measurements. Women were left to fend for themselves concerning budgets, cooking time, the nutritional value of foods, dimensions of cleanliness, and just about everything else. Women (and some men) in the home economics movement lobbied for better education for women, set up science-based test kitchens to determine protocols, and wrote, recorded, and published volumes.

In the introduction to the *Boston Cooking-School Cook Book*, Fannie Farmer says this: "It is my wish that [this book] may not only be looked upon as a compilation of tried and tested recipes but that it may awaken an interest through its condensed scientific knowledge which will lead to deeper thought and broader study of what to eat."[7]

And who was their audience? They were rural, urban, working at home, working outside the home, the very young, and the very old. Maybe they had financial means, but just as important, maybe they didn't. What they needed and were entitled to get was solid, reliable, and accessible information to do the job right.

Fanny Farmer did not disappoint. Well-respected by those involved in home economics, she provided detailed instruction, sometimes to the extreme, so her audience could have repeatable processes with measurable results. Here is how Miss Farmer explained her approach on the first page of the first chapter titled, simply, "Food":

> *Food is anything that nourishes the body. Thirteen elements enter into the composition of the body: oxygen, 62½%; carbon, 21½%; hydrogen, 10%; nitrogen, 3%; calcium, phosphorous, potassium, sulfur, chlorine, sodium, magnesium, iron and fluorine the remaining 3%. . . . Food is necessary for growth, repair and energy; therefore the elements composing the body must be found in the food.*[8]

The book was timely, and well and thoughtfully written, but Fannie Farmer's publisher was hesitant to publish it. Would it sell? Who would even want to read it? So, he required Miss

Farmer to pay the initial printing costs. She did, and in the process she retained the copyright *and* rights to the profits. The book received an overwhelming response, and Miss Farmer became a very wealthy woman.

THE LEVELING REVOLUTION

One of Fannie Farmer's most groundbreaking achievements is so obvious today, it's hard to believe anyone actually invented it. It was her view that throwing a teacup of flour or a spoonful of baking powder of an indeterminate amount into a bowl was unacceptable. There was no way to calculate the outcome—whether the taste, texture, nutritional value, or cost—unless the proportions were measured and known.

From this belief, Fannie Farmer advocated a system called "leveling." Take the ingredients and put them in a cup, teaspoon, or other consistent tool of measurement, then take a knife and run it across the top. The quantity and result would be consistent. Should the task be harder—with, say, butter or Crisco—the process could be adjusted. For this achievement, the venerable Fannie Farmer won the title of "Mother of Level Measurements."

In 1902 Fannie Farmer left the Boston Cooking School to start Miss Farmer's School of Cookery. The classes focused less on theory, as the Boston Cooking School did, and more on teaching women how to cook. As Miss Farmer spent much of her life sick, she was interested in the curative aspect of foods and developed specialty diets recorded in her book *Food and Cookery for the Sick and Convalescent*. Her work was so esteemed that Dr. Elliot P. Joslin, a pioneer in diabetes, whose namesake is the Joslin Clinic, cited Fannie Farmer as "the stimulus which started me in writing about diabetes."

After leaving the Boston Cooking School, Fannie Farmer lectured at her own school each week, always to a full house and widely reported in the press. She continued testing, inventing, and sampling recipes, including those at fine restaurants in Boston and New York City. If she couldn't identify the source of the flavor, or the chef refused to tell her, she allegedly took a sample back to the school and analyzed it to find out. At the end of her life, Miss Farmer suffered two strokes and was confined to a wheelchair. Still, she continued to lecture up until ten days before her death. Her best-selling cookbook became one of the most popular books in America of all time.[9]

Aunt Sammy
Not Really Real, but We Don't Mind . . .

> *I arrange my work so as to spend as little time in the kitchen as possible. There are more important things to do.*—Aunt Sammy, circa 1920s[10]

The twentieth century ushered in a host of spokespersons, experts, and personalities, available 24/7 via the printed word and, increasingly, radio. The most remarkable aspect of these

Aunt Sammy's Radio Recipes, 1926, Wikimedia

advisors was that many weren't real. But nobody knew that.

One of these non-people was "Aunt Sammy." She appeared in the 1920s, at the start of radio's meteoric rise in America. At that time, there were about 10,000 radios, mostly homemade by radio hobbyists. Within five years, roughly 7.5 million people had a radio at home. For farm families, radios were a link to the outside world, fueled by batteries, much more reliable than electricity, even in storms.[11]

Women, in particular, found a friendly voice to accompany them in their demanding and often lonely days. One of the voices was Aunt Sammy. It's hard to imagine that Aunt Sammy was a real person even when she first appeared in 1926 as Uncle Sam's (yes, *that* Uncle Sam) wife or sister (it isn't entirely clear). Likely, few listeners believed it. But that's not the point. Unlike other trusted advisors who represented the interests of corporations, Aunt Sammy represented the interests of the Bureau of Home Economics, which created her under the United States Department of Agriculture. Her audience was rural and town-based and her message about many things, primary among them food. Good, wholesome, and economical food.

Listeners tuned into Aunt Sammy's fifteen-minute segment, the "Housekeeper's Chat," which first aired in 1926 and ran five days a week. She was represented by thirty different women at thirty different stations—a total of 150 actresses over eight years of production. The Aunt Sammys shared the same script but had different regional accents to better reach their listeners. The content was driven by numerous factors, including letters sent by listeners. By 1927, more than a million women were tuning in to the program and had sent 60,000 letters seeking advice. If the questions were pertinent and interesting enough, they were raised on air. If not, the listeners received a personal letter in response.[12]

AUNT SAMMY AND CROSSED SIGNALS

While radio was readily available, it was also scratchy and, at times, incoherent, especially important when delivering recipes. Sometimes, radio signals got crossed. In one production a young husband was trying to copy a recipe for his wife. The connections crossed and he ended up with the following instructions: "Hands on hips, place one cup of flour on the shoulders, raise knees and depress toes and mix thoroughly with one half-cup of milk . . . inhale quickly

Want to Read *Aunt Sammy's Radio Recipes*? You can find it online, at Internet Archive. The price is right (free) and the quality perfect for easy reading.

one-half teaspoon of baking powder, lower the legs and mash two hard-boiled eggs in a sieve . . . lie flat on the floor and roll the white of an egg backward and forward . . ."[13]

Fortunately, Aunt Sammy was also a writer and began producing cookbooks and pamphlets in 1927, published by the USDA and approved by the new government-operated and -funded Bureau of Home Economics. Simply called *Aunt Sammy's Radio Recipes*, the instructions were simple, easy to follow, and deemed foolproof. Aunt Sammy promoted the cookbook on-air, saying: "By the way, some of you have begun to listen in quite recently. You may not have copies of the loose-leaf Radio Cookbook Uncle Sam is sending to homemakers. I want to give Uncle Sam all the credit due to him, but the cookbook was not his idea at all. After he saw how neat it was, and how easily extra pages could be added, he waxed enthusiastic—he really did. His only regret was that he didn't originate the idea himself. Isn't that just like a man?"[14]

Within the first six months of publication, the USDA received 41,000 requests for the publication and soon had printed 100,000 copies. All were gone within the year. In 1931, a new edition called *Aunt Sammy's Radio Recipes Revised* was the first cookbook printed in Braille.[15]

Betty Crocker
Not Real, Not at All Real . . . Then Why Do We Love and Trust Her?

Betty Crocker was as unique as she was popular, and popular she was and still is today. A true powerhouse, she blazed a trail from homemade cakes to cake mixes, from chicken salad to an evening dinner party chock-full of guests, with the greatest of ease. Her personality was steady: not too intimate but not too removed, and always reassuring. Unflinchingly, Betty doled out information to a hungry public and received inquiries, accolades, and honors in return.

Betty Crocker's story began with Washburn-Crosby, later called General Mills, the maker of Gold Medal Flour. In 1921, the company ran a contest for women to complete a jigsaw puzzle, send it in, and win a flower-shaped pin cushion. Washburn-Crosby received thousands of entries and with it letters from anxious homemakers seeking advice. The company seized the marketing moment and soon their staff was busily responding to inquiries, signing their name "Betty (a warmly familiar name) Crocker (the name of a Washburn executive)." And that's when Betty Crocker was born.

Betty went from Washburn-Crosby to General Mills, going from her own Minneapolis radio show, *The Betty Crocker Cooking School on the Air*, to print publications, books, TV ads, and newspaper columns, as reassuring to women at home during World War II as she was throughout the Great Depression. By the 1950s, 99 percent of housewives in America recognized Betty Crocker's name.[16]

BUT WHO WAS THE NOT-REAL BETTY CROCKER?

Betty Crocker was no simple advertising face like, say, Ronald McDonald, or advertising personality based on a real person like Colonel Sanders of Kentucky Fried Chicken fame (not actually a colonel and not from Kentucky). Instead, Betty Crocker traveled in the real world seamlessly, portrayed by a series of actresses who never let on. Betty was more than a homemaker-helper—she was an unmitigated authority doling out information and, according to her PR team, "America's Foremost Cook-

One of the many faces of Betty Crocker
ClickAmericana/Wikimedia

ing Authority." Betty Crocker's *all-new* Gold Medal Flour, for example, was even developed in a home economics–esque test kitchen. In fact, so successful, so hard-working was Betty that the actual real-life scientists and advocates should have been embarrassed at their lackluster performance.

Here's but one small example of what creator General Mills had to say: "The idea of 'kitchen tested' flour belongs to Betty Crocker, nationally known cooking authority, who has found through her work with thousands of housewives in the country that a flour, to assure uniform baking to the housewife, must be 'kitchen-tested' before it leaves the mill." The article goes on to say that "in addition, it is baked in a real kitchen, measured with cups, mixed with spoons, baked in a family-sized oven and treated in every aspect as it is to be treated in the kitchen of the critical housewife."[17]

Through it all, Betty was closely associated with cake and other desserts and still is today. The reason goes straight to the role of cake in the American kitchen. In her own-ish words in the opening of a 1945 Gold Medal Flour recipe booklet, Betty explains: "More cakes are made in American homes than any other type of baked food. They are a real achievement in the art of cooking. And cakes have become the symbol of homelife in our country."[18] The importance of Betty Crocker, and cakes, is played out in the numbers: Betty has sold a staggering 75,000,000 cookbooks since the first *Betty Crocker Cookbook* in 1950.[19]

Amazingly, even as the cakes changed—new flavors, textures, and even mixes—throughout her long tenure (one hundred years and counting), Betty didn't. No menopausal highs and lows, no annoying complaints about the lumpiness of batter or bad weather that ruined the cake, and absolutely no scandal, be it a rocky divorce or misappropriation of funds. In fact, Betty barely aged, ever the woman all women are supposed to be: efficient, undaunted, and calm in spite of the demands placed on women, be they working women or stay-at-home homemakers. American women saw the same young face in magazines for *years*, never questioning it was her.[20]

Ann Pillsbury
The Other "Betty"

Betty Crocker wasn't the only commercial pretend person on the marketing circuit, but one, in particular, was her arch nemesis. In postwar America, General Mills' Gold Medal Flour was the most popular flour, but Pillsbury was a close second. So the company brought out Ann Pillsbury.

A rocker-esque character with a similar demeanor and purpose, Ann was as unapologetically "real" as Betty Crocker. In fact, she was real-er, carrying the last name of the Pillsbury family. Like Betty, she was scientific and innovative. Ann proudly extolled the wonders of no-knead baking, which she herself invented using Pillsbury's flour, which was the "ideal flour for . . . quick-to-mix cakes." Even better, each bag of Pillsbury's flour was packed with "exclusive new Ann Pillsbury recipes, created in the Ann Pillsbury Service Center," sparking visions of white-coated women with test tubes bubbling full of pastel food colorings.[21]

Like Betty, Ann wrote booklets such as *Adventures in Cake Craft* in 1948, which contained twenty-two of her "favorite" cake recipes.[22] Also like Betty, she was a comfort in hard times. In 1945, during food shortages due to World War II, Ann Pillsbury, now "Director of the Pillsbury Home Service Department," provided a set of recipes to "Ration-wise housewives," according to one article of the time. The recipes contain "meat-miser" entrées, sugar-saving recipes, and "short-on-shortening desserts."[23]

Several factors separated Pillsbury from its nemesis General Mills and their spokesperson Betty Crocker. First, Pillsbury came up with something better than a mere booklet. It invented the "Grand National Recipe and Baking Contest," later called "The Pillsbury Bake-Off." This event created a PR and marketing stir unlike any other—and it became the parent to today's bake-offs. In fact, Pillsbury owns the registered trademark for the phrase "Bake-Off" in the United States; hence, *The Great British Bake Off* is called *The Great British Baking Show* here.[24]

In subsequent years, the Ann Pillsbury story gets increasingly stranger. First, the company unceremoniously outed Ann for what she was—a fictional character. It didn't apologize for the deception or even end the career of the nonexistent relation/company director the company so dearly cherished. It simply repositioned her as something else.

For example, in 1958 journalist Cobey Black, of the *Honolulu Star-Bulletin*, got together with Ann for an interview and some helpful baking tips when Ms. Pillsbury was visiting Hawaii. Black reports: "In reality, the capable lady behind the red signature which graces the labels and recipes on Pillsbury boxes is Mrs. Ruth Andre Krause," a Pillsbury employee, war widow, and mother of three. Then she quotes Mrs. Krause as saying: "As a person, there is no Ann Pillsbury. . . . As a personality, helping homemakers in the name of the company, she is thirteen years old." Not a *real person* but a *personality*?[25]

Then, in an announcement for an upcoming bake-off in 1967, *Arizona Republic* food editor Dorothee Polson tells us: "In the glorious décor of the Century Plaza Hotel, 'Ann Pillsbury' is up to her flour-dusted nose in sifters, mixers, blenders, and measuring spoons. . . . Ann Pillsbury is Helen Horton, Consumer Service Director for the Pillsbury Company, and director of the world's most exciting recipe contest: the $100,000 Grand National Bake-Off."[26]

That same year, the *Arizona Republic* tells us there's a "new Ann Pillsbury," Barbara Thorton, "a very tall and slender brunette," who, we learn, "grew up in the company's kitchen." She is quoted as admitting, "I am Pillsbury's spokesman to the consumer." And there, Pillsbury relegated Ann to the status of an employee.[27]

Ann's ultimate fate differed from Betty Crocker's, however. That occurred in 1970. One newspaper article opened with this headline, which both gives Ann Pillsbury a new title and provides some sad news: "Consumer Aid Ann Pillsbury to be Retired." Consumer Aid? OK, never mind. More important, Pillsbury is "retiring" Ann Pillsbury. Got it? No, actually, you don't. It's too complicated. The article goes on to say: "Ann Pillsbury the *symbol* of the Pillsbury Company's consumer activities services is leaving the field to the town's other celebrated home economist—the ubiquitous Betty Crocker."

The article goes on to explain that the *name* Ann Pillsbury is being retired. But even that is not the case. Actually, the aforementioned Barbara Thorton, now "director of Ann Pillsbury Consumer Service Kitchens and a company employee for 17 years," is resigning "to work as a private food consultant." OK—so, Barbara's retiring. But what about Ann? For her, the announcement was actually an obituary. Ann Pillsbury was done. Over. Yielding to the supremacy of her archrival, Betty Crocker, Ann will provide baking tips and introduce new recipes no longer.

Yet, the announcement/obituary ends with this further confusing disclosure: "Ann Pillsbury, since her inception, has never been used in company advertising or as a brand name—unlike her more intrepid colleague at General Mills." *What??* Did we miss something? Then, there's this concession—a sad revision of Ann's blockbuster career: "At one time, however, directions on various baking mixes carried the Ann Pillsbury signature as did answers to some customer correspondence."[28]

Ann was replaced by a new Pillsbury representative who had been part of the Pillsbury scene since 1965: the Pillsbury Doughboy. He was a creation of Burnett Advertising and Disney Productions.

Portrait of Aunt Jemima, circa 1890s, *AB Frost, Wikimedia*

Nancy Green
The Face of Aunt Jemima

Another breakthrough in the world of cake mixes occurred with a very different kind of cake, one that actually isn't a cake but still enjoyed at parties and fundraisers. It's a pancake. That particular story started in 1888 when Chris Rutt and his friend Charles Underwood bought the Pearl Milling Company. A year later, they had an abundance of excess flour to unload. So, they added additional ingredients, bagged it, and called it "Self-Rising Pancake Flour." And there, on the bag, the made-up woman known as "Aunt Jemima" got her start.

Soon, Rutt and Underwood were in hot water, unable to get the capital they needed. They sold the business to a larger milling company that added rice flour, corn sugar, and powdered milk to the mix, making it the nation's first, home-grown "ready-mix." This in turn was bought out by Quaker Oats in 1925. During this time, when Betty Crocker was barely a whisper, Aunt Jemima went from being a face on a bag to an entire brand.[29]

Like Betty Crocker and Ann Pillsbury, Aunt Jemima was played by numerous women over time. The first, Nancy Green, debuted at the Chicago World's Fair of 1893 where she sat beside a twenty-four-foot-high flour barrel. All the while, she operated a pancake-cooking display, singing and telling stories about the happy days of a South where life was good for blacks and whites. Surprising? Upsetting? Humiliating, perhaps? Yes. But at the World's Fair, a whites-only event, no one seemed to mind.

Also like Betty Crocker and Ann Pillsbury, Aunt Jemima went on tours, gave advice, and was received by a welcoming audience. But that's where the similarities end. Betty and Ann dressed in mainstream clothing of the time, suitable for a well-heeled, middle-class homemaker, while Aunt Jemima wore the head scarf and clothing of enslaved workers. Betty and Ann spoke in accent-less English, measured and reassuring. Aunt Jemima's word use was in the realm of minstrel shows, postcards, and cartoons that portrayed African Americans as foolhardy caricatures. One newspaper ad announcing the arrival of Aunt Jemima's Pancake Mix in 1906 offered a free doll in exchange for box tops. The doll was a grotesque version of the archetypal "mammy," complete with bandana and apron, what they called "cute, kinky, laughing little pickaninnies." "I'es your honey," the doll was quoted as saying.[30]

Thirty years and many Jim Crow laws later, little had changed. One newspaper ad in 1938 tells readers: "Famous Colored Mammy Will Bake Pancakes at Burns Grocery Saturday" and that "Aunt Jemima is a popular Negro mammy of the old Southern days." In terms of her appearance, the article quotes Aunt Jemima as saying, "Sho am 'portant."[31] All very unlike Betty and Ann, both of whom were likely too busy in their test kitchens to attend.

Gradually, things changed for Aunt Jemima. Other mixes caught up, including selections from Betty Crocker, who also came out with premade frosting. Aunt Jemima's dialect vanished in favor of written advertising text. Yet Aunt Jemima was still . . . well, Aunt Jemima, the title, as was "uncle," given to elderly enslaved workers who were not permitted to use "mister" or "missus." Just as important, the ads persisted in references to the "old time Southern" appeal of Aunt Jemima and the good old days of Southern living when African Americans were enslaved laborers.[32]

As for Nancy Green, she was born into slavery in Kentucky. After the Civil War, having lost her husband and children, she moved to Chicago, where she worked as a domestic for the family who recommended her for the Aunt Jemima part. She was fifty-nine at the time. After twenty years of playing the part, she was fired for refusing to attend the Paris Exhibition and was replaced by the company and forgotten. A longtime activist and proponent of equal rights for African Americans, Nancy Green returned to her previous life as a domestic and lived with relatives. When she died at the age of eighty-nine, she was buried in an unknown grave with no headstone.[33]

ABOUT THE PANCAKE MIX

In 2020, Quaker Oats, owner of the Aunt Jemima brand, decided enough is enough. The name "Aunt Jemima" did indeed reflect a racist depiction of African-American women and everyone thought so. So, the company returned the mix to its roots (after centuries of buyouts and acquisitions), calling it, once again, "Pearl Milling Company."

This Is Entertainment!

Dinner Parties: Deviled Eggs, Poached Oysters, and Plenty to Eat

Remember that hospitality has been defined as "making your guests feel at home even though you really wish they were."—Irma Rombauer and her daughter Marion Rombauer Becker, *The Joy of Cooking*, 1953[1]

THE FIRST-EVER DINNER PARTIES

The earliest dinner parties are hard to track, but plenty of people have tried. Some consider the Last Supper the first dinner party. No, that was Passover. Others point to the parties of ancient Romans.

We think of the ancient Roman parties as ruckus affairs, full of torrid sex and never-ending goblets of wine. Actually, they were more tempered. Called "conviviums," as in *convivial* gatherings, they were held at the relatively tame (albeit sumptuous) homes of influential Romans. There, hosts would show off their wealth, network with the similarly powerful, and intimidate their enemies. Some *did* have riotous goings-on, no doubt, so no disappointment in that regard. As for the famous vomitorium, where guests went to expel their food to make room for more? Never happened.[2]

Do-It-Yourself Roman Banquet

Interested in hosting a Romanesque dinner party? Here are some ideas of what to make.

ANCIENT GARUM

Mix dried, aromatic herbs such as dill, celery, mint, and oregano and place at the bottom of a 26- to 35-quart container. Place a layer of sardines or other fatty fish over this, then a layer of

> **Want to follow specific directions, no matter what?**
> Luckily you can still find the Roman cookbook *Apicius de re Coquinaria*, possibly the oldest existing cookbook in history. Even better, it's translated into English, and even available online so you can get guidelines aplenty. Look for *Cookery and Dining in Imperial Rome*, translated and annotated by Joseph Dommers Vehling, first published in 1936. Plenty of other translations are out there as well.

salt two fingers high. Repeat these layers until the container is filled. Let it rest for 7 days in the sun, then mix the sauce daily for 20 days, when it will become liquid. Use on everything you can. Or, google modern recipes for garum. Not quite the same, but the preparation makes more sense. Or, use whatever fish sauce you like.

MULSUM WINE

Mix wine with honey. Modern preference: $^1/_2$ cup of honey with a bottle of somewhat dry wine.

EGGS

Romans loved eggs. In fact, they were the favorite appetizer at a Roman meal. Here's what you do: Mix pepper, lovage, and soaked pine nuts. Add honey and vinegar and mix with garum fish sauce. Pour over peeled medium-boiled eggs.

What is "passum"?

Passum is an ancient Roman raisin wine. To make it right, you have to grow the grapes a certain way, pick them at a certain time, then prepare them a certain way. Very stressful for some of us. Or follow a modern-day recipe and get on with your life: boil grape juice until reduced by half, then add sugar. Or just get a bottle of sweet wine.

SEASONED MUSSELS

Mix garum, chopped leek, cumin, passum, savory, and wine. Dilute with water and cook the mussels in it.

PEAR PATINA DESSERT

Grind boiled and cored pears with pepper, cumin, honey, passum, garum, and a bit of oil. When the eggs have been added, make a patina, sprinkle pepper over, and serve.[3]

When in doubt, improvise. Throughout history, that's pretty much been the point.

DINNER PARTIES IN MODERN AMERICA
Welcome to the Ball

Before restaurants became a haven of culinary entertainment, people entertained at home. What these meals entailed depended on the location, the income of the hosts, and the presence of maids as helpers.

Of all the dinner parties of the past, however, the one that was the most illustrious and heavily planned was the ball. This event wasn't exactly a dinner party, but it wasn't a dance either. It had music and dancing, but food as well. It was an event unto itself, not for the common folk, but a means of shaping and satisfying everyone else.

The Words and Wisdom of Henry Davenport Northrop

The balls of the past were different from any social event of today. To get it right, hosts needed advisors and, fortunately, there were advisors aplenty, guiding women at home through books, newspapers, and magazines. One authority on the subject was Henry Davenport Northrop, editor of the *Household Encyclopedia*, late 1800s. Here are some questions he was surely asked, and his ready answers.

The Ball, by James Tissot, 1880, *Wikiart*

WHY SHOULD AMERICANS HOST BALLS?

"Having no aristocracy of blood or wealth, we form our own aristocracy of education refinement and good society." Of utmost importance, Northrop says, is "to be able to appear well upon social occasions." And what better place for these social skills to be cultivated than at a ball where "society is on its best behavior." OK. Good.

HOW DO YOU HOST A BALL?

It goes without saying that the host's primary duty is to select the right guests. According to Northrop, you have a choice: either imitate the "vulgar among the higher classes" and have a crush—inviting one and all—or, in better taste, limit the number of guests so everyone can be "accommodated for." The choice is obviously not a choice (who wants to be *vulgar*?), so great care must go into the guest selection.

Once guests are selected, Northrop provides detailed instruction as to how to create an appropriate invitation (made at a stationery and opening with "Mrs. —— requests the pleasure of ——'s company . . ."); invite the appropriate companions for said guests (unmarried ladies should be accompanied by their mothers); choose the décor (square room, light, lofty and well-ventilated); prepare the floor (no roughness, polished is best); and select the music (orchestra—top of room).

At long last, we come to the most important part. The food.

WHAT FOODS DO YOU SERVE?

What food do you serve? Not so fast. Food is a well-planned affair where guests may partake in refreshments in not one but two rooms. It's best to understand the difference.

Room #1: The Refreshment Room. The "refreshment room" should be close to the ballroom, as doing otherwise would be inconvenient and dangerous. The danger comes from ladies who get overheated from dancing and will be daunted by stairs requiring further efforts on their part. Besides, it's "most destructive" to their dresses.

As for the food: lemonade, tea and coffee, biscuits, wafers, cakes, crackers, bonbons, and, for some, wine. A lady should drink very little wine and certainly not more than one glass of champagne. The gentlemen should likewise be on guard as "nothing is more odious or

"Sweets Are Never Forgotten," 1901, *Mrs. Beeton, Wikimedia*   "Meats A' Plenty," 1923, *Wikimedia*

MENU
(Planned for 6)
Tomato-Salad Appetizer
Spring Dressing
Cherry-Glazed Baked Ham
Baked Bananas   Relishes
Asparagus
with Lemon Butter
New Potatoes
Mustard-Water-Cress Sauce
Salt Sticks
Crème Brûlée
Coffee

"Meat Rich Courses," 1948, *Ladies Home Journal*, 1948

contrary to the usages of modern society than any appearance of excesses in this particular." Got it. Don't get drunk.

Room #2: The Supper Room. The supper room opens at midnight and remains so until the last guest has left. The food depends on the host and the availability of resources. Ordering from a good confectioner is apparently the simplest, albeit most expensive, option. If made at home (by servants, it goes without saying), let it be done of a liberal but not a "vulgarly profuse scale."

   As for the substantive fare, ham, tongue, fowls, turkey, and other birds are "absolutely necessary." These should be cut up beforehand and held together by ribbons. Optional are jellies, light cake, blanc-mange (a sweet, pudding-like dessert), trifle, and so on. Then, there's the "French fashion" addition—hot soup. Very pleasant. Other lighter soups are also an appropriate option—Julienne, gravy, and vermicelli among them.

Between that and the refreshment room, guests are bound to be comfortably full (but not overly so) as an evening full of dance comes to its conclusion at the break of dawn.[4]

THE FORMAL DINNER PARTY

Why it should be so I don't know but convention has always set certain dishes aside and labeled them dinner party dishes.—Advice columnist and socialite Emily Post, 1933[5]

Like balls, "formal dinners" emphasized strategic invitation lists, appropriate attire, and correct table settings, each fork, glass, and spoon with an appointed purpose. Today, we cook. Then, they molded decorum. As for the food itself, most dinner parties had these basic courses, give or take a few plates and platters: an array of appetizers, the main course (typically laden with meat), then dessert and a closing beverage. That beverage may have been alcoholic in nature. Eventually, the libations included cocktails, which opened and closed the meal as well, especially important to *distinguished* guests.

Cocktails for the Tongue

The chief virtue of cocktails is their informal quality. They loosen tongues and unbutton the reserves of the socially diffident. Serve them by all means, preferably in the living room and the sooner the better.—The Joy of Cooking, 1953[6]

As glamorous and delicious as cocktails are today, they likely got their start for far less glamorous reasons: to disguise the taste of bad alcohol. Ancient Egyptians used fruits, such as dates, to cover the taste of beer; the pagans of England made wassail with various spices mixed into rather intense hard cider; and the Romans, always at hand to offer up a good time, added honey, spices, herbs, and what-have-you to flavor their wine. No question, these flavorings

Want to try early cocktails?
Why not get the first recipe book on the subject, *How to Mix Drinks, or the Bon Vivant's Companion*, written by bartender Jerry Thomas in *1862*? Word of warning: don't expect paper umbrellas or grenadine. This is about mixed drinks, and the drink part is mostly alcohol.

had other benefits such as treating illnesses, aiding in digestion, restoring energy and well-being, and so on. The same could be said of cocktails today.

Closer to American history are the remarkable assortment of drinks mixed by the early European immigrants. Starting in the 1600s, these newcomers drank such concoctions as sack posset, a blend of ale, sack (sherry), eggs, cream, sugar, and herbs, including nutmeg and the red skin that covers it, what we call mace. Others included sherry sweetened with raspberries, toddies, slings, and a variety of punches.

These drinks may have been made at homes or in taverns, such as Cato's Road House, the first tavern to open in the would-be United States in 1712. The proprietor, Cato, an enslaved worker who bought his freedom, sold New York Brandy Punch, South Carolina Milk Punch, and Virginia Eggnog.[7]

By the late 1700s, Americans were drinking far more than anyone could wish for—four times more than in the early twenty-first century. Around that time, someone posed a question to the *Balance and Columbian Repository* of Hudson, New York: What is a cocktail? The response: "Cocktail is a stimulating liquor, composed of spirits of any kind, sugar, water, and bitters—it is vulgarly called a bitter sling." And therein lay the first public acknowledgment that the cocktail existed. Sipping mixed drinks from frosted glasses, with well-placed olives skewed on a toothpick amid the hum of polite and well-heeled conversation? That took decades to evolve.[8]

THE ORNATE COCKTAIL

Too much of anything is bad, but too much of good whiskey is barely enough. —Mark Twain[9]

Cocktails got off to a slow start in the early 1800s but gained speed after the Civil War. The 1890s marked the golden age of cocktails, which remained a regular feature at dinner parties and social gatherings with only a break for Prohibition.

The specifics of each drink are another matter. *The Joy of Cooking* tells us that mulled wine, once a colonial drink, is fine for an after-theater party. The Old Fashioned deserves to be decorated with a twist of lemon, a thin slice of orange, and a maraschino cherry. A dry martini gets but a dash of orange bitters. Add an onion and the drink becomes a Gibson. As for the quantity of alcohol per drink, whether gin, whiskey, rum, or rye, always keep the alcohol content to 60 percent of the drink, never less than half. Drinks are a before-meal appetizer and should not be weighed down with sugars, eggs, or creams, which dull the appetite for the meal that follows instead of stimulating it.[10]

One of the most popular drinks is one that is least served at dinner parties—the Bloody Mary. A mid-twentieth-century drink, it is a mixture of spices, vodka, and tomato juice that, more or less, put Eastern European vodka on the American map. The cocktail may have been introduced by Broadway columnist Dorothy Kilgallen in 1939, when she called it the "newest hangover cure to entrance the head-holders."[11]

Who could say no to a Bloody Mary?, *Susan Benjamin, Courtesy True Treats*

Behold the Appetizer!

Appetizers were far more than tasty morsels leading up to a gargantuan meal. Their job was to whet the appetite. These deliciously culinary morsels covered a variety of foods—soups, salads, small portions of fish, and various fruits, vegetables, and nuts.

Like just about everything else, they had a medicinal side, not exactly *tasty* but with the same name and purpose. In 1840, for example, in an ad titled "Glad Tiding to the Afflicted. Hampton's Vegetable Tincture," the concoction was described as an "appetizer and purifier of the blood."[12] Cheatham's Chill Tonic of 1900 touted itself as a "perfect strengthener and appetizer" for "persons of enfeebled health and invalids." This particular appetizer came in two varieties: bitter and tasteless, neither exactly appealing. As for the ingredients: pure soluble iron concentrate and pure amorphous quinine.[13]

One of the most compelling and yet sobering advertisements was from Row's & Cos Depot, which proclaimed such truly mouth-watering dinner options as "oysters of the finest quality from New Haven, grouse from the prairies, venison from the woods, and varieties of aquatic fowl from the waters above." From this poetic description, they had this to say about appetizers: "And then there are condiments suited for every kind of dish with appetizers to make a sick man hungry."[14]

A few decades later, medicinal "appetizers" vanished, morphing into the purely culinary variety. Your basic oysters on the half shell became the illustrious palate-prepping Oysters,

Tabasco, Horseradish Sauce, with Wafer. Others were enduringly simple, especially in the early twentieth century. Two regularly featured appetizers, enjoyed by food snobs and easy-eaters alike, were celery and grapefruit. It's worth taking a look at these remarkable, and yet unremarkable, foods.

THE ELEGANT YET WILD GRAPEFRUIT

For decades grapefruit was a sign of elegance, served on a plate with segments neatly divided for easy lifting or served with its own beveled "grapefruit spoon." Or, sometimes, both. Where the fruit originated is mired in mystery. All citrus plants evolved from Asia—except grapefruit. Their origin was the Caribbean, as recorded in 1664 by a Dutch physician visiting Barbados, or Jamaica, as witnessed by one Patrick Browne in 1789. The grapefruit is likely a hybrid of sweet orange and pomelo, created either naturally or with a botanist's helping hand. No one knows. What we *do* know is that the tree was wild, *inelegant*, spreading with abandon along the hillsides. Eventually, someone, actually lots of someones, realized that these wild trees could be tamed and enjoyed for their delicious fruit.

How did grapefruit wind up in the United States? Again, a mystery. Some say a Frenchman brought the first grapefruit to Florida in 1823. Others say they appeared with various merchants and explorers. Regardless, by the late 1800s grapefruit trees were growing commercially in Florida, Texas, and Arizona.

In 1910, a worker at a Florida grapefruit grove discovered a tree that was producing *pink* grapefruits. The grove started selling pink grapefruits, people loved them, and in 1929 the official Ruby Red grapefruit was born.[15]

Grapefruit lurched into popularity in the early 1900s as an appetizer, breakfast food, dessert, and drink mix. Cookbooks devoted entire sections to grapefruit. Some chefs, such as the esteemed master chef Louis P. De Gouy in the *Gold Cookbook* of 1947, recommended numerous grapefruit recipes—the Grapefruit Rainbow alone took a page to describe.[16]

Fannie Farmer's *Boston Cooking-School Cook Book* offered more-accessible recipes, such as broiled or baked grapefruit appetizers. Here's what you do: Put 1 tablespoon of brown sugar and, if desired,

Grapefruits Clustered on Branch, 1803, Michel Garnier

1 tablespoon of French dressing or (as commonly suggested in other recipes) 1 tablespoon of sherry or brandy in each grapefruit half. Bake or broil and serve as a first course or dessert.

Then there's the more complicated Grapefruit à la Russe: Wipe three grapefruits, cut in halves crosswise, and remove the seeds and tough portions. Sprinkle with granulated sugar and chill in the refrigerator. Beat 1 cup of heavy cream until stiff and add 2 tablespoons of powdered sugar, a few grains of salt, and $1/2$ teaspoon of maraschino. Make a border of the cream (using a pastry bag and tube) on top of each half in the form of a square. Garnish at each corner with a glacé or maraschino cherry. Serve in double cocktail glasses, having the larger ones filled with crushed ice.[18]

By the mid-1900s, grapefruit had become trendy, with advertising that stretched the value of grapefruit from renegade tree to requirement for entertaining, especially among the smart set.

Recipe for the Exhausted Host
Exhausted from preparing that dinner party? Make this refreshing and simple grapefruit cocktail from 1912 and you'll recover—being sure to include the last ingredient!

Cut a chilled grapefruit in halves and with a thin, sharp knife remove the seeds and cut out each section of fruit, and serve the pulp with the juice in dainty glasses. Two teaspoons of sugar and one teaspoon of sherry may be added to each glass or either or both may be omitted.[19]

CELERY—ALL YOU WANT

Tremendous demands for Paine's Celery Compound, the wonderful remedy that makes people well. Sells above all others because it cures!—Article/ad in *Evening World,* 189420

Not the most inspiring food in the contemporary kitchen, celery was once the vegetable of choice for all things culinary. In the early 1900s, recipes included rice and celery soup, cream of celery soup, celery coquettes, sautéed celery, celery and cabbage (mixed with onion juice and French dressing), and celery relish, to name just a few.[21] Special vases, aptly called "celery vases," were centerpieces on Victorian-era tables, an edible centerpiece with leaves and all, later replaced by long celery bowls.

Stuffed celery, *Susan Benjamin, Courtesy True Treats*

Naturally, as with everything else, celery was used for medicinal purposes. In the late 1800s, newspapers were crowded with advertisements for medicines, such as "Paine's Celery Compound . . . the Wonderful Remedy that Makes People Well."[22]

Celery remained a tasty food, equally at home in lunch boxes and as luncheon appetizers, through the 1960s. Today, it still appears at parties, in its incarnation as a retro food.

FROM SOUP TO NUTS

To make a good chowder and have it quite nice
Dispense with sweet marjoram, parsley and spice;
Mace, pepper, and salt are now wanted alone.
—"Chowder," author unknown, 1834[23]

Radishes were another common appetizer, considered tasty *and* multipurpose, as, for example, a thirst quencher when dinner parties were accompanied by dancing.[24] As for nuts, these may have included almonds, peanuts, or mixes, roasted and salted. And soups? They were pretty basic, like the fancily named "Consomme a la Royal" in 1898[25]—basically clear broth—or strained chicken gumbo in 1921. In the 1970s, as fancy dinner parties became less formal dinners, "Beef Bullion in Cups" was served, as were chips, dips, and other foods straight from the packet.

With all these foods came explicit instructions. These were no mere friendly suggestions but rules that could pitch you to the lower rungs of hosts should you ignore them. Here's what Emily Post, the consummate advisor on all things manners and literal good taste, had to say on the subject of olives, another favorite, and more:

> One last word on the subject of olives for which I receive more letters than I can count. I might explain that olives are usually offered with tomato juice or other cocktails in the living room before dinner, either plain or stoned and wrapped in bacon. . . . If served at a table, olives and celery are passed with the soup. Salted nuts are put on the table, a little dish at each place, and eaten throughout the dinner until the table is cleared for dessert, when nut dishes should be removed. The expression "From soup to nuts" applies to the old fashion family dinners which ended with nuts (in shells) and raisins.[26]

Behold the Oyster!

Oysters are, without a doubt, the most versatile American food, enjoyed in bawdy colonial taverns and inns and at prim luncheons, elaborate picnics, and beachfronts, sold at stalls and pushcarts and eaten, the shell dripping with seawater and ice, standing up. Native Americans ate oysters as well—some as a regular part of their diet,

Oyster with Tabasco
Susan Benjamin, courtesy True Treats

others on special occasions. At formal dinner parties, the oysters were all dressed up, served with a lemon wedge, cocktail sauces of some sort, a dab of Tabasco, and a tiny fork with prongs so thin one could easily lift the saltwater-rich mollusk without ever having to touch the shell.

The Illustrious (and Meat-Rich) Main Course

The main course varied depending on the dinner party, but meat, fish, chicken, or poultry—or all of the above—were typically featured, often with potatoes or another starch and a matching vegetable. Granted, the meats weren't exactly broiled steaks and were served on platters, not plates. Of all the main courses, the ones from the 1800s were the most opulent, such as this lineup from 1898: boiled cod shoulder and head, sauce hollandaise, potato balls, cucumbers with French dressing, roasted capon with chestnut stuffing, cranberry sauce, and rice croquettes.

A menu from 1935 offered up a filet of sole, sliced cucumbers, roast chicken with Virginia ham, buttered potato balls, cauliflower with lemon butter sauce, and grilled tomatoes.[27] By the 1970s, the menu had slimmed down, and the intense preparation mercifully dimmed. One main course may have consisted of veal Smitane, white and wild rice, whole green beans with butter sauce, and sliced cucumbers with cherry tomatoes. Easy yet elegant. Done.

THE OTHER DINNER PARTIES

Gradually, dinner parties changed. Once reserved for the well-to-do, they became a gathering place of friends and families, whether native-born Americans, recent immigrants, or generational families. While the dinner party foods were diverse, depending on region and finances, they were also shared. No dinner party foods represent this better than the omnipresent pigs in a blanket and deviled eggs, both timeless appetizers that double as picnic snacks and light fare at luncheons. The history of both is controversial and, no question, rather odd.

All About Whatever They Are in a Blanket

The history of pigs in a blanket is strange and, at times, confusing, although it should be simple enough. Humans have eaten meats wrapped in bread or related substances for time immemorial. Ancient Aztec women carried tamales—meat wrapped in corn husks—which they heated in a fire to feed the warriors they followed into battle. British laborers carried sausage wrapped in bread in the 1600s for nourishment during the workday. And more recently Japanese workers wrapped their foods in seaweed, a dish we now call sushi.

So why are pigs in a blanket, aka pigs-in-a-blanket aka pig in a blanket, so confusing? Even food historians are confused. Some historians believed the food evolved from "angels on horseback"—broiled skewers of bacon-wrapped oysters that were popular in the late 1800s. Oysters or not, pigs in a blanket has a lot of variations by other—and in some cases no—names.

Many food historians say that the first pig in a blanket appeared in Betty Crocker's cookbook in 1957. Not so. One of the first sightings was actually in 1925 when Mrs. M.B.D. wrote to the *Fresno Bee* newspaper's food advisor, Mrs. Wilson, asking for the correct way to make "Pig in a Blanket." It seems her children insisted that it was made of sausage. True? Mrs. Wilson confirmed that, yes, sausage it is. What you do is take freshly scrubbed potatoes, scoop out the centers with an apple corer, and insert the sausage into the potato. Then, add a little oil to the skin, so it doesn't break, and bake.[29]

A year later, Mrs. L.L.H. wrote to newspaper columnist Prudence, also asking for a recipe for pigs in a blanket. Prudence recommended using fried oysters, dipped in beaten eggs, coated with cracker crumbs, then rolled in bacon before cooking. This sounds like "angels on horseback" . . . but she does say: "Quite a variety of dishes use this name [pigs in a blanket] for a *disguise*." She doesn't say *what* they are disguising or even why.

The story gets even more convoluted by the fact that a 1938 recipe for "Pigs-In-A-Blanket" was not wrapped in bread. And no sausages. Or, for that matter, oysters. According to a recipe in the *Idaho Statesman*, this pigs in a blanket was made of squares of *cheese* completely wrapped in bacon strips and cooked on a stick over coals.[30]

That same year, we learn from another newspaper that pigs in a blanket is a *man's* food. Got it? The appetizer was even featured in a cookbook, *The Stag at Ease*, the stag, in this case, being men. In it, author Marion Squire supplied men with nourishing, easy-to-make foods such as turnip greens with hog jowl, beefsteak, oysters, and pigs in a blanket. What was in this particular version of pigs in a blanket? She doesn't say.[31]

But Miss Squire may have been on to something after all. It seems the Sunshine Bakery of Santa Rosa, California, made 600 pigs in a blanket for a Valentine's Day party thrown for soldiers stationed in the area at the onset of World War II. These treats consisted of *hot dogs* wrapped in a special bun.[32]

Then there's Ann Pillsbury, the fictional spokeswoman for Pillsbury and a fierce rival of the presumed pigs in a blanket creator, Betty Crocker. Pillsbury advertised their own creation—Pig in a Blanket—in 1945, well before Betty Crocker's 1957 "invention." Theirs *were* hot dogs and they *were* wrapped in dough . . . in this case, made from Pillsbury Pancake Mix.[33]

Whatever.

Ideas for Your Pigs in a Blanket

Irma Rombauer and her daughter Marion Rombauer Becker suggest these pigs in a blanket fillers:

Cooked shrimp

Stuffed olives

Pickled onions

Watermelon pickle

Sautéed chicken livers

Skinned grapefruit sections

Dates stuffed with pineapple

Note: These varieties were wrapped in thin slices of bacon and held together with toothpicks.[28]

Deviled Lots of Things

One of the most perplexing aspects of deviled eggs is the name. Why "deviled"? The answer is easy and in no way sinister. "Devil" refers to the hot and spicy nature of foods, first used in Great Britain in the late 1700s. Soon after, deviling became a verb for making things spicy. Some were uncomfortable with anything that evoked the name of Satan and preferred to call the appetizer "mimosa eggs," "stuffed eggs," "dressed eggs," or "salad eggs," as, I'm sure, some still do today.

THE FIRST DEVILED EGG

Deviled eggs first appeared as an appetizer on the tables of ancient Romans. Other versions appeared in thirteenth-century Spain, where egg whites were filled with a mix of egg yolk, cilantro, pepper, coriander, and onion juice, then beat with muri (a sauce made of fermented barley or fish), oil, and salt. Unlike our open-faced eggs, the two halves of the eggs were put back together and held by a small stick. Over the next few centuries, a variety of deviled egg–like recipes showed up. In one, boiled eggs were filled with raisins, cheese, parsley, mint, or other herbs, then fried and topped with a sauce or powdered sugar.[34]

THE AMERICAN DEVILED EGG: MID TO LATE 1800S

When deviled eggs first appeared on the American culinary landscape is up for grabs. Deviled other things appeared, such as deviled ham, deviled tarpon, and deviled crabs, in the mid-1800s, and deviled lobster, ham, turkey, and tongue were showcased by the Boston Tea store in Fort Wayne, Indiana, in 1875. Like deviled eggs, these items were meant for bite-size eating. Says the ad: "These relishes are very fine for tea tables, picnickers, excursions, or travelers."

Deviled *eggs* appeared in the late 1880s, but not as we imagine them. They were made with boiled eggs, yes, neatly cut in two with the yolks taken out and mashed in a bowl. But that's where the similarities end. A typical recipe involved half a teaspoon of mustard; then a large tablespoon of cold ham, tongue, or any other minced meat; *then* a tablespoon of butter or olive oil with salt and pepper to taste.[35]

THE AMERICAN DEVILED EGG: 1930S

By the 1930s, deviled eggs had become common fare in picnic baskets, but made with mustard, vinegar, salt, pepper, and butter, along with other standard variations. It wasn't until the late 1930s that mayonnaise appeared.

The mayo-based recipes are like ours today, only with a flourish. Some called for onion juice, minced green pepper, mustard, chopped parsley, then *three* tablespoons of mayonnaise. Others entailed adding caviar and lemon juice to the egg yolk, moistening it with mayonnaise or cream, then, once returned to the waiting egg white, garnishing it with sliced stuffed green olives. Don't like caviar? No problem. A great substitute was the "combination filling," where you add liver sausage, deviled ham, or chopped meat to the egg yolk; season with salt and pepper; and smooth to a paste with a hearty amount of mayonnaise.

By the 1960s, deviled eggs were in virtually every picnic basket and lineup of appetizers. The creative possibilities had only expanded, and the options were staggering: chicken liver deviled eggs, tuna and caper deviled eggs, lobster deviled eggs, herbed deviled eggs, and deviled egg picnic platters with cold cuts. In the 1980s, when healthy eating became a requirement and not just a sidebar for nonconformist eaters, deviled eggs could be made with yogurt, which "trims calories without cutting taste."[36]

Potluck deviled eggs, *Susan Benjamin, Courtesy True Treats*

DINNER PARTIES FOR EVERYONE: THE MAIN MEALS

Folks usually stand up to eat it at big community suppers and other affairs—the bowls of stew and cups of iced tea rest on high, temporary tables which are simply wide boards nailed to waist-high poles. You will get big mounds of spoon bread as long as it holds out.
—*The Country Cookbook*, 1959/1972

It wasn't just the food that was diverse, but the *kind* of dinner party Americans attended. The *Country Cookbook*, brought to you by the editors of the *Farm Journal*, describes a popular feast, called the "famed coon supper," popular in Illinois. To prepare the raccoon, the main feature of the meal, here's what you do:

Roast Raccoon

The recipe calls for three or four raccoons, about four to six pounds each. Skin the raccoons and cook them, using the smaller bits for gravy and the legs and back for meat, which you dust with salt and pepper and dredge in flour. Then brown in a skillet, transfer to a roaster, and cover and cook for two hours. Invite neighbors and friends and have a coon supper dinner party.

Then there's a "one-dish meal for the entire neighborhood" called, variously, Brunswick stew or Appalachian squirrel stew.

Brunswick Stew (Appalachian Squirrel Stew)

Everything about Brunswick stew defies the conventional dinner party. It is held outside. It involves squirrels. And you don't need to dress up—in many cases, you don't even sit down to eat. All the cooking is done in a single "dish" with about seventy squirrels that you must clean, dress, and cut up—quite an effort given their size. The hard work may be broken up by the relatively easy task of cutting up two large stewing chickens and two and a half pounds of chopped salt pork. Or not, as you desire.

To prepare the meal, add the chicken and squirrels to four gallons of boiling water. Then fry the pork and add that, and the drippings, to the boiling mixture with beans, potatoes, tomatoes, carrots, and freshly picked corn and cook until the vegetables are tender. Next, add cabbage and seasonings until the flavors, as the recipe says, are well-blended, then remove the kettle from the coals to a serving area and hook the kettle on a heavy pole. Helpers must be available to help carry the pot, which contains a full fifteen gallons of bubbling hot stew.[37]

And Don't Forget the Fruit!

Fruit at dinner parties, regardless of who was holding them, was no afterthought. They may have been on the table setting—one-part ornament and one-part snack. Most certainly, fruit would have been a dessert, served with nuts, possibly chocolates, and whatever sweets the host decided to serve.

WHAT BECAME OF THE DINNER PARTIES?

Recently, dinner parties dwindled to yearly get-togethers, typically potlucks. Simply put, dinner parties are too demanding—the elaborate planning, the expense, and the hard work are simply too much. Besides, why go to all the trouble when restaurants are ready-to-serve with space enough for any invitation list?

The Early Days of Eating Out

In the early 1800s, eating out was all about chop houses, oyster bars, and taverns where men drank, caroused, and steadied themselves with a nominal amount to eat. Women rarely went in, except to work there in whatever capacity. For actual meals, customers went home or, if traveling, to an inn whose meals were home-cooked in a way—but not an especially good one. The dining room was typically a side room, more an afterthought than a comfortable eating area, where travelers were served at set times, with no choices on the menu; in fact, there were no menus. Eat a little, eat it all, or don't eat any—no matter. The meal was included in the price of lodging, and you took what you got.

The Delmonico Way

If Delmonico had literary ambitions, he might easily have appointed a historian to note the wit and wisdom of his ten thousand dinners. What a story it would have been for our children.—New York Daily Herald, August 27, 1876[38]

Delmonico's is considered the first, if not the most influential, restaurant in the United States. Even better, it was the first *fine-dining* restaurant. The Delmonicos weren't actually French—they were Swiss—and the founder, Giovanni Del-Monico, wasn't a chef but a sea captain who retired in 1824 and headed to New York to open a wine shop. Two years later, he closed shop and returned to Switzerland, where his brother, Pietro, had started a successful candy and pastry shop. The two considered their futures, especially one in the less-than-civilized culinary plains of the new United States. No question, opportunity awaited.

Back in New York, they opened Delmonico and Brother, a small café/pastry shop selling classically prepared pastries, chocolate, bonbons, orgeats, bavarois, wines, liquors, fancy ices, and Havana cigars, to the delight and relief of their customers—recent European transplants hungry for the finer foods of their past. The shop itself had six small pine tables, with matching chairs, and a counter spread with white napkins and the day's picks of food. Giovanni's wife worked as a cashier—a woman among an entirely male clientele.

As the café became increasingly popular, the brothers became increasingly American: Giovanni became John; Pietro, Peter; and Del-Monico, Delmonico. But the two brothers couldn't go it alone, and in 1931 their nephew Lorenzo arrived from Switzerland. In the coming years, Lorenzo learned every aspect of the restaurant business and was the driving force behind its impeccable standards of both product and service—important as John was not a trained restaurateur and Peter was a pastry chef but not an actual all-around chef.

In 1837 the Delmonico family opened the first American restaurant that was actually called a "restaurant." The food was French. So French, even the menu was written in French. Not that the brothers were necessarily fond of the French or even French cooking. French food meant "European food," which, from the seventeenth to nineteenth centuries, was rooted in Parisian fare adapted to the location, availability of foods, and chef who was creating it.[39]

It wasn't just the food that was so compelling—it was the eating *experience*. The staff was courteous, the settings inspiring, and the variety unique, consisting of subtle French sauces and eggplant, endive, artichoke, and other unique vegetables, many grown in their own gardens. The dishes were served on fine china. Even better, the diners could select individual items, individually priced, from a "bill of fare." Delmonico's bill of fare was the first American "menu." Printed in 1838, it was eleven pages, in French with English translations. The company added new restaurants and opened the Delmonico Hotel, the first of its kind, where rooms and meals were billed separately.[40]

The menu was compelling and suitably high-priced—no riffraff or after-hour revelers here. These guests were so celebrated and exquisitely rich that their fame lives on today: Theodore

DELMONICO'S.
BEAVER AND WILLIAN STREETS, OPPOSITE THE COTTON EXCHANGE.

Delmonico's, New York, 1903, *Wikimedia*

Roosevelt, Mark Twain, "Diamond Jim" Brady, the great actress Lillian Russell, Charles Dickens, Oscar Wilde, J. P. Morgan, Commodore Matthew C. Perry, the Morgans, the Astors, the Goodyears, the Grand Dukes of Russia, Napoleon III of France. There they discussed financing, presidential campaigns, arts, culture, strategy, themselves, and certainly other people.

The foods matched the renown of the guests, where such notables as Lobster Newburg, Baked Alaska, and Eggs Benedict got their start, as well as Delmonico steak, the best cuts the restaurant could offer that day. Today, Delmonico steak refers to a well-marbled rib eye. Oysters Rockefeller did not originate at Delmonico's—that would be New Orleans—but was introduced to the influential New York food society there.

The restaurants endured fires, the changing tastes of the American landscape, and the depression of the 1870s. Regardless, the Delmonico family continued to grow and expand their locations and influence, with children and grandchildren stepping in to fill the gap when an elder died. At various times there were at least ten true Delmonico restaurants and countless others who used such names as Delmonico's Steakhouse or Little Delmonico's, plus a litany of other food-related Delmonico's such as the Mon Lay Won advertised as the "Chinese Delmonico," the Delmonico Billiard Hall in Kansas, and the new and improved tin can opener christened the "Delmonico." If imitation is the purest form of flattery, then Delmonico was basking in the attention.[41]

THE DEATH AND REBIRTH OF DELMONICO'S

In 1923, almost one hundred years after Giovanni Del-Monico set up his wine shop in New York, Delmonico's family-owned restaurant closed. There were numerous reasons for its demise. In the late 1880s, food science advocates, such as the powerful women in the home economics movement, convincingly argued for the value of healthy eating. Another was the newly implemented income tax of 1913, lessening the disposable income well-to-do customers had to spend on extravagantly pricy food. Then in 1919 Prohibition arose, and along with the force of the recent Spanish flu epidemic, devastated countless restaurants, not to mention dance halls, cafés, and taverns that relied on sales of wine, whiskey, and other libations for their profits.

A few years later, in 1926, Oscar Tucci bought the defunct restaurant and turned it into a speakeasy. All the while, he was braced and ready for Prohibition to end. When it did, Tucci purchased the third liquor license in New York. With that, Delmonico's, now named Oscar's Delmonico, rose again. Tucci adopted the original menus and recipes, and the rich, powerful, and most definitely famous again claimed the dining tables, including Lana Turner, Marilyn Monroe, Rock Hudson, Lena Horne, Elizabeth Taylor, Elvis, and JFK.

Oscar's Delmonico had a good run, closing in the late 1900s, with attempts to resurrect it lasting into the 2000s. The countless Delmonico's imitators still abound thanks, in part, to a judge who ruled the name was common property, so integrated into American life as it was. "Delmonico's" was open to all.[42]

Join Us at Noon: Salad Days, Sandwiches, and Jell-O Delight

The luncheon party is basically a woman's world: when you hear that someone gave a luncheon, the scene that leaps to your mind is a tableful of women having their own special kind of party. . . . And because of this, a luncheon lets the hostess really shine.
—The General Foods Cookbook, 1959[1]

If nothing else, luncheons were hosted by women for other women. Men were invited, too, but more of an afterthought or a matter of convenience. The difference between ordinary lunches and luncheons is the food (upscale and artful in its own way), the purpose (geared to impress), and the conversation (gossip). Or so they said.

LUNCHEONS BY MANY NAMES

Through time, luncheons have gone by many names, each representing a different stage in its full, culinary development.

Dinner. Before the Industrial Revolution, the midday meal was the most substantial one people ate. That's because workers in our early agrarian culture needed food more at midday to sustain their energy than at night. Besides, nighttime dinners were difficult to cook and eat in the dark, so often consisted of leftovers from lunch.

Lunch. During the Industrial Revolution, more Americans left the fields and went indoors to work at factories and mills. There they ate hurriedly and in cramped quarters. These midday meals were smaller than before, often consisting of leftovers. This became lunch.

Luncheons. While men ate at work, many women ate at home, often joined by other women. Gradually these get-togethers became an invitation-based affair, a mini dinner party, held in the afternoon. The early luncheons of the well-to-do were complete with maids and butlers to handle unsavory tasks such as hanging coats.

The author of the column In Woman's World, circa 1900, advises that a luncheon should be a "warm cozy affair," which begins with fruit and is followed by fish, meat, salad, and, at last, sweets. Ices were always a plus when dessert came along, and why not? According to the author, women love ices. However, and this is important, when serving jelly omelets or some other "toothsome" dish, ices are neither necessary nor appropriate. Frozen custard smothered in whipped cream or pink-hued ice cream (thanks to a few drops of vegetable food coloring) was also an excellent addition.

Regardless, the full menus were rich with variety and looked like this:

Cream of Asparagus Soup.
Salmon Croquettes. Sauce Tartare.
Brown Bread and Sandwiches.
Baked Sweet Breads. Tomato Sauce.
Green Peas. Finger Rolls.
Pim Olas.
Creme de Menthe Punch.
Lobster Salad. Cheese Fingers.
Fruit Ice Cream. Fancy Cakes.
Salted Nuts. Bon Bons.

Luncheon Protocol or Blush

Any event—be it a formal dinner or a luncheon—was wrapped and protected by protocol. The number of guests at a luncheon should never go beyond the number of matching china sets. The invitation should be written and mailed or given verbally depending on the formality of the event. And, as the In Woman's World column of 1900 recommends: "Hats must not be removed. Gloves are also worn to the table where they are taken off."

If you think these protocols are mere suggestions, think again. Infractions are serious business, as embarrassing as a hostess absentmindedly appearing in slip and bra to greet the guests. One example had to do with a misused dinner gong.

The gong, as you may know from old-timey movies, is how well-to-do hosts called their dinner guests to the table. But a luncheon? No. One does *not* use a gong. Unfortunately, one hostess had the poor judgment to replace her regular maid, who was out sick, with an untrained substitute. The newspaper columnist explained: "Imagine the hostess's dismay when the hoarse clang of the Japanese gong clanged forth. . . . The gong seemed to fairly roar: 'Luncheon, luncheon, luncheon!' The hot cheeks of the hostess did not cool for the entire meal." One guest tried to put the hostess at ease by saying, "What a dear old gong. I mean to have one before I am a week older." But to no avail.[2]

Eventually, luncheons became less demanding, more about appetizers than actual sit-down, fork-in-hand meals. Sandwiches made an appearance, but not the standard sandwich-cut-in-half that nestled in lunch boxes and buckets. By the 1920s, the appropriate way to serve a luncheon sandwich was to cut the bread in strips, diamond shapes, or neat squares, filled with delights of the host's choice, be they olive butter, currant jelly, cream cheese, orange marmalade and nuts, or other tasteful options.

SALAD DAYS

A perfect luncheon is light and simple but satisfying.—Fannie Farmer, *The Boston Cooking-School Cook Book*, 1896/1941[3]

In the 1920s, salads started making an appearance at luncheons, with more fanfare than the earlier version of garnish lost on a plate. The "light" meal may consist of a fruit cocktail, shoestring potatoes, breaded sweetbreads, cake, ice cream with chocolate sauce, bonbons, salted nuts . . . and, significantly, a lettuce salad served with dressing, most likely Thousand Island.

Salads even rose to the top of the menu as an actual entrée, usurping even sandwiches. One menu from 1930 featured stuffed tomato salad as an entrée, complemented by pimento cheese and goose liver sandwiches, and a dessert of fresh berries, cookies, and iced tea.[4]

Gradually salads grew more innovative, as expressed in a household column, this one called the Brides Cooking Primer, in 1940. Says the author, Josephine Gibson, "Salads serve as refreshing interludes, as an appetizer, main dish, and often a main meal." One recipe she recommended was "Frozen Fruit Salad," which entailed mixing 2 slices of canned pineapple, 1 orange (diced), 1 banana (sliced), $1/4$ cup maraschino cherries, $1/2$ cup mayonnaise, and 1 cup sweetened whipped cream. Should you want to try it, here's what you do. It's easy!

Instructions for Frozen Fruit Salad:
1. Moisten the fruit with mayonnaise.
2. Fold in the whipped cream.
3. Mix in the fruit and freeze.
4. Three hours later, slice and serve on a bed of lettuce with a dollop of mayonnaise on the side and a cherry on top.

Granted, other favorite salads were *meat* salads or salads made with other mealtime foods: egg salad, ham salad, and salmon salad, to name a few. The hostesses didn't dispense with vegetables exactly: celery, olives, and minced onions may have been added to the mix, and certainly were resting on a bed of lettuce leaves as garnish, which may, or probably may not, have been eaten.

Another salad worth mentioning was called "Molded Vegetable Salad," made with diced celery, cooked peas, shredded cabbage, and shredded carrots, plus sugar, salt, and vinegar added to unflavored gelatin. This particular favorite was also known as "Perfection Salad," the winner of Knox Gelatin's salad contest in 1905.[5]

The Timeless Waldorf Salad

One of the all-time favorite salads, today sold at grocery deli counters, is the Waldorf Salad.

This once-venerable vegetable dish was created by Oscar Tschirky, who was not a chef but a maître d'hôtel at the likewise venerable New York Waldorf Astoria in 1896. It's not clear how he came to create the Waldorf—it seems he just thought it up, its creation such a non-event that no one bothered to write it down. Decades later, the salad was considered a revolutionary combination and the origin of fruit salads.

Here's the original Waldorf Salad recipe from Tschirky's book, *The Cookbook by Oscar of the Waldorf*, 1896:

> Peel two raw apples and cut them into pieces, say about $^1/_2$ an inch square, also cut some celery the same way and mix it with the apple. Be very careful not to let any seeds of the apples be mixed with it. The salad must be dressed with a good mayonnaise.[6]

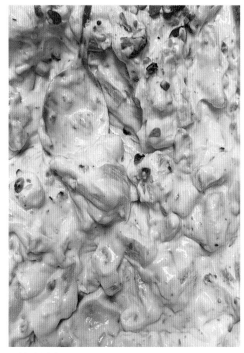

Over the years, with growing veracity, the Waldorf Salad became standard at luncheons, tea parties, and other events, rising to the top of must-make salads. Iterations were prominent, with recipes calling for walnuts, raisins, marshmallows, diced and cooked ham, smoked tongue, leftover chicken and turkey, shredded cabbage, and lemon-flavored gelatin spiked with vinegar.

Some Waldorf recipes suggested adding milk or cream (claiming this was the "original Waldorf"), while others suggested wine as a mayo replacement, which, if you think of it, isn't that bad. But it wasn't just the ingredients but the presentation that mattered. Waldorf Salad appeared in hollowed-out pineapple skins, cored apples, and, in rare cases, a bed of lettuce as Tschirky originally intended.

Waldorf Salad, *Susan Benjamin, Courtesy True Treats*

By the 1970s, the Waldorf became an item distinct from its older self. The versions are endless, some hardly recognizable as Waldorf Salads at all. No question, the Frozen Waldorf will amaze and delight—one-part popsicle and one-part luncheon salad.

Put the signature mayo away for now and combine atop a double boiler, 2 eggs slightly beaten, $1/2$ cup of sugar, $1/8$ teaspoon salt, $1/4$ cup lemon juice, and $1/2$ cup pineapple juice and cook, stirring until thick. Then remove from the heat and let the mixture cool. Next, add $1/2$ cup chopped celery, $1/2$ cup well-drained pineapple, $1/2$ cup broken nut meats, and, at last, two unpeeled finely chopped apples, then fold in 1 cup heavy whipped cream. Freeze the blend in one large or eight individual molds. Serve on a bed of lettuce with a garnish, should you desire, of mayonnaise.[7]

Don't Forget the Jell-O!

Perhaps the most glamorous of all salads wasn't actually salad. It was gelatin, and the most glamorous of all gelatins was Jell-O. This "wiggly" food-like substance could equally match a platter or home décor, and the variety of Jell-O colors could fit any occasion. The molds were seemingly endless—perhaps they actually *were* endless—and the room for creativity immense.

Today, Jell-O is less of a marvel than it was back then. The artificial garish colors, the gelatin made from animal hooves, and undoubtedly its ties to the past made it a relic, not a culinary event as before. Still, Jell-O salads do show up at festive events, as indeed they should. Are you vegan or vegetarian? Plant-based alternatives exist as well.

GELATIN: THE ORIGINAL JELL-O

The first written record of gelatin was in the 1600s, although it's likely that humans have always boiled, baked, or prepared marrow from animals; even today, many among us consider bone marrow healthy. In pre-Revolutionary America, gelatin was a status symbol, primarily because it was so exhausting to prepare that only the wealthy few with their cadre of workers, enslaved and otherwise, could enjoy it.

MEET KNOX—THE NEW GELATIN

A perpetual feast of nectar'd sweets.—John Milton, *Comus*, 1634

Gelatin became popular because, basically, you didn't have to make it. Someone else did—in this case, companies that sold *instant* gelatin. In 1845, the J and G Company of Edinburgh, Scotland, was the first to market this food marvel, which they called "Cox's Gelatin" or "Cox's Sparkling Gelatin." The gelatin wasn't exactly instant—it required some heating and straining, and a handful of caveats, such as the firmness of their gelatin, could depend on the weather. Regardless, there you have it. No daylong boiling process, tired muscles, and frayed nerves.[8]

A few years later, Peter Cooper, an American industrialist and inventor of the first American steam locomotive, invented his own "Portable Gelatin." The only problem was, he was trying .

to make glue. Disappointed as he must have been, Cooper patented the result, then ignored it.[10] No matter, others eventually followed, including Charles Knox's instant gelatin of 1889, the most successful of the batch. As legend has it, Knox was inspired by watching his wife, Rose, labor away in the kitchen making the homemade version. He was determined to save her the toil, and save her he did. The truth behind the story is questionable, though, as plenty of other instant gelatins were available at the time, much like his.

Charles Knox's success was due to many things, his prowess as an aggressive and creative marketer chief among them. He hired door-to-door salesmen to demonstrate the wonders of instant gelatin to his target audience of housewives. In 1905, his company sponsored a cooking contest. The

Knox Gelatin recipe booklet, 1929, *Wikimedia*

third prize went to Mrs. John Cooke of New Castle, Pennsylvania, for her aforementioned "Perfection Salad."

When Charles died in 1908, Rose took over the company, launching Knox's gelatin to near-unrivaled success. She set up test kitchens and published hundreds of free Knox Gelatin booklets loaded with recipes, a popular giveaway at the time. Rose Knox, who once herself labored over a stove of boiling animal hooves, went on to become the first woman business owner in New York State, and in 1929 the first woman on the board of directors of the American Grocery Manufacturers Association. Above all, Rose Knox was one of the few women to own a company producing a product made for other women.[11]

THE RISE OF JELL-O

Jell-O, America's Most Famous Dessert.—Tagline on Jell-O recipe booklet, 1928[13]

In 1895, Pearle B. Wait, a cough-syrup manufacturer in LeRoy, New York, was down on his luck. His cough syrup wasn't selling. So, he tried his hand at the food industry, making a gelatin-based dessert food. He and his wife, May, experimented, adding strawberry, raspberry, orange, and lemon fruit syrups to high volumes of sugar, with, of course, instant gelatin. They hoped women at home would love their creation—and love it they did. By the early 1900s, it was used widely, even at banquets and formal dinners. Only by that time the Waits, who lacked enough funding to market their invention, had sold the formula to their neighbor Orator Francis Woodward. He also bought the rights to the name May had thought up, which was Jell-O.

After a bumpy start, in which Woodward tried selling his newly acquired Jell-O business for $35, his fortunes

Three-tier Jell-O, *Susan Benjamin, Courtesy True Treats*

changed . . . and evolved. Like Knox, Woodward marketed heavily, and like legions of other companies, created millions of free Jell-O recipe booklets no homemaker could resist. Even better, his company developed a slew of advertising slogans with spokespersons, real and illustrated, such as the Jell-O girl in 1904, with her very own slogan, "You can't be a kid without it"; the "There's Always Room for Jell-O" campaign of the 1960s; Mr. Wiggle, introduced in 1965, who helped transform adult Jell-O into a kid's dessert/lunchtime favorite; comedians Jack Benny, Lucille Ball, and Andy Griffith, who promoted and underscored the Jell-O brand through the mid-1960s; and Bill Cosby, who was the face of Jell-O pudding for decades.[14]

EVEN MORE REASONS FOR JELL-O'S SUCCESS

No need to wrinkle your forehead over the perpetual question, "What shall we have for dessert tonight?" For here's Jell-O! . . . always ready with an answer to your menu question . . . a tempting new dessert, a piquant original salad. Watch your family's eyes brighten to match Jell-O's radiant sparkle.
—Jell-O recipe booklet: *Jell-O Brings DOZENS of Answers,* 1928[15]

Jell-O salads were dainty and refined, but affordable too. No mere dessert, Jell-O was gorgeous, especially when squeezed into a mold, brightly colored with fruits, marshmallows, and a litany of other treasures suspended within. They were more than desserts—they were a chance for women to create edible artwork that would dazzle and amaze. Even better, they were "healthful, attractive, economical," as the company liked to claim.

Besides, the possibilities were boundless, from Plum Pudding, made with Jell-O, walnuts, prunes, citron, cinnamon, and cloves, to Prune Whip, which speaks for itself, to Glorified Rice, made with lemon Jell-O, whipped cream, and rice. And then there's Tropical Dessert, made tropical by the addition of six figs, twelve dates, and a banana, and strawberry or raspberry Jell-O (neither actually tropical) with whipped cream. Half a cup of sherry can be used in place of an equal amount of water.

Imaginative gelatin, with maraschino cherries and mayo, *Susan Benjamin, Courtesy True Treats*

Old Glory: Prunes!

At restaurants today, you may order a pudding made with dried plums, or get a plum pastry. What you're really getting is prunes, but the bakers won't let on. Aside from a rare presence in such pastries as prune Danish, prunes have been relegated to a remedy for constipation. Yet, for well over a hundred years, prunes were prunes—delicious, versatile, and sweet. Sweeter, in fact, than the non-dried version. Here's a recipe that proves the point, Jell-O's fabulous Prune Whip:

1 package orange Jell-O
1 pint warm water
¼ teaspoon salt
1½ cups stewed prune pulp
¼ cup sugar

Dissolve Jell-O in warm water and add salt. Chill until cold and syrupy. Place the bowl in a larger bowl of cracked ice or ice water and whip with a rotary eggbeater until fluffy and thick like whipped cream. Fold in prune pulp and sugar. Pile lightly in sherbet glasses and chill until firm. Serves 6.[16]

LOOKING FOR A TRULY ORIGINAL GELATIN RECIPE?

This preparation is a very agreeable refreshment on a cold night but should be used in moderation; the strength of the punch is so artfully concealed by its admixture with the gelatin that many persons, particularly of the softer sex, have been tempted to partake so plentifully of it to render them somewhat unfit for waltzing or quadrilling after supper.
—Jerry Thomas, 1862

In 1862, Jerry Thomas included an alcohol-based gelatin drink in his book *The Bon Vivant's Companion; or, How to Mix Drinks,* the first bartender's book in the United States. Called "Punch Jelly," this recipe is based on a concoction made by General Ford, the commanding officer of Dover. Thomas cautions the reader that the alcohol is "artfully concealed" by the gelatin.

The movie *The Wizard of Oz,* produced in 1939, used six horses, each sponged down with Jell-O to create the horse of changing colors.[17]

To You from Jell-O

If you love the possibilities of Jell-O, then you'll surely love the simple, easy, imaginative recipe booklets such as *Jell-O Brings DOZENS of Answers*, circa 1928, and this recipe for Cherry Sponge.

1 package cherry Jell-O
1 pint boiling water
12 marshmallows, finely cut
Dash of salt
6 drops almond extract

Dissolve Jell-O in boiling water. Add marshmallows and stir until dissolved, then add salt and almond extract. When slightly thickened, beat with a rotary egg beater until consistency of whipped cream. Turn into one large or six individual molds and chill until firm. Unmold and serve plain or with cream. Serves 6.[18]

Cover of Jell-O recipe booklet, 1932, *Susan Benjamin, Courtesy True Treats*

To make it, first separate the peels from the lemons, rind and all, and boil them with lump sugar to make essential oil. Then squeeze the lemon and boil it with sugar until the sugar is dissolved. (You always have the option to buy lemon extract and skip those steps.) Add the extract and adjust to taste—don't forget to add cognac and Old Jamaica Rum, stirring as you go. Bottle immediately and store in a cool cellar.

As for the quantities, General Ford's original recipe called for three dozen lemons, two pounds of lump sugar, and "to every three quarts of the mix, add a pint of cognac and one of Old Jamaica Rum." As you're probably not looking to serve a platoon or legions of friends, Thomas gives you an out by telling you to adjust the flavor to taste.

Finally, to every pint of General Ford's concoction (above), add an ounce and a half of isin-glass (fish gelatin) dissolved in a quarter of a pint of water. Another option: add orange, lemon, or calf-foot gelatin instead. Even better, modern Jell-O should do the trick. Either way, take out your favorite molds, pour in the mixture, and let it set.[19]

GARDEN PARTIES: FUN, FOOD, AND FASHION

Just before the dog days comes the season for lawn parties, and the dwellers of the rustic regions revel in them to their heart's content.—Newspaper column, 1893[20]

The variety of garden parties in the early 1900s ran the gamut, as did the foods that were served. The only prerequisite—the garden party must take place outside, although even that requirement was waived. There were lawn parties for pleasure and for profit; private lawn parties and public lawn parties; large lawn parties and small lawn parties. Here are but a few that stand out.

Traditional At-Home Garden Parties

Many of us think of garden parties as British/royalty-inspired, flourish-infused affairs. With Americans' adoration of all things British, the American Revolution aside, that was true . . . but only for the well-to-do. These events could only succeed in gardens where guests were suitably awed by the blooming flowers, sumptuous background, and, even better, a sputtering pond. In other words, large gardens set on very British-ish lawns late 1800s style.

The food and drink were understated, but the *dress*? "The garden party dress, while not strictly speaking 'full dress' is nevertheless very elaborate," said one expert on the subject in 1901. "It is a dress that calls for a hat and the hat is part of the gown and the two go together continually, and no gown can be a garden party success unless the hat contributes its share of beauty."[21]

For anyone intimidated by high-fashion requirements, smaller affairs with a handful of friends were an option. Regardless, most guests were women who supposedly used the gathering to gossip. The food may have been a cup of tea, chocolate, or coffee with sandwiches or wafers, olives, and salted nuts with, maybe, cold meats, ices, salads, and jellies. Entirely up to you.

Beth enjoying a backyard garden party, 2022, *Susan Benjamin, Courtesy True Treats*

Lawn Parties

Hosted by a society, band, or club, lawn parties were festive, even carnivalesque, much like today's community fairs. Some hosts charged a fee, usually as a fundraiser, while others didn't. They were held in a grove or field with enough room for an entire neighborhood, plus friends.

A perfect example is one sponsored by a Masonic lodge in 1923. They dispensed with the bright breezy music, sandwiches, tea, and polite conversation of classic lawn parties for an experience "just as fun as a circus for the kiddies. There will be balloons, cake, candy, hot buttered popcorn, the red lemonade of childhood days, the hot dogs, and best of all, a fishpond."[22] The possibilities were endless.

Porch Parties

Naturally, porch parties took place on a porch, so guests could escape the heat of a summer's day while still viewing the garden. These parties were made even more delightful thanks to refrigerators, which became increasingly common in the 1930s. One such refrigerated dish, refreshing and tasty, was the Frozen Fig Salad, circa 1934. It's an easy-to-make medley of cream cheese, lemon juice, mayonnaise, figs, a dash of salt, and whipped cream, all mixed together. Place in the freezer. Wait a bit. Serve and enjoy.[23]

Casual Get-Togethers

In the 1950s, garden parties became more relaxed, offering beer and cocktails, with a grill for burgers to replace the standard crustless sandwich fare. Still, plenty of traditional garden parties existed, with menus that reflected the ones of old with a shot of zeal. Jellied fresh fruit, relishes, a variety of radishes, assorted sandwiches, and stuffed tomatoes were still on the menu. But so were tuna soufflé sandwiches, buttered green peas, crusty rolls, fruit with custard sauce, and coffee or milk. In fact, tuna soufflé was such a hit that it was the headline for a how-to on successful garden party food in 1951. Here's the headline and the recipe, should you be so inclined to serve it.

Cocktail Delight, *Susan Benjamin, Courtesy True Treats*

Garden Party Menu Features Tuna Soufflé Sandwiches

8 slices bread

1 cup flaked tuna

¼ cup finely chopped celery

¼ cup finely chopped green pepper

½ cup shredded American cheese

1½ cups milk

3 eggs, beaten

1 teaspoon salt

½ teaspoon paprika

Trim crusts from bread and put four slices in a baking dish. Combine tuna, celery, and green pepper and spread over slices of bread. Sprinkle cheese over all. Top with the remaining four slices of bread. Combine milk, eggs, and salt, mixing well. Pour over bread, and sprinkle with paprika. Bake at 325 degrees F for 40 minutes.[24]

Grocery-Store Garden Parties

Like all things in the food world, garden party take-out food has become increasingly prevalent. Today, just hop over to any supermarket or corner store to see the fixings—potato salad basking in mayo, Waldorf and Watergate salads leisurely swimming in a chilled bowl. Cold cuts ready for sandwich-making, but not yet sliced, lie indifferent to the grinding meat cutter behind them. Starting around the 1950s, these delis and grocers were supplying basic sliced roast beef as well as such pseudo-elegant selections as "Famous Chicken a la Tramp" and "Jumbo, French-Fried Fan-Tailed Shrimp." Who could resist?

Actually, society maven Amy Vanderbilt could resist and, in fact, had much to say on the subject in 1969. She reminded us that the garden party's most salient feature was comfort and refinement. Vanderbilt's venue was her "city garden," lit by torches to keep the bugs away, a fountain humming and tiny lanterns gently accenting every table. As for the menu: "Vermont cheeses with cracker. Eggs Cardinal. Shrimp with a variety of dips. Cocktail Tomato." Those were the hors d'oeuvres. As for the entrées: "Cold sliced Vermont ham. Smoked Nova Scotia salmon with dill. Homemade potato salad with boiled dressing and sliced, sweet gherkins." And the list. Went. On. Granted, many of these dishes *are* available as takeout, and a bit over the top for a garden party. But don't tell Amy. As for the drinks, they included cold beer, chilled Anjou rosé wine, and coffee. And tea? No tea.[25]

PICNICS

It's the spirit, not the food, that makes this meal special.—Food Timeline[26]

What did people eat at picnics? Why did they host them? Go to them? Just take tea parties, garden parties, cookouts, fundraisers, and fairs, blend them together, and you have picnics. Even more to the point, you have American picnics. And, like most things American, picnics started somewhere else.

An American Picnic

The US model for picnics likely started in British medieval hunting feasts. The food—pastries, hams, baked meats—foreshadowed what we have today, albeit more illustriously. The truly romantic picnics, however, came about in the Victorian era, reflected in literature and the sumptuous works of artists such as Monet, Renoir, and Cézanne in the 1860s.

American picnics started taking off around that time as well. Unlike the European model, American versions were egalitarian and either overlapped or were lumped together with such other social gatherings such as barbecues, tea parties, cookouts, and garden parties. Gathered around the quintessential picnic baskets were families, friends, lovers, and numerous cause-related groups and politicians hoping to make money or win supporters.

One such group was the Labor Council, which hosted a Labor Day fundraiser in 1897. The events included a potato-picking match, a mule race, a concert by the Saxton Band, a spot for dancing, a goat race, and refreshments. "All work and no play," their near full-page newspaper ad reads, "makes Jack a dull boy. Take this to heart and see the sports at the Labor Day picnic." As for the food, the refreshments were "light," such as lemonade and

Woman with a Picnic Basket, 1890, Raimundo de Madrazo, Wikiart

ice cream, and, combined with the entertainment, valued at "$5.00 worth of fun for only .50." In the true spirit of the picnics-for-the-people, the event was actually a fundraiser for miners. "The Labor Council will send the miners nearly all they make on the picnic Monday," the ad said. "Miners average less than $15.00 a month in wages and $3 and $4 must go to powder, tool sharpening, etc. Help them by attending the Labor Day picnic." And so they did.[27]

Featuring the Sandwich

At the heart of most picnics, regardless of purpose or persuasion, was the food, and the food invariably contained sandwiches. Unlike today, with our more-or-less set approach to sandwiches—i.e., bread, meat, possibly lettuce and tomato, a dash of condiment, and done!— the picnic sandwiches of the past were innovative.

Yes, they featured the quintessential American cheese sandwich, but also American cheese with anchovy sandwiches, minced chicken liver and lobster sandwiches, oyster and lettuce sandwiches, and sandwiches stuffed with canton ginger, caviar, celery, and uncooked cabbage, to name but a few.[28]

Unlike tea parties, cookouts, and garden parties, the menu at picnics was closely tied to the demands of transportation. To have a picnic, you have to get there. Advice columnists such as Mrs. Mary J. Lincoln in 1904 weighed in, offering spill-proof ideas:

> It is wise to provide some receptacle in which a greater variety of foods may be carried. Small fruit jars, with glass covers and rubbers, which may be tightly sealed—tiny tumblers for a small portion of stewed fruit, or soft pudding, tiny custards, puddings and timbales, meat or fish, salads and many other foods, will all find a place in the lunch box prepared by one who is willing to give some thought and time to this duty. Waxed paper is almost a necessity, if things are to be kept separate and in attractive condition. Plates made of wood as thin as pasteboard are cheap and especially convenient for picnics and travelers, where no table is procurable; and a cheap knife, fork, and spoon add little to the weight, but much to one's comfort.

Naturally, her recommendations included sandwiches, such as chicken sandwiches, served with tiny rice puddings, peaches, and milk. Other easy-to-carry options such as stuffed eggs with a side of buttered rolls and oranges or fish balls, Graham bread and butter, prune whip, and lemonade were most certainly included.[29]

By the mid-1940s, when most families had cars, picnics expanded to offer a gender-inclusive picnic concept, or at least that's how some people saw it:

> When it's a picnic in the wide-open places that your family craves, a simple box lunch of sandwiches, a refreshing salad in covered watertight cartons, a tasty hot creamed dish, baked beans, or soup in a vacuum jug . . . may be your choice. . . . However, if men were given a choice, most of them would probably vote for the picnic . . . over the open fire.

Lucky for them, folding portable grills that "burn charcoal of briquets [and] can be purchased for a reasonable sum" were available.[30]

Picnic Beverages: From Dreary to Dramatic

By the 1950s, picnics were changing. Sandwiches were still in, but so were broiled steaks with smothered onions or kabobs with grilled sweet potatoes and ginger cake. The menus also included beverages, most familiar and uninspired: lemonade, tea, and increasingly often coffee.[31]

Then, enter the picnic delights of the 1960s for new and deliciously entertaining libations to supplement your lemonade cache. If you're thinking of wine . . . well, yes, but these picnics had a bevy of drinks meant to embolden, delight, and satisfy. And face it—who would say no to a thermos of Bloody Marys that accompanied sliced roast beef and corned beef sandwiches, or a thermos of martinis—yes, a *thermos* of *martinis*—to help wash down a Bermuda onion sandwich on handmade bread. Not to belabor the point, but should you serve caviar with the meal (and who wouldn't?), definitely pair it with chilled vodka, as culinary taste sensation James Beard recommended in 1960,[32] or chilled champagne, or—why not?—iced vodka.[33] It wasn't that picnickers merely drank these tempting libations, but they ate them, too. Recipes called for wine-poached trout,[34] chili con carne in red wine on polenta squares,[35] and so much more.

By the 1970s, alcohol from your basic beer and white wine to your chilled Southern Comfort was fully entrenched in the American picnic basket. That is not to say people didn't drink the nonalcoholic options, they did, but alcohol added a certain zing that made the picnic ever more memorable—or forgotten, depending.

Today, the average picnic-lover enjoys their favorite outdoor setting three times a year—averaging a total of 94 million picnics. Above everything else, we have sandwiches to thank for the picnic's duration. They're easy to make, possible to order out, and remind us of the importance of nature. So, it's ever so slightly ironic that the favorite picnic food is . . . potato salad.[36]

Teas: High, Low, and Floral

To understand the origin of tea parties, or any tea-associated get-togethers, we must, of course, understand the history of tea. Food historians have amazing stories to tell—involving heroism, bold business moves, and innovation. Amazing stories, but pretty much none of them are true. So, to clear the air, let's look at the prevailing myths and realities—it's likely you've heard a few.

> Today, tea is one of the most popular beverages in the world, second only to water.[1]

MYTH AND REALITY OF TEAS

What is tea?

Myth: When we talk about tea, we usually refer to black tea, sometimes green tea, and now and then white tea. We probably believe these varieties grow in fields, decoratively laid out, in even rows.

Reality: The most common varieties of tea come from only one plant, *Camellia sinensis*, an evergreen shrub with beautiful white and yellow-centered flowers.

Who invented black tea?

Myth: The story of black tea goes back to 2737 BC when Shen Nung, emperor of China, accidentally discovered the pleasures of drinking tea. It seems the emperor regularly drank boiled water, which he believed promoted good health. One day, as the emperor's servants were boiling water for his drink, leaves from a nearby *Camellia sinensis* fell into the pot. The emperor drank the water anyway, and declared that it produced vigor of body, contentment of mind, and determination of purpose. Besides that, it tasted great. As it happens, Emperor Shen Nung was also a botanical explorer. In his quest for knowledge, he accidentally poisoned himself eighty-five times. Each time, he was cured by the wonderful *Camellia sinensis* brew.

Reality: No one knows who sipped the first cup of tea—but this unlikely legend has circulated for millennia. It's so fascinating, why bother to replace it?

Who introduced tea drinking to North America?

Myth: Americans have Peter Stuyvesant to thank for tea and tea drinking in the United States today. Stuyvesant, the Dutch director-general of New Amsterdam, brought tea to North America from Europe in 1650. No one knows exactly what he intended to do with it. Sell it? Serve it? No matter—not too long after, New Amsterdam was ceded to the British, who named the colony New York.

Reality: Native Americans drank a variety of teas. These were largely "botanical," used for health, medicine, ritual, and, of course, flavor. Yaupon comes closest to black tea and has a milder, but equally satisfying, taste. As for black tea, newcomers from Holland, Britain, and Portugal all took tea with them on ships sailing to North America. And possibly, Stuyvesant was one of them.[2]

Who invented iced tea?

Myth: Iced tea was at the St. Louis World's Fair in 1904. The place was the India Pavilion, where Richard Blechynden, commissioner of Indian tea, was promoting the teas of India and Ceylon (now Sri Lanka). Unfortunately, the weather was swelteringly hot and there were few takers. Out of desperation, Blechynden poured ice into the tea. People *loved* it and have loved it ever since.

Reality: There's no evidence that Blechynden sold iced tea at the St. Louis World's Fair. Besides, even if he had, he didn't invent it. Iced tea had already been sold at the Chicago World's Fair of 1893. And . . . iced teas, or at least cold teas, aka "punches," were around since the early 1800s, heavily enriched with alcohol.

Kentucky Tea: The Recipe

Here's a tea recipe from the 1839 cookbook *The Kentucky Housewife*, by Mrs. Lettice Bryan. Don't have yesterday's loaf sugar? Use today's 2½ cups white sugar instead.

Tea Punch—Make a pint and a half of very strong tea in the usual manner; strain it, and pour it boiling (hot) on one pound and a quarter of loaf sugar. Add half a pint of rich sweet cream, and then stir in gradually a bottle of claret or of champaign [*sic*]. You may heat it to the boiling point, and serve it so, or you may send it round entirely cold, in glass cups.[3]

Where did sweet tea originate?

Myth: Sweet tea is from the South.

Reality: Sweet tea is not tea with heaps of sugar spooned into it. It's tea with sugar added when it's hot, so the sugar dissolves, and the presweetened concoction is later poured over ice. There's no evidence that sweet tea started as a Southern drink, although it later became one. In fact, iced tea wasn't readily available to the general public until the 1920s, when cars and electric iceboxes became common.[4]

And one more myth/reality . . .

That would be about Earl Grey tea. For many, it's considered the upper crust of teas and for good reason. Earl Grey is high-quality black tea, made even better by being flavored with bergamot oil. As for Earl Grey himself? He was Earl Charles Grey, prime minister of England from 1830 to 1834. While Earl Gray was in China, he saved the son of a tea blender from drowning. In return, the grateful father named his prized tea blend after him. Or, say some, he actually created the tea as a thank-you to him. Or . . . whatever . . . because this too is a myth. Yes, Earl Charles Grey was indeed a British minister, but . . . he never went to China. He probably didn't save a drowning boy either. But he was around when his namesake (we think) tea was invented.[5]

BOTANICAL TEAS: SIPPING FOR THE REST OF US

While some scoff at the mere suggestion that tea is anything other than the leaves of *Camellia sinensis*, true tea drinkers feel differently. Call it what you may, the rituals of tea drinking are rich with leaves, roots, and barks going back through the ages. And, like black tea, they were considered medicinal, healthful, and culturally significant. Here are some of the most prominent.

Petals and Peels

Chamomile. A standard alternative to black tea at tea parties, garden parties, and other affairs, chamomile was enjoyed by the colonists. It is a perfect blend with other botanical teas and pairs well with cakes . . . and just about everything else. One of the most ancient medicinal herbs, chamomile was considered a panacea for a universe of ailments.

Hibiscus. Fragrant and delicious, hibiscus is compelling on its own and perfect in mixed drinks, punches—both alcohol-based and botanical—and other party beverages. Plus, it's thought to be rich in antioxidants, relaxing, and good for sweet sleeps.

Classic blue teapot, *Susan Benjamin, Courtesy True Treats*

Hops. Originally a tea, hops were used from ancient Greeks to colonists.

Related to hemp, it is a relaxant and rich in antioxidants. While pleasant with milk and plenty of sugar, many think hops are best left for beer.

Jasmine. Subtly sweet, with bitter undertones, most jasmine tea is made with a green tea base. It is enjoyed for its relaxing and delicious scent, and thought to improve health and strengthen the immune system.

Lavender. This floral-flavored tea with earthy undertones is a great mix with other teas and in cocktails, ice cream, hard candies, chocolate, and atop ice creams and puddings. Lavender has been long used to boost appetite, relieve stomach upset, and ease stress.

Lemon/orange citrus peels. The dried peels of lemons and oranges have a citrusy flavor—not sweet like the fruit or as bitter as the fresh peel. They were used by colonists for tea, sweets, and good health. A great addition to black tea, desserts, and lemon- and limeade, citrus peels are rich in vitamins and fiber.

Marigold. With its floral, refreshing flavor and slightly bitter undertones, marigold is enjoyed with milk, honey, or sugar. It was used by Aztecs, European monks, and others for magical, religious, and medicinal purposes. How can you beat that?

Rose. Prized since antiquity as a symbol of love and beauty, rose has an amazing floral flavor and also mixes well with other botanicals. It is a tasty addition to lemonade, limeade, and cocktails and is high in vitamin C and antioxidants.

Marigold tea flowers in a traditional cup and saucer, *Maryann Fisher, Courtesy True Treats*

Mid-twentieth-century teacup, *Maryann Fisher, Courtesy True Treats*

Roots and Barks

Ginger. With its spirited flavor, ginger is the perfect blend with lemon and mild botanicals. It has long been used for spiritual and physical health and protection against evil spirits, in addition to an aphrodisiac and remedy for upset stomach, nausea, and congestion.

Licorice. From the plant's root, the licorice flavor has a subtle spiciness to it. It is delicious with milk, sweeteners, or on its own, assuming you like licorice. Native Americans chewed the root to treat everything from coughs to dental issues. The root also doubled as a kid's penny candy from the 1800s to the mid-1900s.

Marsh-mallow. The origin of the marsh-mallow, made by ancient Egyptians, the flavor of marsh-mallow is sweet and somewhat earthy. It contains mucilage and has a smooth texture when hot but

Marsh-mallow flowers, *Susan Benjamin, Courtesy True Treats*

thickens when cold. It is thought to calm coughs and relax aches, and has beautiful white and pink flowers.

Sarsaparilla. The sarsaparilla root has a sugary-sweet flavor, a little like licorice and root beer, which makes sense since it was part of the original root beer recipe. It was gathered by the Apache and grown in the colonies. As a remedy, it was thought to cleanse the blood, treat colds, and much more.

Leaves and Stems

Blackberry. Blackberry has a pleasant, fruity flavor as a tea—good hot or cold—and mixes well with other teas, plus whiskey, wine, and even as a mojito. It has been used as a medicine for over 2,000 years and is now considered a "superfood," rich in vitamins and minerals.

Dandelion. Earthy and nutty in flavor, dandelion is enjoyed as a tea and blends well. You can even use the dried leaves sprinkled on salads and other dishes at a tea or garden party or even formal dinner. It has been revered for millennia for its esthetic, culinary, and medicinal value.

Mint. Mint makes a tasty, refreshing tea. The original was spearmint, which formed a natural hybrid with water mint thousands of years ago to create peppermint. It is excellent in punches and cocktails, and has long been used to ease stomach upset, stress, and the common cold.

Raspberry. With a tangy, black-tea flavor, raspberry is also good in lemonade and limeade. So valued, the ancients thought Olympian gods discovered it. Rich in minerals and vitamins, raspberry is helpful for women's issues from menstrual cramping to pregnancy.

Rose hips. The remains of a rose once the petals have fallen, rose hips have a floral, slightly sweet, slightly bitter flavor. They are good as a tea or in a tea blend, and as an addition to jellies, syrups, and cakes. Rich in vitamin C, rose hips have long been used to soothe stomach, chest, and other ailments.

Strawberry. Somewhat like black tea, enjoy it with lemon, mint, and clove. It is excellent in a festive punch and has long been enjoyed by Native Americans and later European immigrants. Strawberry is rich in antioxidants and calcium, and contains a number of vitamins and minerals.

Mixes for Fun!

Chai. A centuries-old South Asian blend of spices such as cinnamon, cardamom, cloves, and allspice, chai is a delicious tea, festive and spirited. Add milk and sweetener to taste.

Mulling spices. These traditional spices date back to the second century and were used by the Romans for mulling—the parent to wassail. They are delicious all year as a tea and in wine, juice, or gin.

THE BOSTON (SALTWATER-LESS) TEA PARTY

As we all know, the colonists had a penchant for tea from their ancestral land. In fact, apothecaries in Boston were selling green and black teas as far back as the 1690s. When the British put a tax on tea as a fundraising device, leading to the famous Boston Tea Party, the colonists drank hot chocolate instead. Since then, chocolate has been a sidekick at tea parties, as has champagne and wine.

The first evidence of American tea parties was an instruction book on the subject, printed in Boston in 1827. Here's what it said to do: Pour the tea into cups, which are handed out on trays with jugs of cream, bowls of sugar, and plates of cakes, toast, bread, and butter. When the first cup of tea is finished, wash the cup, and return it before more tea is poured.[6] Not much has changed since then.

OVER IN ENGLAND: INFLUENCERS OF AMERICANS

Meanwhile, over in England, Anna Maria Russell, the Duchess of Bedford, was getting peckish in the long span between early breakfast and 8:00 p.m. dinner, as was the custom in 1840. So, she started taking tea and light fare in her boudoir mid-afternoon. Before you knew it, Anna was inviting friends to her house for afternoon tea. The event took off among others in high society, held in elegant rooms, set with fine china, hot tea, and small sandwiches.

Teacups of the 1700s

Eighteenth-century teacups were handle-less, set in a deep saucer. The idea was to pour the tea into the saucer where it quickly cooled, and sip from there. Seen here is a period cup with hibiscus flowers yet to be brewed.

1700s teacup with hibiscus tea flowers
Maryann Fisher, Courtesy True Treats

Among the highest of society was Anna's good friend Queen Victoria, who enjoyed the tea parties and started holding her own. Victoria, ever the trendsetter, instantly made tea a tradition. The middle class soon joined in with their own tea parties—inexpensive, easy to prepare, and a great way to create a social gathering with relatively little mess to clean up in the end.[7]

THE GREAT TEA DIVIDE

Whether the tea is simple or elaborate, teatime is the time to bring forth the very finest that the family treasure chest holds in silver, linens, and china.—Los Angeles Times, 1936[8]

Tea parties have traditionally fallen into two categories—afternoon tea and high tea. Some teas took place outdoors, a way to show off hats and flowing flowery dresses, but most were indoors in living rooms and parlors accented with vases of flowers. The table setting was more important than the food and, to be honest, rivaled the tea itself.

Afternoon Tea

The front daylight heightens the informality of afternoon tea. It seems to say: "Here is no pretense but the meeting grounds of friends and all agreeable people."—Omaha Daily Bee, 1890[9]

Afternoon tea was "the least expensive, least troublesome, and one of the most popular forms of social entertainment," said author Anne Seymour in her *A-B-C of Good Form* in 1915. And why was it so easy and inexpensive? The food. There wasn't much of it. The limited selections

The Cup of Tea, 1880, Mary Cassatt, Wikiart

entailed thin sandwiches, thin cookies (and not too many of them), thin triangular pieces of toast, little cakes . . . and even your odd candy, maybe a chocolate. One piece.

Whatever the selection, Seymour reminded readers it should be in good taste:

> *The English muffin, toasted, is, unhappily, not a thing that we have much success in making, nor is the nice Scotch scones. . . . There is something cavalier in offering one's friend crackers bought in boxes, as for the sawdusty little bits of sweetness that are often made to answer the place of a bite of nourishment, they are delusions and snares. Anything in the world except stale sweet crackers.*

Instead, she recommends small, scalloped cakes fresh from the oven, either sugared or frosted, baked in little tins, and delightful bonbons or finger-food-sized caramels or fudge displayed on a plate.[10]

Over the years, the selections changed. Mayonnaise and gelatin, for example, had an increasing presence, and themed

The more formal of the informal afternoon teas, says Lucy Allen in her 1927 book *Table Service*, entail "cut sugar or rock crystals, a pitcher of cream, a small dish of sliced lemon." As for the food: "Plain bread and butter sandwiches or sandwiches of the simplest kinds—olive, nut, or lettuce, also, of course, small cakes or wafers."[11]

tea parties replaced traditional ones. Among the endless varieties were tennis teas, card game teas, and bridal teas. Many included musicians playing such instruments as harps (one of the few places people actually got to hear them) and quartets playing Vivaldi, especially at the height of spring or Christmas time.

High Tea—Rich and Sumptuous

> *The five o'clock tea table has come to be as much of an institution in the United States as it is in England, where no well-to-do home is without its tea service. . . . The art of making and pouring tea gracefully is one that every woman may acquire and should practice until perfection is reached.—Economy Administration Cook Book, 1913[12]*

Unlike the relatively sedentary afternoon teas, high tea was rich and sumptuous. The event evolved out of newly industrialized Britain where workers, now in factories, couldn't stop long enough for a decent teatime. Instead, teatime came after work, at the end of the day. By then, they were good and hungry, so the food was more substantive than the afternoon fare. These teas eventually morphed into high teas, aka "supper."

Meanwhile, the *other* high teas, the ones for pleasure and social hobnobbing, weren't exactly about mutton and gravy. In 1933, author Margaret House Irwin described the menu as containing "Scalloped Oysters, (host serving), Baked Stuffed Tomatoes, Jellied Fruit Salad, Onion Juice Sandwiches, Fruit Meringues, Coffee . . . or Jellied Veal, Stuffed Baked Potatoes, Hot Rolls, Currant Jelly, Fruit-and-Ginger-Ale Salad, Angel Food Cake Stuffed with Strawberry Ice Cream, *Coffee*."[13]

As you might imagine, the possibilities of high teas were limitless. In one "7:00 Tea," as reported by the *Sioux City Journal* in 1890, men were given a character portrait when they arrived. Then each gentleman, as his assigned character self, invited a lady to take tea with him. After the fine meal was served, each character was asked to give a small speech, indicating who they were. The party was a hit, as the author assured us: "The evening passed all too soon for the guests who were given much to enjoy." At another Sioux City 7:00 tea, guests had to prepare the meal themselves. The moment they arrived, they were "soon busy with the following good menu: turkey with dressing, pressed veal, chicken salad, hot rolls, coffee, pickles, celery, ice cream, caramel cake, fruit cake, and orange cake."[14]

The Great High Tea–Low Tea Caper, according to Emily Post

Emily Post, syndicated advisor on all things etiquette, had strong feelings about high tea. In her column of 1946, where she answered questions from readers, she had this to say about high tea:

> *A church committee of women asked me if a "high" tea . . . would be a good idea for their money-raising party. . . . The answer is that it would not do at all. The menu of a high tea is even more substantial than that of a formal dinner. It means a table groaning with hot foods—creamed or fried oysters, fried chicken Maryland, hashed creamed potatoes, coffee, tea and chocolate with whipped cream, several varieties of hot breads and, of course, waffles! A buffet supper would be simpler and an afternoon tea the simplest, since this last exacts nothing but tea, sandwiches, and cookies.*[15]

By the mid-1900s, something remarkable happened. High teas morphed into low teas, although no one seemed to notice. The sumptuous meals simply became thin, crustless sandwiches, salted nuts, and on occasion, a few olives. Emily Post, who so belittled high tea, may have been a harbinger of the change. At the very least, she explained it.

TEA BISCUITS

Sometimes, it's great to sit down with a friend for a cup of tea. Not afternoon, not high, just . . . tea. These informal get-togethers also call for a teatime staple: biscuits. The timeline of biscuit history is parallel to other sweets we might have at tea, such as cake. Both started in the Neolithic age as humans began cooking grains to make them easier to digest.

Later, the Romans made their own version of biscuits, called rusk, which was something like biscotti. These biscuits, used by the military and travelers on long treks, were later eaten by sailors in the Royal Navy in 1588 and by soldiers in the American Civil War. Called "hardtack," these biscuits were baked *four* times for ultimate durability and were as enjoyable as eating rocks.

The functional biscuit became the culinary biscuit around the fourteenth century, when both sweet and savory versions, including the wafer, appeared. The role of the newer biscuit was one-part pleasure, one-part digestive after a meal. In the seventeenth and eighteenth centuries, biscuits became ever more popular due to the increasing availability of cane sugar, and that, of course, was because of enslavement.

In the American South biscuits were particularly popular. Only one problem: baking soda and powder had yet to be invented and yeast was expensive, which meant the dough had to be beaten by hand with a mallet or rolling pin for over an hour. That difficult duty fell upon enslaved women—once enslavement ended, biscuits fell out of favor.

Biscuits did return, however, in the late 1800s, largely due to innovations of African-American chefs and caterers. One was Alexander Ashbourne, who was born enslaved in Philadelphia and, in 1875, applied for a patent on his invention—a spring-loaded biscuit cutter. By the late 1800s, as Queen Victoria's teas became an American ritual and tea parties an American pleasure, biscuits were evolving. Their popularity grew in the 1900s to become a staple of most American kitchens. But, by then, biscuits already had a place on plates alongside teapots, where they remain today.[16]

TEAHOUSE DECORUM

The teahouse phenomenon may have started in Boston, but it took off nationally in the late 1800s. "The tea house is here to stay," said one newspaper reporter in 1897. "It is a convenient place to drop in. It is English and it is elegant. It is a cheap and capital way of entertaining" and, said the author, filled with "talkative, tea-tippling femininity."[17] Whatever.

No question, tearooms were egalitarian. Who can resist the classic three-tiered arrangements of food, trays typically in descending size? The contents have changed just a little since the afternoon teas of old: little cakes, scones, crustless sandwiches—and, yes, *cucumber* sandwiches—cookies, and the odd vegetable, albeit nothing with oysters and a scarce, if any, representation of olives.

Best of all, tearooms showed up in a variety of places. No surprise they had a presence in well-heeled hotels and department stores, frequently in spacious courts held by faux Roman columns and adorned with imported billowing palms. No mere teas settings, these venues hosted tea dances, complete with full orchestras. By the 1930s, tea dances were occurring in ballrooms, town halls, community centers, and hotels where young people showed up to enjoy tea, sandwiches, cakes, and each other as they danced to Big Band music, all for a small fee.

Other teas took place outdoors on porches, decks, or lawns or inside, in country farmhouse settings, some furnished with gorgeous antiques. In fact, in more than one, guests had the option to purchase the table where they enjoyed their tea or buy the hooked rug where they were standing.[18]

As automobiles became more prevalent in the 1920s, giving new meaning to a Sunday drive, teahouses became a chosen destination. Tearooms also morphed into way stations for weary travelers, popping up alongside gas stations and hotels or at campsites. Even candy stores, which were being replaced by wrapped-and-ready candies in every pharmacy and grocery store, added teahouses to their property for extra revenue.

Tea parties, teahouses, and other assorted tea gatherings have remained an American tradition, but like the lavish dinner parties, the community barbecues, and other food-centered events, they are smaller and less robust. There are holdouts, though, especially in older, swankier hotels and modern wannabes.

In 1918, teahouses gave Russians fleeing their country's revolution an opportunity to set up shop, with hot tea, a slice of lemon, and a maraschino cherry, served in a tall glass with a handle.[19]

Looking for a Tea-Time Excursion? Here's Some Advice

Determine your budget in advance. Fancy hotels, especially, have classic tea menus, meaning not much food. So, plan to have enough money available to eat out afterward. The cost per person can be around $85-plus.

Book a reservation for a small teahouse. These places usually don't have the bandwidth for unexpected guests, as they are often in small inns or B&Bs, and their hours can be sketchy. The service may be mercifully high tea-ish, with scones, a variety of sandwiches, cookies, and even spreads and cheeses.

Think out of the box. In this case, out of the box means museums, be they art museums, botanical gardens, or historical homes. Either way, the experience will likely be authentic, and the profits go to a good cause.

Tea reflected in window glass, *Susan Benjamin, Courtesy True Treats*

ALICE IN WONDERLAND

> *"At any rate I'll never go THERE again!" said Alice as she picked her way through the wood. "It's the stupidest tea-party I ever was at in all my life!"*—Alice's Adventures in Wonderland, 1865[20]

We can't end any discussion of tea parties without the Mad Tea Party in Lewis Carroll's book *Alice's Adventures in Wonderland*. The chapter was perplexing (Alice was offered wine, although they had none), even stupid (what Alice called the tea party), but it became the foundation of many a girl's tea party fantasy. Well, that *plus* America's fascination with all things British royalty, *plus* Disney's practically unrelated re-creation of the tea party in its theme parks and movies.

How to Create a Real Alice in Wonderland Mad Tea Party

So, what was served at the original party? And how do you create a more-or-less accurate rendition? In the story, Lewis Carroll's characters enjoyed tea and toast with butter, which, as you know, was common fare. They also discussed treacle (although they didn't serve it), which is a British relative of molasses. You can enjoy treacle as syrup or candy, which comes in hard candy or toffee form, or use molasses instead. From there, you can fill in with other pleasures of a mid-1800s tea party, such as lemonade, sandwiches, chocolate (gritty, if possible), and biscuits.

To be *truly* loyal to the original, dispense with adherence to all things polite, and be perfectly frank and rude if you feel like it. Then, afterward, explain to the kids that this behavior is actually *not* OK in real life.

Let's Celebrate with Cake!

Go to any top-ten list of favorite desserts, and at least a few cakes fill the spots. The beauty and deliciousness of cake is undisputed. Perhaps that's why cakes have endured so long: they're one of the *oldest* desserts. Ironically, in their most popular form as birthday cakes, they're also one of the *newest*. But not because of cake. Because of birthdays. But first—a cake timeline.

Beth's birthday cake for Sandy, *Susan Benjamin, Courtesy True Treats*

THE OFFICIAL CAKE TIMELINE

8000–7000 BC: Humans started cultivating grains. Grains being difficult to chew, let alone digest, required intense amounts of cooking, making, essentially, a grain "stew." From that stew came bread and from bread came cake.[1]

5000–3000 BC: The first known cake was made by Egyptians. Amazingly, that ancient cake sounds palatable and well worth a try for curious cooks. Here's what you do: Just mix whole-grain flour, honey, dried fruits (sugar), yeast, milk, eggs, and spices and bake on hot stones. Or, you could also use an oven. The quantity of each ingredient is up to you. The idea of using specific measurements wouldn't come along until the nineteenth century.[2]

2000 BC: In Crete, cakes appeared at religious events, rituals, and even dinner parties. These cakes were early versions of today's sweet rolls, sponge cakes, flatbreads, pastries, twists, and even layered cakes, all coming in a variety of shapes and sizes.[4]

300 BC (roughly): Ancient Celts made cakes to celebrate the beginning of spring. In this ritual, revelers rolled a cake down a hill, reflecting and *ensuring* the movement of the sun. Should the cake break at the bottom of the hill, whoever rolled it would die that year. Otherwise, all would be well.[5]

Mid-1600s: Cakes evolved over time, getting their biggest boost from new, more reliable ovens, more readily available sugar, and the existence of pans and hoops. Best of all—icing appeared. No rich, cloudlike frostings with room to nestle sugary flowers, these icings were a mix of boiled sugar, egg whites, and occasional flavorings. The mix was poured on the cake and heated in the oven to form a crisp, glossy glaze.[6]

Mid-ish 1800s: Bakers replaced yeast with eggs, separated and beaten for long periods to infuse the cake batter with air. The whites formed a mountain of foam, forcing the batter to rise when heated. This process spawned new and improved cakes, such as sponge cakes

> ## What? Yeast in ancient cakes??
>
> Believe it or not, yeast, so neatly packaged in supermarkets for home cooks, has been around for millennia. The ancient Egyptians used yeast when baking bread in 1300–1500 BC, and the Chinese from around 500–300 BC. As for yeast used to brew beer and make wine? That started in Sumeria, Babylonia, and present-day Georgia around 6000 BC.[3]

and ladyfingers, whose name and appearance promised a soft, sponge-like consistency but were actually dry and airy.

Mid–late 1800s: Cakes were given a boost when white flour, sugar, and, above all, baking powder appeared on kitchen shelves. In rapid fashion, a range of cakes entered the American landscape, eventually taking on prominence in household desserts and events, such as birthday parties and weddings, and, eventually, lunch boxes.[7]

1900s: Upper-class and even the most wealthy families began celebrating events with ice cream and cake. As time went on, the cakes grew ever more ornate. For birthdays, professional bakers and caterers began

Ladyfingers, *Susan Benjamin, Courtesy True Treats*

inscribing messages on the frosting. "Many Happy Returns of the Day" was one, but "Happy Birthday" was not. That only occurred when the hard-to-sing but ever-popular song "Happy Birthday to You" appeared in 1924, ushering in the birthday cake.[8]

BIRTHDAY CAKES AND HAPPY RETURNS . . .

What's remarkable about birthday cakes is what's remarkable about birthdays themselves, and even more remarkable, the history of *time*. For most of human history, time was based on broad concepts—seasons that came and went and the rise and fall of the sun and moon. A person's birthday was as irrelevant as their age.

Then, in the 1800s, came the Industrial Revolution, bringing clocks, often one per village, that chimed loudly for all to hear. Those living in rural communities would have to wait for decades for time-telling, but at least that was a start. As the nineteenth century progressed, household clocks and pocket watches became more readily available. At the same time, record-keeping became more and more prevalent, and with it our awareness of the day we were born.

In the mid-1800s birthday parties started taking off, especially for kids, but it wasn't until the early 1900s that birthdays were celebrated more broadly. For some, their birthdates remained a mystery for decades more.[9]

How Cake Became the Birthday Cake

Cakes had long appeared at celebratory occasions, so it makes sense that they became popular at birthday parties as well. But the real reason for their existence was the "Birthday Song." That story began in 1893, when Mildred Hill and her sister Patty Hill, both schoolteachers in Kentucky, wrote a song called "Good Morning to You/All" for students to sing before class. It went like this:

> Good morning to you,
> Good morning to you,
> Good morning dear children,
> Good morning to all.

Make no mistake: the Hill sisters were no cute, little old ladies with limited talent where lyric-writing was concerned. Patty, a valedictorian of Louisville Collegiate Institute, was a critical part of the progressive education movement. Mildred was an accomplished organist, composer, and "Negro music" scholar. The reason for the song's simplicity was so kids could sing it, remember it, and greet each day warmly.[10]

From Good Morning to Happy Birthday

Sometime in the early 1900s, the Hill sisters' melody began appearing in numerous songbooks with birthday-themed lyrics. Who changed the lyrics? No one really knows. But by 1921, the new version became wildly popular across the United States, the quintessential celebratory song, at the quintessential American celebration. And such a celebration deserves a cake, complete with candles, compliments of the ancient Greeks.

The only problem: the song had no attribution. Plenty of people were making money from the song, but the Hill sisters weren't among them. Lawsuits ensued, of course, and eventually the Hill sisters settled for a one-third share of all revenues generated by the song at the time . . . but none moving forward. The ownership debacle continued, and today Warner/Chappell Music Inc. owns the rights to "Happy Birthday (to You)." They charge movies, radio spots, and ads anywhere from $1,500 to $50,000 to use the song, the reason why the lyrics have been changed in many productions or, more likely, the song simply isn't sung. As for the cake: still in the domain of everyone.[11]

> "Happy Birthday to You" became the most popular song of the twentieth century and the most recognized one in the English language. It has been translated to eighteen languages and performed billions of times, including by the astronauts of the Apollo 9 mission.[12]

WEDDING CAKES

The American wedding cake has long been festive and flamboyant, but not necessarily with a towering mass of white frosting. And, as with so much else in the fun food kingdom, its history is riddled with myth, marvel, and mayhem.

Ancient Weddings

Wedding cakes, like so many celebratory foods, were influenced by the British, and the British were influenced by the Romans. The Roman "cake," in this case, was actually a wheat- or barley-based bread, which, legend has it, was broken over the bride's head at the end of the wedding as a symbol of good fortune. The couple then ate a few of the crumbs, a custom called *confarreation*, aka "eating together." Guests later gathered up the remaining bits as tokens of good luck. At some point, the guests also received handfuls of mixed nuts, dried fruit, and honeyed almonds called *confetto*, which they showered over the bride and groom with abandon.[14] Luckily, those treats were replaced with rice, flower petals, and colored paper, later showered over newlyweds around the world.

Wedding Cakes of the Modern World

By the 1840s, the wedding cake morphed into three cakes: the bride cake, the groom cake, and a less consequential third cake. Essentially, the groom cake was a dark fruitcake, with no icing. It was small and unadorned. The bride cake was stacked and white, sometimes adorned with flowers and other decorations.

A household advice column of 1894 explains that at the wedding, the two cakes should be placed side by side on a table, each with a knife, tied in white ribbon, lying beside it. Before the bride and groom cakes are cut, they should be passed to the bride and groom, respectively. Then the bride should take a slice from her cake, the groom a slice from his. The guests would then enjoy a slice of the bride cake, as is the tradition today. The groom cake may have been eaten at the wedding or taken home by guests, slices wrapped and ready at the end of the event. Many couples saved the third cake as a tasty remembrance of the ceremony.[16]

How to Make a Wedding Cake, circa 1685

One early wedding cake is the "bride's pye," which appeared in *The Accomplisht Cook* of 1685. Author Robert May described this festive dish as a large round pie with a decorated pastry crust covering a filling made of oysters, pine kernels, cockscombs, lambstones (testicles), sweetbreads, and spices. That particular mixture was reserved for the wealthy few. Everyone else indulged in the less expensive versions containing the more palatable minced meats or mutton.[15]

The Future Inside a Wedding Cake

The twentieth-century wedding cakes were an event unto themselves. To grasp the true nature of the wedding cake, including serving instructions, design protocols, and flavor, we must turn to Martha Grey, head of the Home Economics Department of the *Chattanooga Daily Times*. In her 1934 article "How to Plan and Serve the Feast Inexpensively and with Appropriate Appointments," she first dismisses the groom cake. It's nice but unnecessary. Irrelevant, if you will. As

Wedding cakes, *Susan Benjamin, Courtesy True Treats*

> Why are wedding cakes white? The white color symbolizes purity and virginal attributes—a notion brought to you by the Victorians. Before then, most bride cakes were white for a more practical reason—status. Ingredients for the bride cake were expensive, especially the sugar for the icing. White icing meant the finest refined sugar, a symbol of the family's wealth.

for the bride cake, that consists of a white cake, either angel food or butter, "dazzling white icing with decorations, either flowers or grill work and often with a small figure representing the bride in her wedding gown—a figure which is removed before the bride cuts the cake."

The cutting occurs after the main course, where the bride cuts and divides the first piece into two mini-slices—one for her and one for the groom. Then the bride's maids, seated at the table, cut slices for themselves. "What fun this cutting of the bride's cake is," says Ms. Grey, "for the person who makes the cake usually is careful to insert various little objects in the cake to foretell the future of the person who gets it." A bright, shiny dime means riches lie ahead. A gold ring represents marriage. A thimble? A future "old maid" gets that piece. As for the ushers, there are fewer tokens—a button, for example, indicates whether the gentleman in question will marry and a dice whether he will obtain wealth. Differentiating between the two is a challenge for the baker, who must indicate which side is for the groom and which for the bride "so there will be no such catastrophe as a bridesmaid getting a button intended for an usher."[17]

Gradually, the number of wedding cakes whittled down to one: the bride cake. The groom cake did have a resurgence in the 2000s, and the reason for its return, according to one article, is that "a groom cake traditionally represents something masculine, providing a contrast to the oft-feminine features, such as floral bouquets and frilly gowns."[18] Good to know.

THE CHRISTMAS FRUITCAKE

There is only one fruitcake in the entire world, and people keep sending it to each other.
—Johnny Carson, *The Tonight Show*, date unknown

Cut This Out for Your Receipt Book . . . Take four cups of flour, two of butter—and to make a long bother short, take your pocketbook and go to Morse and Stoddard's Fancy Bakery . . . and buy a fruit cake there.—Minneapolis Star Tribune, 1874[19]

Without a doubt, fruitcake is the most loved, loathed, misunderstood, and conflicted cake of all time. Still, we all agree on the fundamentals:

1. Fruitcake is dense; in fact, the ratio of fruitcake to mahogany is 1:1.[20]
2. Fruitcake, at least *good* fruitcake, contains an appreciable amount of sugar and alcohol.
3. Fruitcake has a long shelf life. In fact, the sugar, alcohol, and low-moisture ingredients make fruitcakes among the longest-lasting food in the world.
4. Fruitcake is about Christmas, and Christmas, for better or worse, contains fruitcake. But *that* particular fact hasn't always been the case.

The Oldest Fruitcake Ever

The oldest fruitcake in existence is 4,176 years old, discovered in an Egyptian tomb. Now on display in a Swiss food museum, the cake, and others like it, was meant to provide sustenance in the afterlife. Mostly, though, fruitcakes were used as sustenance during war. For ancient Romans, that meant bread with pomegranate seeds, pine nuts, raisins, barley mash, and honeyed wine, durable enough for soldiers to carry into battle and high enough in calories to see them to the end.

While the Roman empire fell, fruitcakes remained. During the Crusades, knights used fruitcakes made of stale bread, honey, spices, dried fruit, and mead to get through the months-long trek to the Holy Land. Eventually, early fruitcakes morphed into such delights as the Italian panettone and the British plum pudding. The bright, glistening fruit of today's variety appeared around the fourteenth century with glacé—fruits heated in sugar syrup, which doubled as a preservative and tasty treat.

By the 1800s, a typical fruitcake was chock-full of citrus peel, pineapples, plums, dates, pears, and cherries, all drenched in sugar, sugar, sugar. Fruitcake seeped into Victorian Christmas rituals as well, which became the seeds of today's American Christmas extravaganza.[21]

Christmas Cake vs. the Christians

Christmas-like as it was, Christian leaders had a mixed relationship with fruitcake, mainly because of the lavish, alcohol-infused ingredients. The Crusaders ate it, the Catholic Church banned it. England bakers baked it, the European Church turned against it. In the 1400s, the Catholic Church prohibited bakers from using butter for cakes during Advent. Butter was an important ingredient in fruitcakes, but all was well. The butter-less fruitcake brought us stollen, still popular today. The fruitcake back-and-forth disappeared in Europe for good by the mid-1800s, just in time for Queen Victoria's wedding fruitcake.[22]

But the church's love-hate relationship was nothing compared to that of the Americans'. Fruitcake arrived with European colonists in the 1700s and took hold over the next century. During that time, it was popular and esteemed. So important, a good maid could make one that would last a year. Important, yes. Esteemed, yes. But it was also exhausting to make. The

Homemade Mennonite fruitcake, Hagerstown, Pennsylvania, *Susan Benjamin, Courtesy True Treats*

fruit had to be cleaned, dried, and de-pitted; the sugar weighed; the butter softened; and the eggs beaten—and that was just the *preparation*. By the late 1800s, professional bakers rushed to ease the pain women (primarily) experienced making them at home. They made various versions of fruitcakes, each one far superior to the competition's.

CAKES: BEYOND UNKNOWN

The style of cakes depended on the circumstances of the cook, of course. While most narratives reflect cakes made by homemakers in households with stacked cupboards and comfortable kitchens, plenty of cakes were made with the wonders of improvisation and hard work. Here are two examples.

Pioneer Women

Pioneer women faced months of hardships along their westward journeys—harsh winters, limited supplies, little food, and then an exhausting and lonely life once they reached their destinations. When the 1851 edition of *Directions for Cookery* went into print, a pioneer woman was making a cake for her daughter's birthday as follows:

There was no flour to be had, and corn was ground on a hand mill. The meal was carefully emptied from one sack to another, and fine meal dust clinging to the sack was carefully shaken out on paper; the sack was again emptied and shaken, and the process was repeated laboriously time after time until two cupsful of meal dust was obtained. The rest of the ingredients were as follows: $^1/_2$ cup of wild honey, 1 wild turkey egg, 1 teaspoonful of homemade soda, 1 scant cupful of sour milk and a very small amount of butter, to all of which was added the meal dust. The batter was poured into a skillet with a lid, and placed over the open fire in the yard, the skillet lid being heaped with coals. To a little girl's childish taste the cake was very fine, but looking back through the years, the honoree said reflectively, "It was none too sweet."[23]

Enslaved Bakers

Enslaved bakers were an echelon of experts, although their contributions were primarily experienced by those who enslaved them. Nellie Smith, one of the former slaves interviewed in *Born in Slavery: Slave Narratives from the Federal Writers' Project, 1936 to 1938*, describes one of them (colloquialisms from the original text):

Well, Child, two of the best cake-makers I ever knew used them old ovens for bakin' the finest of pound cakes and fruit cakes, and everybody knows them cakes was the hardest kinds to bake we had in those days. Aunt Betsey Cole was a great cake-baker then. She belonged to the Hulls, what lived off down below here somewhere, but when there was to be a big weddin' or some 'specially important dinner in Athens, folks most always sent for Aunt Betsey to bake the cakes.[24]

Enslaved workers also made other cakes for themselves. The quantities were dictated by the availability of food and cooking necessities, the recipes passed down orally through the revolving community of enslaved workers. Here are two with the likely ingredients:

Flannel Cake
1 quart flour
1 pint meal
1 teacup milk
3 eggs
2 teaspoons salt
Blend well together and let it rise to usual time in a warm place.

Another former slave described how he, and other enslaved workers, used molasses to prepare a cake:

We had thick, black lasses and sometimes we got a piece of bread and dug a hole inside uf it an' den filled dat hole wid lasses, an' dat wus jes' like cake to us. All de cake we eber had to eat wus made wid meal an lasses.[25]

HALL OF CAKES: THE FAVORITES

Cupcakes

No surprise, the term "cupcake" refers to the size—made in a cup. Some called them "tea cakes" as well, but the point is the same. In what might be the first mention of these mini-cakes, Amelia Simmons referred to cupcakes as "a light cake to bake in small cups" in her book *American Cookery* (1796). In 1828, "tea cakes" appeared in Eliza Leslie's *Seventy-Five Receipts for Pastry, Cakes, and Sweetmeats*. The connection to today's cupcakes was moderate: they were small, but not necessarily transportable, and unlike today's cupcakes, expensive and enjoyed mainly by the well-to-do.

Early American Cupcake Recipes

Here are two early cupcake recipes, taken directly from their sources.

Amelia Simmons's Cupcake Recipe, 1796

A light Cake to bake in small cups.

Half a pound sugar, half a pound butter, rubbed into two pounds flour, one glass wine, one do. [glass] Rosewater, two do. [glasses] Emptins, a nutmeg, cinnamon and currants.[26]

Eliza Leslie's Tea Cakes Recipe, 1828

5 eggs.

Two large tea-cups full of molasses.

The same of brown sugar, rolled fine.

The same of fresh butter.

One cup of rich milk.

Five cups of flour, sifted.

Half a cup of powdered allspice and cloves.

Half a cup of ginger.

Cut up the butter in the milk, and warm them slightly. Warm also the molasses and stir it into the milk and butter: then stir in, gradually, the sugar, and set it away to get cool. Beat the eggs very light and stir them into the mixture alternately with the flour. Add the ginger and other spice, and stir the whole very hard. Butter small tins, nearly fill them with the mixture, and bake the cakes in a moderate oven.[27]

Tea cake at a tea party, *Susan Benjamin, Courtesy True Treats*

Hostess then and now, *Susan Benjamin, Maryann Fisher, Courtesy True Treats*

ENTER HOSTESS CUPCAKES

Have You Tried Les Petits Gateuax Hostess, Hostess French Pastry Cream-Filled Cup Cakes. New! Super Rich! Super Delicious! You Cannot Beat This Cup Cake Treat!—Hostess ad, 1949

Cupcakes did have a presence on the American culinary landscape throughout the 1800s, but the real breakthrough came in 1919. World War I had ended, Prohibition was beginning, and Hostess introduced its wrapped and ready cupcake. The invention fulfilled numerous needs. Women no longer had to bake cupcakes to get them in the kitchen—a quick trip to the grocer's took care of that. They were affordable, in 1919 selling at 20 cents a dozen, less than dough-nuts at 25 cents and more than cookies at 15 cents. And, like other cupcakes, they were easier to store than full-size cakes, a real boon in the evolving family car rides as well as traditional picnics and other getaways.

Over time, Hostess cupcakes acquired their vanilla-esque filling and white swirl. Plus, the company launched an impressive array of advertising claims, such as Hostess cupcakes were prepared with "the famous secret-blend flavor of chocolate from the African gold coast and the Blue-Green jungles of Brazil." If that weren't enough, they supply "54% quick energy . . . 46% reserve energy . . . continuous energy for 4 hours."[28] And convenient? So convenient that Hostess reminded readers that millions of women pick up extra packages when shopping.[29]

The many flavors of Hostess cupcakes, *Susan Benjamin, Maryann Fisher, Courtesy True Treats*

These days, bakery-based cupcakes are a luxury item, made by hand and sold in glassy-shelved stores, at eye-wateringly high prices. As for Hostess, it too has ebbed and waned. But as of this writing, Hostess cupcakes have a place on supermarket shelves, in more colors and flavors than even Hostess could have imagined.

Chocolate Cake

Barring wedding cakes, which are persistently white and light, chocolate is the most popular cake flavor. Yet today's chocolate cakes took about a hundred years of morphing to become what they are today. Here's a brief timeline.

First quarter of 19th century: a yellow or spice cake meant to accompany a chocolate-based drink.

Second quarter of 19th century: a white or yellow cake with chocolate icing *on* it, not in a cup beside it.

Mid-19th century: chocolate as an ingredient in cakes, not to mention cookies.

Early 20th century: today's chocolate cakes!

One of the first chocolate cake recipes was published by Eliza Leslie in her *Lady's Receipt Book*. The chocolate was true to the cacao bean's actual flavor—bitter. Once chocolate cakes became a common dessert, options followed. Even today, we have rich, so-called molten lava cakes, essentially filled with chocolate pudding, and flourless chocolate cakes, so dense and dark they rival fudge in intensity.

One of the most popular offspring of the plain chocolate cake is devil's food cake. When this cake first appeared in the late 1800s—a rich, dark cake, chocolaty without being bitter—it was simply called "chocolate cake." Whether you were eating plain old chocolate cake or "devil's food cake" you never knew.

> The name "devil's food cake" refers to the cake's rich chocolaty texture and flavor, so delicious it's "sinful."

Carrot Cake

How carrots became carrot *cake* is anyone's guess. But we do know about carrots. These crunchy delights originated in Afghanistan, where the locals enjoyed carrot pudding—a dish that spread to Europe and eventually wound up in North America with European immigrants. So a better question might be—how did the pudding morph into the cake? Europeans had been using carrots when sugar and other sweeteners were hard to find. Was that the connection?[30]

No one knows for sure, but some things are certain: Carrot cake has been around since the 1800s. In the mid-twentieth century it took hold as a "healthy" alternative to other desserts, what with the carrots, nuts, and cream cheese icing, arguably the best part of the cake. Today, this cake of unknown origin, and most likely not what you'd call a "health" food, is one of the top cakes enjoyed by Americans.[31]

Tenth-Century Carrot Pudding

Here is the original recipe for *T'Khabis al-jazar* (sweet carrot pudding):

Choose fresh tender and sweet carrots. Peel them and thinly slice them crosswise. For each pound of honey use 3 pounds of these carrots. Boil the honey and remove its froth. Pound the carrot in a stone mortar. Set a clean copper cauldron with a rounded bottom on a trivet on the fire and put in it the skimmed honey and carrots. Cook the mixture on medium fire until the carrots fall apart. Add walnut oil to the pot. For each pound of honey used add ⅔ cup of oil. Pistachio oil will be the best for it, but you can also use fresh oil of almond or sesame. Add the oil before the honey starts to thicken. However, you do not need to stir the pot. You only scrape the bottom gently when mixture starts to thicken to prevent it from sticking to it. To check for doneness, use a stick or a spoon to see whether the pudding is thick enough or not yet. When pudding becomes thick, put the pot down, and spread the dessert on a copper platter. Set it aside to cool down before serving. It will be firm and delicious.[32]

Coconut Cake

The most fascinating aspect of coconut cake is the coconut. The nuts are buoyant and able to travel great distances on the sea, thereby dispersing themselves without human intervention—a rare feat in the botanical world. Of course, coconuts aren't going to appear ready to sprout in such places as Maine. That involved sailors, whether old-world explorers or cargo ships carrying goods. Either way, that's a good thing for coconut cake lovers everywhere.

As for the origin of coconut cake? It's not as amazing as the cake's flavor. Coconut cakes are typically white or yellow round layered cakes, although the variations are endless. Most have coconut frosting, although some use coconut flavor in the cake instead. Some have layers of white coconut-laced frosting; others use pastry cream, lemon curd, or cream cheese (think cheesecake). Basically, cake with coconut. Why need more?

Cheesecake

The cheesecake story is truly a tale of two cities—one is Philly and the other is New York. Although cheesecake probably originated in Italy, it was German immigrants who brought cheesecake to Philadelphia in the early eighteenth century. In fact, a favorite gathering place for German immigrants was the Cheesecake House, situated in the middle of a pleasant garden, shaded by cherry and apple trees.[33]

Cheesecake didn't become *New York* cheesecake until around 1872. If you're thinking of bustling New York City streets with bakeries jam-packed with eager customers—forget it. This cheesecake's origin was actually *upstate* New York. The story goes that William Lawrence of Chester, New York, accidentally developed a type of cheese while trying to make the French Neufchatel. Not too long after, a New York dairyman made a silky version of Lawrence's cheese for the Empire Cheese Company, later to be known as Philadelphia Cream Cheese. And that groundbreaking, albeit humble, cheesecake is considered the crème de la crème of American cheesecakes—especially among American Jews.[34]

CAKES: THE OUTLIERS

Throughout history, a variety of cakes have come and gone, some quirky, some delightful, some really strange. Of these many cakes, some are still with us and we enjoy them today. Here are a few that have passed.

1234 Cakes

Naming cakes for the quantity of each ingredient dates back to the eighteenth century, possibly earlier. The reason had to do with literacy: as most people couldn't read, the simple name made it easier for them to remember recipes. The basic 1234 ingredient list consists of 1 cup butter, 2 cups sugar, 3 cups flour, 4 eggs.

It's likely whoever was baking added other ingredients, whether nuts or flavorings, based on taste, tradition, or instruction passed down orally. Two 1234 cakes you have enjoyed are pound cake and cupcakes.[35]

Chiffon Cake

OK, chiffon cakes are still around, but not enough, in my option. I love the very concept of chiffon cake, even the name. How light and airy sounding can a cake's name get? Made with vegetable oil, a lot like angel food cake, the best thing about chiffon cake is that it was served with *grapefruit*, of all things, at Hollywood's Brown Derby in the 1930s. The cake lives up to its name. So elegant, so enticing, even Betty Crocker joined in.

Betty Crocker's chiffon cake, *Ladies Home Journal*, 1948

Mayonnaise Cake

The mayonnaise cake is a miracle of cake-composition. A divine union of nuts, seasonings, flour, chocolate, mayonnaise, and inspiration.—Hazel Lim, food writer, 1940.[36]

Strange as it may seem, cookbooks of the 1930s and '40s regularly contained recipes for mayonnaise cake, whether plain old mayo cake, chocolate mayo cake, or mayo cake with custard sauce. Some recipes appeared among a bevy of other mayonnaise-based foods such as chipped beef with a "creamed" mayonnaise sauce. Granted, many of the recipes were slightly embarrassed about having mayonnaise on their ingredient list. The author of one recipe from 1945 reports: "This cake bakes out very chocolate-y looking and is as light as frou-frou and bears not even the slightest suggestion of being born of mayonnaise."[37]

So, who invented this marvelous, albeit strange, creation? The answer is unclear. Many believe it was Hellmann's/Best Foods. But Hellmann's brand rarely appeared in most recipes for mayonnaise cake. Instead, the main ingredient was generic, tasty, and utilitarian mayo. The price was right—especially in shortages of the Great Depression when mayo replaced relatively expensive milk and butter. Besides that, the shelf life was over a week. And the texture was smooth and creamy. By 1981, Hellmann's was still trying to convince readers that mayonnaise was more than a spread for sandwiches and assorted picnic salads, calling it the "amazing ingredient" with a place in just about every food, including applesauce, raisins, and cheesecake.[38]

Soapy Cake

Soapy cake mix was an attempt by Proctor & Gamble to edge its product out of the sink and into the batter. Evidently, it never gained traction, and probably for good reason. Here's what a *New York Times* article reported in 1938:

> Use of soap in baking cake has been developed by the Proctor & Gamble Company of Cincinnati, it has revealed in a patent (No. 2,123,880). . . . Soap added to the baking mix, the inventors say, will prevent the cake from falling or turning out flat. The final product is described as fluffier and lighter than other cake. Addition of the soap also permits the use of more sugar in the mix, so that the cake may have more sugar than flour. As little as twenty-five one-thousandths of 1 percent of soap is added to the mixture. This small quantity does not adversely affect the flavor of the cake, it is asserted. The soap is mixed in with the batter. Any soap may be used.[39]

The cake never took off.

MIX-'EM-UP CAKE MIXES

Many of us think of Betty Crocker as being the mother of cake mixes. Her name is still splashed on cake mix boxes to this day, and her advertising was a work of art. But—Betty Crocker didn't invent cake mixes and, in that regard, was relatively late to arrive in the rush-rush competitive world of instant foods. Here's a cake mix timeline you don't want to miss.

> *1837:* The cake mix market was launched not with cake mix but custard powder made by Alfred Bird, an English food manufacturer and chemist. Bird's Custard Powder was a ready-to-go mixture—just add milk, heat, and pour.[40] As for eggs, a standard component of most baked goods? Unnecessary. In fact, Bird created the mix so his wife, who was allergic to eggs, could eat custard like the rest of us. But the eggless-ness may have been the undoing of Bird's custard creation in the United States. As one reporter claimed, the mix challenged Americans' loyalty to their "hens." In other words: women *wanted* to add eggs.[41]

> *1888:* Journalist Chris Rutt and his friend Charles Underwood bought the flour man-ufacturer Pearl Milling Company. A year later, they had an abundance of excess flour to unload. So, they added additional ingredients, bagged it, and called it "Self-Rising Pancake Flour." And there, on the bag, the woman known as "Aunt Jemima" got her start. American women followed her lead, making everything from biscuits to waf-fles with Underwood's mix.

1920s: For decades, women had been describing life in the kitchen as "drudgery." By the 1920s, the drudgery factor had taken its toll. Fewer women were baking bread at home, more were buying at stores, and the flour companies were anxious.[42] Then, in the early 1920s, Mr. McCollum of New Brunswick, New Jersey, developed a mix for corn muffins and piecrusts. Other companies joined in, such as Mills, Pillsbury, Occident, Ward Baking Company, and the Doughnut Corporation. Easy-to-use mixes were a success, so it only made sense the grandest mix of all—cake mixes—would follow.

1930s: Ironically, cake mixes appeared because manufacturer John D. Duff had a surplus not of *flour*, as you'd expect, but *molasses*. So Duff, the owner of a Pittsburgh-based molasses company, figured out a way to dehydrate his molasses, which he then mixed with flour, sugar, dried eggs, and other ingredients to create gingerbread mix. All home bakers had to do was add water. As for the flavor, definitely molasses-intense. Each hundred-pound bag of wheat flour called for a hundred pounds of molasses. Strong, intense, and not delicious.[43]

1933: Regardless of the ginger cake failure, John D. Duff continued experimenting with mixes, finally patenting one in 1933 that contained dried eggs. He discovered something that Bird had learned decades earlier: women disliked products with dried eggs of any sort, in this case because it made adding fresh eggs redundant. *And women wanted to add eggs.* But—the reason had nothing to do with their

> Here's what John D. Duff wrote on his patent application of 1933: "The housewife and the purchasing public in general seem to prefer fresh eggs and hence the use of dried or powdered eggs is somewhat of a handicap from a psychological standpoint."

loyalty to the American farm system or, for that matter, hens. The reason had everything to do with guilt. Cake was all about love. It was about family, warmth, tradition. Or, anyway, it should be. Using a cake mix where no effort was involved—even cracking eggs—wasn't actually *baking* a cake. It was a cheap trick foisted on those they loved best. So, Duff made a mix that *required* eggs, a strategy still used by food mix manufacturers today.[44]

1940s: Big flour companies spent their time supplying mixes for the GIs overseas during WWII while revving up for the cake mix demand at home once the war was over. Their foresight was right: many women at home had little desire to become in-house bakers and turned to mixes as an out. By the late 1940s, hundreds of small companies got into the cake mix market, introducing new flavors and promises. For all their enthusiasm, these businesses eventually were bought up by the bigger companies or went under.[45]

1947: Betty Crocker created "Gingercake Mix," which the company called "a cake in a box." What followed was the "Party Cake Mix"—a layer cake, where the recipe "was all measured out." As for eggs? Betty was conflicted. In one advertisement, she proclaimed that her mix demanded nothing but water. As for cracking eggs? Nope. Unnecessary. Her mix came complete with dried eggs.[46] Yet, in other ads Betty assured women, "None of my mixes contains dried eggs. Fresh eggs mean superior cakes."[47] Betty?

Duff's Ginger Cake Mix ad, *Ladies Home Journal*, 1948

1951: Duncan Hines entered the cake market with the tagline "An adventure in good eating." The company was true to its promise with its "Three Star Surprise Mix." Made with three flavors, the mix captured 48 percent of the market in a matter of weeks. Duncan Hines mixes called for eggs.[48]

Mid-1950s: The cake mix market expanded like an industrial balloon, but by the mid-1950s it started deflating. The reason was not about eggs this time but frosting. Eggs or no eggs, women still felt a detachment from the cakes they were baking. The answer, cake manufacturers realized, was to give them creative control not on the interior of the cake but the exterior. Enter premade frostings and an ever-increasing array of cake decorations. Birthday cakes became cake-shaped football fields. Graduation cakes were decorated with hats and scrolls. The possibilities were limitless, and women at home loved it.[49] Cake decoration made cake mixes complete. Homemakers didn't have to sift flour, measure baking powder, or worry about the consistency of butter. That out of the way, they could tap into their creative selves, making the cake, boxed and corporate, their own.

About Duncan Hines

Duncan Hines wasn't a real person, but he wasn't entirely made-up either. Duncan Hines was a food writer, restaurant and hotel reviewer, author of guidebooks, and a businessman who produced over 250 products branded to bring high-quality food to the American kitchen. However, he was not a cook and he never invented cake mixes. He did license the use of his name for products and the usual ads, advice, and endorsements. Duncan Hines, the real one, died in 1959 at the age of seventy-eight. The licensed one lives on.[50]

2020: By now, 186.18 million Americans used dry cake mixes, and more people ate cakes from mixes over scratch. And 32.49 million Americans used Betty Crocker—more than any other brand. Betty Crocker mixes still call for eggs.[51]

Pies: Apple, Cherry, and in Your Face

The term "American as Apple Pie" originated in a 1924 advertisement in the Gettysburg, Pennsylvania, Times for men's suits that bucked English fashion trends.—Smithsonian Magazine, September 2019[1]

Pies are undoubtedly a quintessential American dessert, which, being American, had roots elsewhere. That elsewhere is largely the Middle East and Mediterranean. Pies were different then. Those flaky crusts we love today were actually *holders* for the ingredients inside—too hard and unappetizing for actual consumption. The ingredients within weren't exactly apples, cherries, or blueberries with sugar, maybe a dash of vanilla. No matter, they got the pie-ball rolling, bringing us where we are today.[2]

"Every American is born with an appetite for pie," a New York newspaper opined in 1895. As for the immigrant, the paper wrote, "his Americanism, in fact, may be tested in his taste for pie."[3]

A BRIEF TIMELINE OF PIES

Early pies: Pies originated in the Neolithic era, around 6000 BC, when humans were settling into their first established villages. These freestyle pies were made with oats, wheat, rye, or barley and baked over hot coals. By 1237 BC bakers had incorporated nuts, honey, and fruits into the bread dough. As if predicting the importance of pie later in history, drawings of early pies appeared on the tomb walls of Ramses II.[4]

Enter piecrusts: The ancient Romans made piecrusts with flour and oil. Later, medieval Europeans created a version closer to today's crusts, using cooking fats such as suet, lard, and butter.[5]

Pies as pyes: "Pyes," as they were called, appeared in twelfth-century England—essentially meat cooked within a crust-based "coffyn," aka "box" or "container." The fancier varieties contained fowl whose legs hung over the side of the dish and were used as handles.[6]

Emergence of fruit pies: The sixteenth-century British enjoyed sweet fruit pies or tarts, no doubt influenced by Elizabeth I, who was partial to cherry pie. By the seventeenth century, fruit pies had become commonplace.[7]

FLYING BIRDS AND HIDDEN MIDGETS: A SEVENTEENTH-CENTURY TREAT

Think only of the nursery rhyme most of us remember from childhood—"Sing a Song of Sixpence." In the unlikely event you don't know it, here it is:

Sing a song of sixpence,
A pocket full of rye.
Four and twenty blackbirds
Baked in a pie.

When the pie was opened,
The birds began to sing;
Wasn't that a dainty dish
To set before the king?

The king was in his counting house,
Counting out his money;
The queen was in the parlour,
Eating bread and honey.

The maid was in the garden,
Hanging out the clothes,
When down came a blackbird
And pecked off her nose.

And shortly after that,
There came a little wren,
As she sat upon a chair,
And put it on again.

When the pie was opened . . . , *The Boyd Smith Mother Goose*, 1920

Dainty dish, indeed.

This actually happened. Well, half of it did. The nose snipping and replacing business—not true. The living blackbirds baked in a pie? In the 1600s, British royalty and the well-to-do did, in fact, bake pies filled with living creatures—blackbirds, rabbits, frogs, and other small animals.

The story may seem grisly enough—living creatures slowly being cooked to death to the amusement of humans who were about to eat them. But that isn't quite accurate. Once the pie was cooked, it was cut open, releasing blackbirds and leaping frogs to the astonished pleasure of the guests. Of course, the creatures must have been all the worse from their piping hot imprisonment, and the pie a mass of feathers and droppings. The guests weren't expected to eat the contents—a separate pie was prepared at the time for their consumption.[8]

Blackbird Pie

Should you, or any of your friends, want to try blackbird pie—or even if you don't—it's always good to know what to do. From the English-translated version of *Epulario* (The Italian Banquet), published in 1598:

> To Make Pie That the Birds May Be Alive In Them and Flie Out When It Is Cut Up—Make the coffin of a great pie or pastry, in the bottome thereof make a hole as big as your fist, or bigger if you will, let the sides of the coffin bee somwhat higher then ordinary pies, which done put it full of flower and bake it, and being baked, open the hole in the bottome, and take out the flower. Then having a pie of the bigness of the hole in the bottome of the coffin aforesaid, you shal put it into the coffin, withall put into the said coffin round about the aforesaid pie as many small live birds as the empty coffin will hold, besides the pie aforesaid. And this is to be at such time as you send the pie to the table, and set before the guests: where uncovering or cutting up the lid of the great pie, all the birds will flie out, which is to delight and pleasure shew to the company. And because they shall not bee altogether mocked, you shall cut open the small pie, and in this sort you may make many others, the like you may do with a tart.[9]

Small people, then called "dwarfs," were also set in a pie, either alone or with blackbirds. The dwarfs broke through the crust with the expected amount of fanfare, then walked down the table entertaining guests by reciting poetry, doing tricks, sketching the guests, and other amusements.

One of the most famous dwarfs of all was Jeffrey Hudson. He got his start at a dinner for England's King Charles I and his wife, fifteen-year-old Queen Henrietta Maria. Seven years old, and only eighteen inches tall, Hudson rose from a pie in a suit of miniature armor then stood beside the enthralled queen and bowed low.

Later called "Lord Minimus," he served as the Queen's Dwarf, one of a lineup of curiosities and pets, including William Evans, a giant Welsh porter. So favored was Hudson that the famous seventeenth-century painter Sir Anthony Van Dyck painted his portrait with the

Young Lord Minimus and Queen Henrietta, *Sir Anthony van Dyck, 1633*

queen, a monkey resting on his arm. Hudson later had a difficult, albeit interesting, life. After being kidnapped by pirates, he participated in the English Civil War, killed a man in a duel, was captured by pirates a second time, lived as a slave in northern Africa for about twenty-five years, spent years in jail . . . and through it all, doubled in size and thoroughly disowned his previous, frivolous self.[10]

The jumping-out-of-pie tradition remains today, when "bachelor" parties feature a barely clad woman jumping out of a cake. Evidently the same holds true—or did—for pies.

PIES IN NORTH AMERICA

Early settlers brought pies to North America. For fillings, they used native pumpkins, pears, quince, blueberries, and whatever made sense. There were plenty of advantages to making these pies, but festive eating wasn't one of them. Pies demanded less flour than bread, didn't require an oven, and could adopt whatever provisions were available into the mix. As for crusts, no flakiness here: still dense and questionable from a culinary standpoint, they were made of rough flour and suet. As with earlier crusts, these were more holders for the fillings than a flaky finish to each bite of pie.[11]

Colonial Pies

Most colonial pie fillings were unlike what we know and love today. In Martha Washington's cookbook, the ingredients were more French than North American—no native pumpkins, pears, quince, or blueberries but rather almonds, rosewater, and Damascus prunes, first bought to England by the Crusaders.[12] Of course, Martha's cookbook was from the early eighteenth century, passed down to her from her mother-in-law as a wedding present.

One of the pies in Martha Washington's cookbook was "Pie of Sweetbreads." Granted, sweetbreads sound like crumbly cinnamon and sugar baked treats but actually refer to the thymus gland, found in young lambs, piglets, and calves, as well as the general pancreas, ovaries, or testes. The pie itself was more like today's oyster stew, consisting of boiled sweetmeats, of course, and oysters, stewed until their edges curled, then mixed with butter, flour, cream, and well-beaten egg yolks. All of this was put in a pie shell and covered with crust.[13]

As the country grew, so did the options for sweeteners. Maple syrup, hickory syrup, corn syrup, and sugars derived from fruit were among those native to North America. Others, such as cane sugar and its derivative molasses, sorghum, and beet sugar, were imports, as was honey brought by Europeans in the early 1600s.

Apple Pie

The apple pie grows in every section of our beloved country, varying in thickness and toughness of crust, it is true, but always characteristically American.—Sacramento Record Union, 1889[14]

While Pie of Sweetbreads was not exactly your all-American apple pie, apple pies *did* exist in the early days of the nation. In fact, Martha Washington's cookbook included an apple pie called a "Codling Tart." "Codling" was a type of apple used for cooking and "tart" referred to a small pie. These apple pies were direct descendants of the fifteenth-century English apple pie, made from uncooked apples, fat, sugar, and sweet spices mixed together and baked in a crust. These particular pies were also encoded with both American and English DNA: the trees were planted from spores brought by the settlers.[15]

> Pies were a weapon during the Civil War when Southern women gave lethal arsenic-laced pies to Union soldiers.[17]

Mark Twain on English Pie

Mark Twain loved American pies of all sorts—cherry, peach, mincemeat, pumpkin, squash—and was a loyalist all the way. Here's what he said about the English apple pies, from which the American version descended:

RECIPE FOR NEW ENGLISH PIE—To make this excellent breakfast dish, proceed as follows: Take a sufficiency of water and a sufficiency of flour, and construct a bullet-proof dough. Work this into the form of a disk, with the edges turned up some three-fourths of an inch. Toughen and kiln-dry in a couple days in a mild but unvarying temperature. Construct a cover for this redoubt in the same way and of the same material. Fill with stewed dried apples; aggravate with cloves, lemon-peel, and slabs of citron; add two portions of New Orleans sugars, then solder on the lid and set in a safe place till it petrifies. Serve cold at breakfast and invite your enemy.[16]

Assorted pies at a diner, *Susan Benjamin, Courtesy True Treats*

TWENTIETH-CENTURY PIES: THE COUNTDOWN

Pies of the twentieth century were dynamic, but not necessarily how you think. They were loved. Homemade. All-American. And quite possibly deadly. Here's a look at modern pie history through the decades.

1900–1909: Banana Cream Pie

Bananas entered the American marketplace with a bang in the late 1800s. Their entrance was made possible by advanced transportation that delivered bananas to your town and advanced marketing so you knew all about it. In the early 1900s, bananas found their rightful place alongside lemon, chocolate, orange, almond, and pineapple cream pies.

One banana cream pie, circa 1877, called for sliced raw bananas, mixed with butter, sugar, allspice, and vinegar, boiled cider, or diluted jelly baked between two crusts. The caveat, however, was that cold-boiled sweet potatoes may replace bananas, and are "very nice."[18] Another simpler version in 1901 called for putting sliced bananas in a piecrust, covering them with powdered sugar, and, once cooled, topping them with whipped cream.[19] A few years later, the banana cream pie of today came into existence. Here's one recipe from 1906:

> Line a pie pan with crust and bake in a hot oven. When done, cover the bottom with slices of banana cut lengthwise, very thin (two small bananas are enough for one pie). Then fill the pan with a custard made in the following manner: Two glasses of milk, two tablespoonfuls of cornstarch dissolved in a little milk, yolks of two eggs, and one teaspoonful of vanilla extract. Boil in a double boiler until the mix thickens; then pour into a pie crust. Cover the top with the whites of the eggs beaten stiff and slightly sweetened. Place in the oven just long enough to give it a rich brown color.[20]

1910–1919: Pies of Peace and War

> As soon as an American boy goes to any foreign country, he at once begins to languish for American pie. —Boston Daily Globe editorial, 1918[21]

In the 1910s, pies were pretty basic, consisting of sweet potato pie and new arrivals such as Moon Pies. These familiar wrapped treats were made for coal miners in 1917, albeit more of a hand pie and, for that matter, more of a cake. During World War I, Americans had to curtail their use of sugar, wheat, and meat while conserving food. Graham flour was used instead of wheat, and molasses replaced

> World War I soldiers were required by law to eat *only* America-made pies, ensuring their loyalty to US pies once the war ended.[22]

How to make a pumpkinless pie under any circumstances: Scald one quart of milk; use a scant cup of Indian Meal and a little salt. When cold add two eggs, cinnamon and ginger to taste; sweeten with brown sugar. Put a little cream or milk on top and bake.[23]

cane sugar. The result was new and innovative pies, requiring fewer ingredients while remaining tasty.[24]

Many recipes were created by women at home, such as one made by Mrs. E. M. King of East Orange, New Jersey. Named the "Pumpkinless Pie," she sent her creation to the National Emergency Food Garden Commission, where it eventually reached a baker in "Uncle Sam's Navy . . . somewhere in the Atlantic," who served her creation to 500 sailors. The pie was such a hit, Mrs. King went on to invent a ginger-less pie. [25]

1920–1929: Fruit Pies, Meatless Meat Pies, and Shoofly Pie

Shoofly pie, *Maryann Fisher, Courtesy True Treats*

The 1920s, while known for outrageous, Prohibition-era antics, were also a time of fruit pies! The variety seemed endless—lemon, cherry, apple, and even *mincemeat*. This particular pie is a clear descendant of medieval meat pies, containing meat and suet but also raisins, currants, nuts, apples, cider, and even fruit jelly. Many mincemeat recipes left meat out altogether and still do today.

Then there's shoofly pie, which debuted in print in 1926. The pie is considered an invention of the Pennsylvania Dutch, who aren't actually Dutch but descended from Germans. Likewise, shoofly pie isn't German *or* Pennsylvania Dutch, but a descendant of sugar-filled pastries made in the ancient Middle East and medieval Europe. As for who introduced shoofly pie to America, that would be immigrants from many nations.[26]

That said, it *was* the Pennsylvania Dutch who gave the shoofly pie its name. According to some experts, the reason is that the cooling molasses-filled pie attracted flies that had to be shooed away. Others say it somehow derived from an unidentified German word.[27] The Pennsylvania Dutch likely added the pastry dough, too, to make it easier to eat with morning coffee.

Regardless of time, name, people, or place, shoofly pie consists of molasses or brown sugar; flour; spices such as nutmeg, ginger, and cloves; butter; and pastry crust. Here's an example of an early version from 1837, when it was called "molasses pie":

> *Four eggs—beat the Whites separate—one Teacupful of brown Sugar, half a Nutmeg, two Tablespoonfuls of Butter; beat them well together; stir in one Teacupful and a half of Molasses, and then add the Whites of Eggs. Bake on Pastry.*[28]

1930–1939: Depression-Era Pies

The Depression era made way for the greatest range of pie innovation imaginable. Americans had little choice but to be innovative given they were juggling a devastated economy *plus* shortages due to the economy *plus* droughts leading to the infamous Dust Bowl in parts of the United States.

One innovation was "mock" pies such as mock cherry pie, which was made with cheaper and more readily available cranberries; crusts made with saltines, wafers, and other varieties of crackers (but *not* Ritz crackers, as legend has it); and unlikely innovations such as "water pies" made with only a handful of ingredients, including water. The most intriguing of all were "mystery pies." True to their name, mystery pies could be anything that was on hand, such as walnuts and fruit and a soda cracker crust;[29] leftover pork, tomatoes, cracker crumbs, and macaroni;[30] or a jack-o'-lantern shell for Halloween.[31] Newspapers even published mystery pie naming contests.

1940–1949: Sugarless Pies

Sugarless pies of the 1940s were not, by any means, diet pies or even low-cal pies. They were pies without cane sugar. The reason for the "sugarless" part was sugar rationing during World War II. Honey was rationed, if available at all, but not so molasses or corn syrup. So, custard pies were out and apple pie in, sweetened primarily by its own juices.

These sugarless pies were also patriotic: America was off to war and what better pie to eat than American apple pie, no matter how it tasted. Pecan pie made with native pecans was also popular, made with a small amount of sugar (if any) and molasses and/or corn syrup. But, beyond doubt, the most well-suited pie for wartime requirements was the aforementioned shoofly pie: molasses, flour, a dab of butter, and the crust of your choice.[32]

Make Your Own Water Pies

Water pies are better than they sound, and require only a few basic ingredients.

1 (9-inch) deep-dish piecrust, unbaked
1½ cups water
¼ cup flour
1 cup sugar
2 teaspoons vanilla extract
5 tablespoons butter

Preheat oven to 400 degrees F and set the empty piecrust on a baking sheet. Pour the water into the piecrust.

In a small bowl, stir together the flour and sugar. Sprinkle evenly over the water in the crust. Don't stir.

Drizzle the vanilla over the water in the piecrust. Place pats of butter on top of this.

Bake at 400 for 30 minutes. Reduce heat to 375 and cover the edges of the crust if needed to prevent burning. Continue cooking for an additional 30 minutes.

The pie will be watery when you pull it out of the oven but will gel as it cools. Allow to cool completely and then cover and place in the fridge until chilled before cutting.[33]

1950–1959: Grasshopper Pie

Grasshopper pie, which originally *did* contain grasshoppers (in the Philippines), became an industry-created spectacle in the 1950s, essentially a green-colored, mint-flavored mousse pie with a chocolate crumb crust. It may have signaled the beginning of the new pie, a radicalization of an American tradition, but it didn't. Pies haven't changed much . . . *but* their reputation has.

THE GREAT PIE DEBATE—BAD PIE, BAD-BAD PIE!

Believe it or not, the all-American pie was steeped in controversy beginning in the mid-1800s and lasting close to a hundred years. Rumor and misinformation were the primary culprits, much as Halloween apples were erroneously said to contain razor blades but on a larger scale.

Mid-1800s: Pie Posed Serious Health Threats

In the mid-1800s, pie was the equivalent of cigarettes—today a smoke, then a slice. Pie, according to food experts, posed a special threat to the infirm. In 1841, Sarah Josepha Hale expressed this sentiment in her cookbook, *The Good Housekeeper*:

> *Pies are more apt to prove injurious to persons of delicate constitutions than puddings, because of the indigestible nature of the pastry. Those who eat much of this kind of food, when made rich, (and poor pies are poor things indeed,) usually complain of the loss of appetite, and feel a disrelish for any kind but high-seasoned food. It would really be a great improvement in the matter of health . . . if people would eat their delicious summer fruits with good light bread instead of working up the flour with water and butter to a compound that almost defies the digestive powers, and baking therein the fruits, till they lose nearly all their fine original flavor.*[34]

Early 1900s: The Moral and Physical Ineptitudes Related to Pie-Eating

One thing can be said about pie at this time in history: it was controversial. One commentator for the *Chicago Daily Tribune* in 1899 proclaimed that pie was "an article of necessity in every household as much as the bed and cook stove." Maybe, but others considered pie as egregious as alcohol during the height of Prohibition. Elizabeth Fulton, a home economist at Kansas State Normal School, for example, proclaimed that pie, like alcohol, was so ruinous it could lead to divorce. Pie-haters didn't stop at so singular an issue as divorce: they rolled pie into one immoral ball. "Pie really is an American evil," wrote one reporter in 1902. It is an "unmoral food," she said, and those who indulge have "sallow complexions" and "lusterless or unnaturally bright eyes" and "are all dyspeptic. . . . No great man was ever fond of pie."[35]

The anti-pie sentiment eventually reached a pitch of paranoia. Newspapers printed such reports as one, in 1915, claiming that pie was the culprit for an epidemic raging through their town. In but one occasion, a husband (a Civil War veteran, no less!) and wife got a deadly case of food poisoning from eating lemon and squash pie at Gavitt's restaurant. Others survived, but just barely.[36]

Late 1940s: Why Would Anyone Want to Bake a Pie?

Pies rose above the claims that had been waged against them for almost a hundred years, with help from the patriotism of the two world wars. Pies were all-American. And because they were all-American, we must love and eat them. Then, in the late 1940s, pie once again won the ire of the American dessert-loving public, but for different reasons, which came down to this: hardly anyone wanted to make pies. They were too difficult. Too time-consuming. Then, just when pies took yet another downturn, corporate America rushed to the rescue, bringing an arsenal of ready-made crusts, fillings, and even whole pies, as easy to use as their cake mix counterparts. Here are just a few of the companies that showed up.

JELL-O—BEYOND PUDDING

Jell-O pudding morphed easily into Jell-O pie filling, which merely required opening a box, adding an egg yolk and a dash of milk, and stirring. The result was what advertisers in the 1950s called "Nifty Summer Swifties," which were "thrifty, too." Then there was the "Peach Meringue Pie"—"A real peaches n' cream delight made with Jell-O Vanilla Pudding and Pie Filling." Even better, the ad promises, "Here's the *heavenly-est* filling you ever put in a pie shell—fresh peaches happily combined with the delicate flavor of Jell-O Vanilla! Mm, Mm, Mm, that's grand eating—and so glamourous, too!"[37]

THE CROCKER SOLUTION

Betty Crocker's ready-made crust was actually a mix, much like her highly marketed cake mix. Here's how Betty explained it, in a soothing and professional handwritten-ish note in one advertisement: "It's always fun to please your family with something special. But on busy days there sometimes isn't quite enough time. That's when you'll especially appreciate our Betty Crocker pie crust mix, Crustquick, whether you plan a hearty meat pie or glamorous dessert." There, see: pressure's off.[38]

PET-RITZ COMPANY

Pet-Ritz Fruit Pies, Frozen, The Work's All Done. —Pet-Ritz ad, 1959

Pet-Ritz didn't invent frozen pies—that was Clarence Birdseye and later Swanson and Morton. But those were meat pies, not frozen desserts. Pet-Ritz brought to market frozen pie shells *and* whole frozen pies. All the homemaker needed to do? To quote the package: Just heat and serve.[39] And should the homemaker feel the guilt so prevalent among housewives using ready-made foods, the ad is reassuring: "When you first bake a Pet-Ritz Pie, you'll discover there's something very special about pies made the tradition fruit-country way! Heaped high with tree-ripened fruit, the crust tender and golden rich with creamy butter, these are pies you'd be proud to call your own."[40]

Even companies that had only a passing association with pies joined in. Ritz Crackers became Ritz cracker crusts for "Mock Apple Pie" with a crush-it and stir-it preparation plan. Potato chips, normally coupled with dips or a side to burgers, were smashed into a crust-like pie shell, ready for filling. As for Oreo cookies—skip the milk and pound them into a toothsome, if not exceptionally sweet, crust. In the mid-1900s, another no-fuss baking pie filler made its debut—Dream Whip. As for our friends at Hostess, they have their own version of hand pies in all-American cherry and apple flavors, still enjoyed by Americans takin' a lunch break at work.

Hostess fruit pies, classic today, *Susan Benjamin, Maryann Fisher, Courtesy True Treats*

PIES: THE CONTESTS. THE MERRIMENT. THE PRIZES.

Love them. Fear them. Hate them. Pies have always been at the center of merriment, from contests to outrageous pie-in-the-face theater, more than cakes, ice cream, and any other fun food since fun food began. What makes pies a centerpiece in this unlikely arena? No one knows for sure, but the festivities still endure today. And that's a good thing.

Pie-Baking Contests

Yes, we know baking contests from county fairs and other festive events, with beribboned entries lined up beneath well-constructed tents. And, yes, while these contests always were magnificent and community-oriented, they were nothing like the industry-sponsored pie-baking contests when it came to prizes. One contest, sponsored by the Oregon Power Company and *News-Review* newspaper, promised winners a Premier Duplex Vacuum Cleaner or an Automated Hotpoint Electric Range as prizes in 1927.[41]

The contests were generous prize-wise, but precise and demanding when it came to competitors and their pies. The Rotary Club and Michigan Consolidated Gas Company, for example, hosted a contest for "girl contestants no younger than 15 years of age and no older than 19." No creativity allowed here: each contestant had to bake a *cherry* pie, eight and one-half inches in diameter and one and one-quarter inches deep with a lattice crust on top. To enter, contestants had to submit two typewritten copies of the recipe; give a speech, no more than three minutes long, titled "What the Cherry Pie-Baking Contests Has Meant to Me"; *and* furnish her own utensils and supplies . . . except cherries. As for the prize, college-aspiring girls received $175 toward a scholarship. The others received a $50 prize and diminishing prizes going down to $5 for seventh-place entries.[42]

But the most jaw-droppingly impressive event with awards, stardom, and complexity was the Pillsbury Bake-Off. A product of marketing brilliance, the event, if you can call it that, was launched in 1949 to celebrate Pillsbury's eightieth birthday and promote Pillsbury Best flour. As for the prize? Advertisements of the time promised $154,000 prize money for the best recipe and final product.[43] So, it's no wonder the company got thousands of entries from across the country.

> So influential were the Pillsbury Bake-Offs, Lucille Ball, as Lucy Carmichael on *The Lucy Show* (1964), entered a pie-baking contest.[46]

Today, Pillsbury claims they actually gave away a $25,000 prize. Food historians say the grand prize was $50,000. But why quibble?[44] The value of money shrinks compared to the illustrious fanfare that accompanied the event.

To start, the Bake-Off, then called the "Grand National Recipe and Baking Contest," selected one hundred finalists out of the many applicants. They, as with all applicants, could only use Pillsbury Best flour. That was the rule. Actually, Pillsbury's *law*. Some, probably most, finalists had never left their homes, never rode on a train, never stayed in a hotel or eaten a high-class dinner. And there they were, being flown into New York City to stay at the Waldorf-Astoria where the venue was hosted, having breakfast in bed, dining on pheasant under glass, and preparing for a national sensation, hosted by Art Linkletter, an endearing comic sensation and all-American guy. Even more remarkable was that the guest-of-honor at the event, at *their* event, was not their great-aunt Harriet or some local celebrity but Eleanor Roosevelt.[45]

> The first Pillsbury Bake-Off, in 1949, was so successful that it was held annually until 1976 and then every two years until the forty-seventh competition in 2014. Each year, the happy winners jumped, hugged, and cried tears of joy, a happy hysteria no longer part of the many televised cook-offs today.[47]

About the winners: In one sense, they were all winners, as they got at least $100 for their recipe *and* the G.E. electric stove they used in the competition. As for 1949's *big* winner, who received $50,000 or $25,000, depending on the source? That was Mrs. Ralph E. Smafield of Detroit, Michigan. Her entry wasn't a pie, it was bread, but if you're interested, here is the prize-winning recipe:

NO-KNEAD WATER-RISING TWISTS

$^1/_2$ cup shortening

3 tablespoons sugar

1$^1/_2$ teaspoons salt

1 teaspoon vanilla

$^1/_2$ cup scalded milk

2 cakes yeast, crumbled, or 2 packages dry yeast dissolved in $^1/_4$ cup warm water

3 cups Pillsbury All Purpose Flour, divided

3 eggs

$^3/_4$ cups chopped nuts (any kind)

$^1/_2$ cup sugar

1 teaspoon cinnamon

Combine shortening, 3 tablespoons sugar, salt, vanilla, and milk in mixer bowl. Add yeast and mix well. Blend in 1$^1/_2$ cups of the flour and beat until smooth. Cover bowl and let rest for 15 minutes.

Add eggs, one at a time, beating well after each addition. Blend in remaining 1$^1/_2$ cups flour and mix thoroughly. The dough will be quite soft. Let rise in one of two ways: (1) set covered dough in a warm place about $^1/_2$ hour, or (2) tie dough in a tea towel, allowing ample space for dough to rise. Then place in a large mixing bowl and fill with water (75 to 80 degrees F). Let stand until dough rises to top of water, about 30–45 minutes. Remove from water. The dough will be soft and moist.

Combine nuts, $^1/_2$ cup sugar, and cinnamon. Divide dough into small pieces with a tablespoon. Roll each piece in sugar-nut mixture; stretch to about an 8-inch length. Twist into a desired shape. Place on a greased baking sheet. Let stand for 5 minutes. Bake in a preheated 375-degree oven for 12–15 minutes.[48]

Pie-Eating Contests

Pie-eating is sport sublime. / That ancient and honorable pastime, pie-eating.—Poem in
San Francisco Examiner, 1918 [49]

While pie-eating contests aren't as absurd as traumatized blackbirds flying from a pie, they do
lack the grace of a pie-*baking* contest. That's because pie-eating is in a realm of its own, one-
part food and one-part sport, with more humor than, say, a boxing match. The first formal pie-
eating event occurred 150 years ago in Toronto, Canada, and a description in the *Indianapolis
Journal* says it all:

> *A certain number of very luscious and very sticky tarts, say of raspberry or other fruit, are
> placed on low stools, and the game consists in eating them without the aid of the hands, a
> prize being offered to the person who eats the most in a given time. The contestants' hands
> being tied behind them, and they make the assault on their bended knees. The spectacle of
> a row of dignified gentlemen or beautiful ladies with faces besmeared with jelly and bolting
> tarts, with their hands tied behind them, would be one to instruct and amuse.* [50]

Decades later, pie-eating contests became more widespread, held at community fairs, pubs,
men's clubs, church gatherings, and more. The competitors were adults, children, men, and
young ladies of all ages. Many had strategies for eating quickly without killing themselves, and
prizes reached $1,000. Stars rose up, such as Joe "Spider" McCarthy, who ate thirty-one pies
in a competition at Charles Tanby's Saloon in Manhattan. His success encouraged him to pen
a Broadway show based on pie-eating, complete with real-life pie-eaters, but the production
never took place. [51]

By 1895 announcements for pie-eating contests fell beneath bicycle races and other semi-
athletically oriented games such as tug-of-war, greased pole climbing, ring tournaments, and
footraces. The contestants varied—one of them entering a pie-eating contest championship
was described as a "little guy" and "oh can he eat!" (Turns out, he was in seventh grade.)

Like all sports, injury was a possibility, and not just from choking. Said a reporter for
the *San Francisco Examiner* in 1918: "One of the big events was the pie-eating contest. One
contestant finished his plate first of all, but lost because a considerable part of the pie was
attached to his ear. Just as the contest was about to start, a trouble-making bumble bee came
up and jabbed its stinger into his ear. His hands were tied behind him and still that ear had
to be rubbed. So he rammed it into the pie and wiggled it until the sting was gone. And that
cost him the match." [52]

Today, competitive eating is big business, with competitive eaters, both male and female,
considered professional athletes. Pies aren't the only food being so ruthlessly, albeit skillfully,
devoured. The annual Nathan's Hot Dog Competition is broadcast on ESPN, and the competitors are announced with all the grandeur of professional boxers. [53]

Pie-in-Your Face, Pie-in-the-Eye

A Hindoo seer declares that if you tell him what tickles you, he'll tell you what you are. Should that turbaned gentleman chance into an American movie palace and hear the gales of laughter that greet a Chaplin pie-throwing contest, he'll naturally conclude that Americans are a race of custards.—Hutchinson Gazette, 1921[54]

The epitome of pie-as-fun is when it's thrown in someone's face, and for over one hundred years pie-throwing, now known as "pieing," has appeared in cartoons, TV shows, and movies. Its debut was on the vaudeville circuit and soon became standard fare on the big screen, starting with the silent film *Mr. Flip* in 1909. Its ascension in the universe of entertainment had much to do with the efforts of Mack Sennett, aka the "King of Comedy," who founded the Keystone movie studios in 1912. His singular mission was to make people laugh. Among the studio's many now-famous pranks were slipping on a banana peel and the slapstick cop chase.

Sennett's methods were outlandish and often sophomoric, but his reasoning was solid. To maximize comedic potential, he enlisted the right actors for the right roles, including Charlie Chaplin, who, at the time, was fresh out of vaudeville. As for pie-throwing, Sennett had rules for who was pied: mothers in-law, yes; mothers, no. Everyone else—fair game. Sennett's pies were specially made with heavy-duty pastry and syrupy custard. As time went on, filmmakers used custard pies—they were messy, yes, and open-faced, making them less painful than a fully crusted pie.[55]

> ## Pies for Throwing
> Want to try pie-throwing for yourself? Have fun with the kids? Add pizzazz to an amateur production? Here's a pie recipe used for silent film star Buster Keaton: Weld two baked pie crusts together to create a solid base of flour and water. Then, add an inch of thick flour-and-water paste. The rest depends on who is receiving the pie. If the target is a blonde or a man in a light suit, try something colorful such as a chocolate or strawberry garnish. For a man in a dark suit, add lots of whipped cream.[56]

Silent Films Grow Up and Pipe Down

Pie-Throwing . . . and Other Theatrical "Evils" Are Threatening America. . . . In particular, promiscuous kicking and mauling of men and women and the throwing of eggs and pies in their faces . . . not to mention "betrayal and seduction of men and women" and "vulgar exhibitions of underclothing."—"Pie-Throwing Movies Arouse Ire of Reformer," 1920[57]

When talkies came along in the 1930s, pie-fighting was a standard in most comedies. But the one who gave it the highest honors was Charlie Chaplin, whose pie-throwing-infused comedy stunts became part of American culture. One comedic commentary from 1919 said, "Movies are elevating taste because the housewives imitate the sumptuous setting they see on the screen, but we hope they don't carry it too far. They might imitate Charlie Chaplin's pie-throwing and dish-smashing stunts too."[58]

Pie-throwing went on to premiere in such comedies as Stan Laurel and Oliver Hardy's *Battle of the Century* (1927), which used 3,000 pies, and Our Gang's *Shivering Shakespeare* (1930), which climaxes with an auditorium full of people throwing pies. The Three Stooges made good use of pie-throwing in such films as *In the Sweet Pie and Pie* (1941) and *Pies and Guys* (1958), and Lucille Ball, on *I Love Lucy*, had a hilarious pie-throwing scene with her crew of Desi Arnaz, Vivian Vance, and William Frawley in the "The Diner" (1954).

Cookies: Hardtack to Soft and Squishy

The art of making cookies and crackers is that of turning simple ingredients into wonderful things. . . . Like cakes and pastries, cookies and crackers are the descendants of the earliest food cooked by man—grain-water-paste baked on hot stones by Neolithic farmers 10,000 years ago.—Cookies and Crackers, 1982[1]

The numbers are staggering. Today, Americans eat over *two billion* cookies a year, averaging about 300 cookies per person. That's 35,000 cookies in a lifetime . . . quite possibly more. In fact, it would be hard to find a household without cookies in them—experts say 95.2 percent of American households harbor a stash of cookies in their kitchens.[2] Amazing to think cookies started as a test.

THE ORIGINAL TEST KITCHEN

Cookies, like cakes and cereals, started as grains. Too hard to chew, humans in the Neolithic age boiled the grains until they formed a stew. The stews became the cakes and a few hundred thousand years later . . . cookies appeared. Not as food, per se. More like a cooking implement so cooks could test a small amount of batter before committing to the whole cake.

How did the cookie taste? How was the texture? Foremost, though, was determining the temperature of the oven—a consequential matter in the days before thermostats. Once the cookie had done its job, you'd imagine someone would eat it. Take it home for the kids? History doesn't say. As far as cookies enjoyed for eating, they appeared in Persia in the seventh century, in Italy in the fourteenth century, and across Europe thereafter.[3]

THE MOST FAMOUS ANCIENT COOKIE OF TODAY

The most famous ancient cookie of today is biscotti. Originally made by the Romans, the dough was baked numerous times, leaving it hard and flavorless but durable. It provided sustenance, if not joy, to sailors and others on long journeys.

When the Roman empire fell in AD 455, so did biscotti. That is—the *old* biscotti. The new biscotti rose up, most suitably, in the Renaissance. It was softer, more enjoyable, and increasingly flavored with rosewater, lemon, slivered almonds, and dried fruits.[4] While the "new" biscotti is enjoyed throughout the world today, the *old* biscotti never left completely. It's called "hardtack" and was eaten (but not enjoyed) by soldiers, sailors, and explorers throughout US history, with a presence in war rations from the Revolutionary War to World War II. Still not delicious.

COOKIES COME TO AMERICA

Eventually, cookies wound up in North America with English, Scotch, and Dutch immigrants who landed in New Amsterdam, later known as New York, in the late 1620s. The name "cookie" comes from the Dutch *koekje*, meaning "small or little cake." No matter what the name, cookies were popular. In 1703, Dutch residents of New York served 800 of them at a funeral, the first record of cookies in the pre–United States.

Like so much else, early cookies were homemade but, as sweeteners were expensive and hard to find, only enjoyed on special occasions. Gingerbread, easier to bake and relatively inexpensive, was one of the first, enjoyed in numerous iterations: "hard" gingerbread, like the gingerbread men of today; soft gingerbread, as in gingerbread cake; and the molasses-flavored ginger "snap," likely named for the sound it makes when bitten.

Another early cookie, the macaroon, originated in the eighth century, made by, many believe, Italian monks. These cookies threaded their way nation-to-nation with the Crusaders and eventually into North America. They were a special favorite of Jews, as they were made of egg whites and almonds, but no flour, making them acceptable for Passover. The coconut was a later addition.[5]

As for the first *American* cookie recipe, that appeared in Amelia Simmons's book *American Cookery*, written in 1796. The name of her cookies was, remarkably, "Cookies." Here's how you make them:

> One pound fugar boiled flowly in half pint of water, fcum well and cool, add 1 tea fpoon perlafh, diffolved in milk, then two and a half pounds of four, rub in 4 ounces of butter, and two large fpoons of finely powdered coriander feed, wet with above; make rolls half an inch thick and cut to the fhape of pleafe; bake fifteen or twenty minutes in a flack oven—good three weeks.[6]

As the centuries passed, ovens became increasingly easier to use and temperatures easier to navigate. And Americans started making more kinds of cookies. The ingredients and style of the cookie depended on the location, culture, and income of whoever was making it. One good example, circa 1912, is the boiled cookie.

The name "boiled cookie" encompasses both the cookie and means of preparation. To make a boiled cookie Kentucky-style, you "stir in a double boiler on the stove, stirring until steaming hot, 5 eggs, and two capfuls of granulated sugar. Let cook, add $1/2$ teaspoon of cloves, cinnamon, allspice and flour, enough to stiffen, also two teaspoonful of baking powder. Bake in moderate oven."[7] A rendition of boiled cookies made in the Ozarks also contained cocoa, oats, peanut butter or coconut, vanilla, and chopped nuts.[8]

Gingerbread and macaroons: early cookie favorites, *Maryann Fisher, Courtesy True Treats*

What is the difference between biscuits and cookies?

Not much. People in the United States like to think British biscuits are actually American cookies. But, as the 100 percent British writer Shakespeare said—what is in a name?

THE EVER-MYSTERIOUS OMNIPRESENT FIG NEWTON

As sugar prices dropped, industry picked up, marketing took off, and manufacturers started mass-producing an array of products—most importantly, cookies. One of the first mass-produced cookies was the Fig Newton. The backstory of Fig Newtons is clear. Well, *some* things are clear anyway. They were first made in 1891, or possibly 1892, when a Philadelphian (or Floridian), James Henry Mitchell, invented a machine to fill a hollow cookie crust with jam, let's say *fig* jam, quickly and conveniently. The machine was soon snatched up by the Kennedy Biscuit Company, although some say Mitchell convinced the company to use it.

Or, the recipe for the fig filling was the brainchild of Charles M. Roser, a cookie maker from Ohio, who worked in a bakery in Philadelphia and sold his recipe to the Kennedy Biscuit Company, which then bought the machinery. Some say Mitchell had an affiliation with the New York Biscuit Company. Regardless, what really matters is what followed.[9]

So, here's what we know for sure: The Kennedy Biscuit Company was operating out of Cambridgeport, Massachusetts, a national candy-making hub at the time. It started manufacturing Newtons in the late 1800s but didn't invent them. As for the name "Newtons"? The company named its products after towns near Boston, and the suburb of Newton was one of them. The addition of "Fig" came a few years later. In 1889, William Moore, founder of the New York Biscuit Company of New York, bought Kennedy Biscuits (and its Fig Newtons) and seven other companies. In 1898, they merged with the American Biscuit and Manufacturing Company, owning, together, a hundred-plus bakeries, to form the National Biscuit Company, known as the formidable N.B.C., which in 1901 morphed into Nabisco.[10]

You're with me, right? *Because* . . . not long after Nabisco took the reins, businesses were making or carrying Fig Newtons nationwide. Only they weren't *the* Fig Newtons. They were knock-offs. To underscore the point, in 1909 one company advertised, "We have a shipment of Fig Newtons of over a ton which we received from the largest bakers of Fig Newtons in the country. . . . They can make better Newtons at a lower price than any other establishment in the country."[11] In 1908, *another* company boasted that it sold fig, date, and prune Newtons.[12] In 1920 people were making homemade "fig newtons," and in 1923 "Fig Newton Crackers" were being sold for 15 cents a pound at Ohio-based Duckwall stores.[13]

Fig Newtons, *Maryann Fisher, Courtesy True Treats*

Throughout this time, Fig Newtons were referred to as the generic "fig newtons" or "fig-filled cookies," and, of course, your basic "newtons" without regard to whether the "Newton" name was uppercase or lowercase. One advice columnist recommended using them for "Fig Newton a la Mode"; "Fig Newton Parfait," which basically entailed crushing the Fig Newtons and adding whipped cream with a dash of vanilla; and "Fig Newton Pudding," which involved heating them in a covered casserole at high heat (425 degrees F) then serving them hot with light cream. And then there's the pièce de résistance, "Fig Newton Ice Cream." Here's what you do:

> Break fig newtons into half a cup of cream until the fig newtons are well crushed. Add salt. Whip remainder of cream stiff and fold into fig newton mixture and add one teaspoon lemon juice and $1/2$ teaspoon vanilla. Turn into a freezing tray of a mechanical refrigerator and freeze for three to four hours. (6 portions)[14]

The Reign of N.B.C.
In 1898, N.B.C. built an enormous bakery in downtown New York, what is today the Chelsea Market, and, largely through acquisitions, launched an impressive variety of cookies. In 1902 the company introduced Barnum's Animal Crackers in the famous decorative box resembling a circus cage filled with animals, and in 1912 both Lorna Doone shortbread cookies and the unstoppable Oreos. Today, Oreos make an appearance as a cereal, snack bar, and part of the growing family of carnival-esque deep-fried foods. Amazing.

Fried Oreos, fried everything, *Susan Benjamin, Courtesy True Treats*

Today, Nabisco is a $25 billion enterprise owned by the Kraft Heinz Company, one of the largest food manufacturers in the world. Whatever the case may be, Fig Newtons are now called "Newtons," because, let's face it, who eats figs these days? As for the other companies? Other Fig Newton makers are around, in various iterations of the name, but none made in Newton, or Cambridgeport for that matter.[15]

BARNUM AND THE ANIMAL CRACKERS

What we need is a society for the prevention of cruelty to animal crackers.—Medbury Says, newspaper satirist, 1923[16]

Before the National Biscuit Company and Animal Crackers, there were "Animals." These "fancy" cookies were originally imported from England, then made locally by Herfield & Ducker in Brooklyn and Vandeveer & Holmes Biscuit Company in New York. These companies, in turn, were bought by the New York Biscuit Company, which, upon becoming N.B.C., eventually dropped the *s* in "Animals" to create Animal Crackers. They also added "Barnum" for P. T. Barnum, the famous circus owner. For decades, the treat was variously called "Barnum's Animal Cookies," "Barnum's Animals," "Barnum's Animal Crackers," "N.B.C. Barnum Animals," and other iterations on the theme, depending on who was selling them.

According to newspaper satirist Medbury Says, "The only way a lot of kids can learn anything about wild animals is through animal crackers. But one father was so cautious of his baby, he wouldn't even let the kid have an animal cracker for a pet."[18]

Originally N.B.C made these multi-named cookies just for Christmas. They became so popular, however, that the company started producing them year-round. In short order, they found a home in American pantries and picnic baskets for decades.[17]

P. T. Barnum (The Inside Scoop)

P. T. Barnum, the greatest self-promoter in marketing history, had absolutely nothing to do with Barnum's Animal Crackers. He never got a cent for it. Not a cut. Not even a licensing fee. This is what happened: In 1889, the audacious Barnum decided to gather up his circus—animals and all—and literally ship them to England for a European debut. That's *ten* railcars worth of circus. The event was a sensation and, seizing the moment, English animal biscuit makers added "Barnum's" to the name of their products and packaged them in a circus

In total there have been thirty-seven different varieties of Animal Crackers since 1902, among them tigers, cougars, camels, rhinoceroses, kangaroos, hippopotami, bison, lions, hyenas, zebras, elephants, sheep, bears, and seals.[19]

motif. The National Biscuit Company, never one to ignore a poaching opportunity, put Barnum's name on its cookie . . . and on US store shelves.[20]

LORNA DOONE SHORTBREAD COOKIES

There are three truly exciting things about Lorna Doone cookies. One is that they're still around, which isn't exactly amazing except that the cookies have no pizzazz. No sprinkles. No fillings. Not even a morsel of color. Yet, we love them. The second is that no one knows anything about Lorna Doone, the cookie's namesake. Some food historians say the cookie may have been named for the lead character in R. D. Blackmore's romance novel *Lorna Doone*, published in 1869. The other amazing thing is that shortbread—the basis and only dimension of the Lorna Doone cookie—is *really* old.

In fact, shortbread dates way back to sixteenth-century Scotland. Originally, it was baked with oatmeal and butter, staples of those of humble means. Shortbread is also a relic of an ancient New Year cake. This shortbread ancestor was round, symbolizing the sun, with notched edges, representing the sun's rays.[21]

How Does Lorna Doone Measure Up?
Love to bake? Why not host your own taste test with samples of homemade shortbread cookies? Or divvy out the recipes and have each guest bring a version. Be sure to include Lorna Doone.

SHORT CAKES MADE AT YE BATHE
(FROM *THE RECEIPT BOOK OF MRS. ANN BLENCOWE*, 1656)

Take a pound of flower & rube into it a half pound of flouwer butter very fine; then put in half a pound of flo sugar & wet it with white wine to a paste; the rowle it very thick & cut it round with ye top of ye Drudger, & knotch it round with a squef & bake them upon a tin.[22]

SCOTS SHORTBREAD
(FROM *THE CONSTANCE SPRY COOKERY BOOK*, 1956)

Good shortbread must be made of the finest ingredients, fresh butter, castor sugar, and white flour. Traditionally shortbread is decorated with orange or candied peel and almonds. It needs lightness of hand and nice judgement, for if the ingredients are worked too much together the result is tough and chewy, instead of being short and melt-in-the-mouth.

  4 oz. fresh butter
  2 oz. castor sugar
  4 oz. fine flour
  2 oz. rice flour or fine semolina
  orange or citron candied peel
  blanched split almonds
  castor sugar

Cream butter, beat in the castor sugar. Add flours by degrees, working quickly and lightly. Immediately after they are incorporated, pat out with the fist to a cake about 3/4 inch in thickness and 8 inches in diameter. Pinch round the edge with pastry pincers or with the fingers. Prick the middle and decorate with strips of the peel and the split almonds. Dust over with castor sugar. Slide on to a baking-sheet covered with a piece of paper dusted with flour and bake in a moderately hot oven 15–20 minutes. The shortbread must be a pale biscuit colour.[23]

LORNA DOONES (FROM THE COOKIE BOX)

As for Lorna Doones? Not exactly close, but close enough, as presented on the cookie box: unbleached enriched flour wheat flour, niacin, reduced iron, thiamine mononitrate (vit b1), riboflavin (vit b2), folic acid, sugar, canola oil, corn flour, salt, high fructose corn syrup, baking soda, soy lecithin, cornstarch, flavor, wheat, soy. Easy to make, though. Just take them out of the box.

OREOS, PLUS THE FIRST OREOS

The year was 1908. A wonderful new cookie entered the world and would stay there for decades. It was a sandwich-type cookie, with two decorative, chocolate exteriors and a creamy white center. It was a hit. That cookie was not, as you may think, the Oreo. It was actually the Hydrox, invented by Jacob Loose, who started his company in 1882. The name was terrible. It was meant to evoke images of water (hence the "Hydro") and sunlight shining through company factories, but instead evoked images of chemicals. Fortunately, the cookie's name was offset by the company name: Sunshine Biscuits.

Then, in 1912, Nabisco came up with a new cookie, right on the tail of Animal Crackers. It was a decorative chocolate sandwich cookie with white cream inside. Who could imagine such an idea? The name of the creation was originally Oreo Biscuit, which changed in 1921 to Oreo Sandwich, then in 1937 to Oreo Creme Sandwich, and finally in 1974 to Oreo Chocolate Sandwich Cookie. Most people simply called them Oreos. Why Oreo? No one knows.

The two chocolate cookies competed for decades, Hydrox always lagging behind. Today Hydrox, produced by its umpteenth owner, is free from artificial ingredients. It fits nicely on grocery store shelves between prize-winner Oreos and the most recent Hydrox look-alike, Newman's Own, whose "Organic Chocolate Vanilla Crème Cookie" they describe as "original." Which, as it is an *organic* cookie, is probably true. A stretch. But true.[24]

S'MORES

S'mores are everywhere. There's s'mores ice cream, s'mores ice cream toppings, and (God help me) s'mores cereal, which should be labeled as a dessert but is not. Regardless of their evolution, s'mores were the product of food traditions that started in the early twentieth century.

Tradition 1: combination candy bars. Flat candy bars were invented by the British in the mid-1800s and adopted by Americans. Combination candy bars are different. They're stuffed with nuts, raisins, nougats, marshmallows, and other toothsome sweets. More than delicious treats (which they were!), candy bars were in the first rations during World War I; used as an "energy bar" and "inexpensive meal in a bar" in the Great Depression; and a vital source of nutrients and sugar in World War II.

Tradition 2: soft sandwich cookies. From Victorians in England to Americans north and south, soft and squishy sandwich cookies were the rage in the first part of the twentieth century and remain so today. Composed of a cookie shell and a soft cream or marshmallow center, iterations included Moon Pies, Whoopie Pies, Mallomars, marshmallow and peanut butter sandwiches (aka fluffernutters), and, of course, s'mores. A second generation followed in the mid-1900s, with such classics as Scooter Pies.

So, Did the Girl Scouts Invent S'mores?

Yes. The Girl Scouts invented a campfire-esque cookie called "Some Mores," which appeared in the Girl Scouts of America's 1927 book *Tramping and Trailing with the Girl Scouts*. The early version and the one we enjoy today (at cookouts—*not* in cereal) are the same.[25] The 1940 *Girl Scout Handbook* has a similar recipe for "Some Mores" that offers interesting alternatives as well, such as using apple slices cut crosswise in place of graham crackers, or pineapple slices or peanut butter instead of chocolate.[26] When did the name change to "S'mores"? No one knows for sure.

GIRL SCOUT COOKIE MAYHEM

Tomorrow is the day the Girl Scout Cookie sale begins! Good Luck to all of you. . . . Use your ingenuity in thinking up possible buyers and do not forget relatives. Here's 12 boxes each for every scout in every troop!—Message to Girl Scouts before first door-to-door sales, 1939[27]

Girl Scout cookie sales, circa 2023
Susan Benjamin, Courtesy True Treats

The Girl Scout Cookie fundraising tradition started in 1917, just five years after the group's inception. The purpose was to raise money for the Girl Scouts' increasingly valuable endeavors *and* to teach young ladies predatory sales strategies and business acumen. This, by the way, was a *good* thing. At that point, women didn't have the right to vote, and most were saddled with low-wage work with few options for advancement. The cookie campaign was revolutionary.

Originally, the Girl Scout Cookies were made by the Girl Scouts themselves. In the 1930s, big business pitched in, making Girl Scout Cookies available for distribution far and wide. You'd imagine the first would be a cookie version of the Girl Scout's own S'mores. Oddly, no. The first S'more cookie didn't show up until 2017. Other flavors came and went over the years—peanut butter cookies, chocolate mints (now Thin Mints), and Do-si-dos, among many others. Today, cookie sales bring in millions each year.[28]

In the late 1930s and '40s, the Girl Scout Cookie got a shake-up on the home front. Not satisfied with enjoying the cookies with a hearty glass of milk or cup of coffee, Americans (mainly women) were finding new uses for them. The genius of their ideas begs the question: why aren't these recipes a mainstay of American dessert traditions today? Here are some ideas sent to the Girl Scout kitchens:

Pep-O-Mint Roll. Crush Peppermint Stick candy, fold into whipped pastry cream, and spread on Girl Scout chocolate cookies, stacking them sandwich style. Wrap in wax paper, let sit in the fridge for a few hours, slice diagonally, and enjoy. (Suggested by Mrs. Julius Blum)

Hawaiian Surprise. Using four Girl Scout cookies per serving, put together sandwich style with filling of crushed pineapple. Top with sweetened whipped cream and garnish with a maraschino cherry. (Suggested by Miss Katheryn Kemp)

Mock Fruit Cake. Break one-half pound (one box) of vanilla cookies into small pieces. Soak in three-quarters cup of evaporated milk; chop one cup each of dates, nuts, and raisins; and mix together with flour. Add classic Fruit Cake spices to milk. Stir and add fruit. Let bake for $1^1/_2$ hours at 300 degrees. (Suggested by Mrs. Clarence G. Fredericks)

Kiss. Put together two Girl Scout cookies, any flavor, or combine flavors with your favorite cake filling, to which has been added chopped fruit or nuts or both. (Suggested by *Mr.* Bert Swensen)[29]

TOLL HOUSE COOKIES

Deliciously Different Chocolate Cookies . . . Toll House Cookies are as much fun to make as they are to serve.—Suburban List food writer, 1939[30]

Toll House Cookies, aka chocolate chip cookies, are a classic and their origin is relatively straight-forward. They were invented by Ruth Graves Wakefield, who had a degree in household arts, worked as a dietitian and food lecturer, and in 1930 published a cookbook titled *Ruth Wakefield's Recipes: Tried and True*, which went into thirty-nine printings.

Ruth also opened the Toll House Inn in Whitman, Massachusetts, with her husband Ken. The inn, originally built in 1709, had been a stopover for weary travelers where they paid tolls, changed horses, and ate home-cooked meals. About 200 years later, Ruth was also cooking homemade meals and baking amazing desserts in the inn's kitchen. The inn was still a New England destination.

And it was there Ruth had a problem. She was making a batch of Butter Drop Do cookies for her guests but, unfortunately, she ran out of baker's chocolate. So, she cut chocolate bits from a semisweet Nestlé chocolate bar she happened to have and put them in the batter. She expected them to melt, but they didn't. They *softened*, a soft and delicious softening. She named her creation the "Toll House Cookie."

The cookie took off. Newspapers featured it. People *loved* it. Said one journalist, "These delicious cookies . . . are called 'Toll House Cookies' because Ruth Wakefield of New England's famous Toll House Inn originated them. These cookies are sure to delight your family and bridge club, too, they're new and different. Crisp, tender golden-brown cookies, and when you bite into one—*surprise*! There's a rich bite of semi-sweet chocolate."[31]

Chocolate chip cookie, *Susan Benjamin and Maryann Fisher, Courtesy True Treats*

But no one loved Toll House Cookies quite so much as Andrew Nestlé. He loved them so much, he struck an agreement with Ruth. If he could put the recipe on the chocolate's wrapper, she could have as much chocolate as she wanted throughout her life. She agreed. Nestlé got another idea riffing off the Toll House Cookie's success. Score the Semi-Sweet Chocolate Bar and package it with a special chopper, so customers could cut the bar into small morsels.

Then, in 1939, Nestlé had the best idea yet. He created ready-made morsels, what the company called Nestlé Toll House Real Semi-Sweet Chocolate Morsels and we now call "chocolate chips." Ruth's recipe was on the packaging. In 1967 the Wakefields sold the Toll House Inn. Ruth Wakefield died in 1977, and in 1984 the inn burned down. But the recipe still remains on the packaging where it belongs.[32, 33]

Author's note: Did Ruth really invent chocolate chip cookies? People *were* melting chocolate in to make chocolate cookies. Most likely someone, maybe lots of someones, also added chocolate bits as Ruth did. But if they did, they didn't tell anyone, so Ruth gets the credit. Thank you, Ruth.

THE WONDER OF NO-BAKE COOKIES

Also called "faux-cookies," no-bake cookies are precisely what they say—you don't bake them. They descend from ancient Middle Eastern foods made with nuts, dried fruit, seeds, and even flower petals all pressed together with honey, cane, or some other sugar. No-bake cookies were popular during the Great Depression. They were tasty, easy to make, and inexpensive, as they didn't require fuel for ovens, flour, or expensive ingredients. Fat, such as peanut butter, butter, or cream cheese, could even replace higher-priced sugar as a binding agent.

Delicious "No-Bake" Recipes

DATE BALLS (FROM *THE JOY OF COOKING*, 1936)

Stone: 1 pound dates, or use $^1/_2$ pound seeded dates. Put them through a food chopper with: 1 cup chopped pecan meats. Add: $^1/_4$ teaspoon salt. Shape the candy into tiny balls. Roll them in: Powdered sugar.[34]

FRUIT COOKIES (FROM *GRANDDAUGHTER'S INGLENOOK COOKBOOK*, 1942)

1 lb. raisins	1 c. nuts
1 lb. figs	1 lb. graham crackers
1 lb. dates	2 tb. lemon juice
1 lb. cooked prunes	2 tb. honey

Grind fruit and nuts; add lemon juice and honey. Mix thoroughly and make into roll. Keep in refrigerator. Serve thin slices.[35]

RAISIN PEANUT BALLS (FROM *SEARCHLIGHT RECIPE BOOK*, 1952)

$^1/_2$ Cup Peanut Butter
1 Cup Raisins
1 Tablespoon Lemon Juice
$^1/_4$ teaspoon cinnamon
$^1/_4$ Cup Powdered Sugar
$^1/_2$ Cup Shredded Coconut
$^1/_4$ Teaspoon Salt

Plump raisins by steaming. Drain and chop. Roll coconut into fine pieces. Toast to a light brown in moderate oven (370 degrees F.). Mix peanut butter, sugar, lemon juice, cinnamon, salt, and raisins. Blend thoroughly. Shape into small balls. Roll in toasted coconut.[36]

HOLIDAY APRICOT BALLS (FROM *BETTY CROCKER'S COOKY BOOK*, 1963)

1 pkg. (8 oz.) dried apricots, ground or finely cut
$2^1/_2$ cups flaked coconut
$^3/_4$ sweetened condensed milk
1 cup finely chopped nuts

Blend apricots, coconut, and milk well. Shape in small balls. Roll in chopped nuts. Let stand about 2 hr. to firm. Makes about 5 doz. balls.[37]

A SURVEY OF TODAY'S COOKIES

The cookie possibilities are mesmerizing, as are options for food preparation: packaged, very likely; made in bakeries, somewhat likely; made fresh at home, unlikely; made at home with help from, say, Betty Crocker's mixes and the Pillsbury Doughboy's dough, a bit less unlikely; sold at church fairs and rummage sales, very likely and usually very good.

To avoid confusion, here are nine basic types of cookies, based on how the dough is handled:

Bar cookies: dense cake-like consistency, such as brownies and lemon bars.

Drop cookies: dough dropped from a spoon and flattened into a cookie, such as chocolate chip and oatmeal cookies.

Filled cookies: cookie dough that is stuffed with fruit, jam, or other confections; think all the flavors of Newtons.

Molded cookies: made from a stiff dough molded into shapes, such as Christmas wreaths or gingerbread men.

Fried cookies: fried dough, often dusted with powdered sugar.

Many cookies, many uses, *Maryann Fisher, Courtesy True Treats*

Pressed cookies: made from a soft dough using a cookie press (cookie gun) or pastry bag to form into various decorative shapes.

Refrigerator or icebox cookies: a stiff dough that is refrigerated in logs until it becomes hard and then sliced, such as shortbread cookies.

Cutout cookies: made from a stiff, chilled dough, then rolled out and cut into shapes with a cookie cutter, knife, or pastry wheel; limitless possibilities.

Sandwich cookies: rolled or pressed cookies that are assembled as a sandwich with a sweet filling: frosting, ganache, jam, marshmallow crème, and peanut butter crème are popular. Think Whoopie Pie, Moon Pie, Oreo, and most definitely Hydrox.[38]

Sand tart cookies and antique cookie cutters
Maryann Fisher, Courtesy True Treats

Hoot and Holler!

Men on Couches: Chips, Dips, and Football Games

Nowhere is snack food more at home than by the couch. I am speaking of the many chips, dips, meats, and salsas that festoon American coffee tables and kitchen counters when company comes, especially during football season. The range extends from tender chicken wings to crunchy chips with salsa. Central to them all: easy to eat with minimal utensils that only distract from otherwise engrossing TV viewing.

Chips and would-be dip, *Susan Benjamin, Courtesy True Treats*

CHICKEN WINGS

Americans eat around 1.42 billion wings during Super Bowl Sunday.—National Chicken Council, 2022[2]

Americans have enjoyed chicken wings throughout US history for hundreds of years. That's a relatively small amount of time in chicken history, seeing they started life in northern China about 12,000 years ago. They weren't domesticated until 5,400 years ago and left Asia roughly 3,000 years ago, traveling the world thanks to human intervention. As chickens don't excel at flying, swimming, or running, they had no other way to leave. A few showed up in the Americas between AD 700 and 1390, but arrived en masse in the 1600s via the Atlantic, with Portuguese and Dutch slave traders, and the Pacific, with traders from Asia. It wasn't until the 1800s that chicken settled onto the American table, and the late twentieth century that chicken wings, in a culinary sense, took off.[3]

Yes, chicken wings have been eaten in North America for centuries. They were slow-cooked in the South and served at restaurants in Buffalo, New York, where the Clarendon Hotel dished out "Fried Chicken Wings," and in Boston in 1890, where "Fricassee of Chicken Wings" was advertised by the M. Hills Restaurant. Yes, chicken wings were eaten, but remained in the lower echelon of foods, typically relegated to soups and stews along with lowly necks and backs.

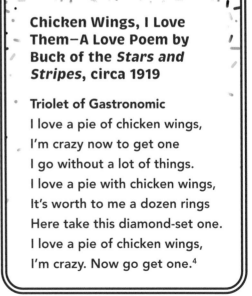

Chicken Wings, I Love Them—A Love Poem by Buck of the *Stars and Stripes*, circa 1919

Triolet of Gastronomic
I love a pie of chicken wings,
I'm crazy now to get one
I go without a lot of things.
I love a pie with chicken wings,
It's worth to me a dozen rings
Here take this diamond-set one.
I love a pie of chicken wings,
I'm crazy. Now go get one.[4]

In fact, by the early 1900s, bureaucrats in meatpacking hubs such as St. Louis, Kansas City, and Chicago considered chicken wings so insignificant, they discarded them. For workers, wings were a culinary boon, free for the taking. By the mid-1900s, most Americans finally agreed, as ever more creative chicken wing recipes appeared in newspapers and magazines. Among the variety were deviled chicken wings in 1924, chicken wings and backs with eggplant in 1930, and chicken wing stew in 1943. One Swanson ad in 1950 gave perspective to the rising popularity of chicken wings with its "New idea for using old favorites—potato salad and chicken wings." Chicken wings an *old* favorite? Good to know. The ad went on to say: "Made for all the chicken wing lovers in your family." Indeed.[5]

Enter Argia Collins

In 1957, Argia Collins rocked the chicken wing world. An African American born in Mississippi, he moved to Chicago when he was young. After serving in the US Navy during World War II, and spending two years at business college, he opened the first of two restaurants in 1950. His forte was barbecue. Only one problem: Chicago sauces were bland and, in his opinion, not worth eating. So, returning to his Southern culinary roots, Collins made a sauce that was a delicious riot of sweet, tangy, savory, sublime flavors. He called it Mumbo Sauce. Today, Collins's mumbo is sold nationwide and is an inspiration for legions of chicken and—most importantly—chicken *wing* favorites.[6, 7]

Two Tales of One City

Many food lovers claim the popularity of chicken wings took off with the Buffalo wing. Who invented them and when remains a source of contention. One thing everyone agrees on—Buffalo wings started in Buffalo, New York.

TALE #1: THE ANCHOR BAR

The Anchor Bar's wings were the intermarriage of churchgoers and quick thinking. The year was 1964, and the Catholic Church's no-meat-on-Friday edict was in full force. Mass ended and hungry parishioners took to the streets in search of a bite to eat. Teressa Bellissimo, owner of the Anchor Bar, was busily at work when the crowds descended. No meat. Hungry worshippers. What to do? She wanted to serve up chicken but had accidentally bought chicken *wings*, not the other more-useful parts. She had no choice but to drum up chicken wings. So she did, serving fried, broken pieces tossed in hot sauce she happened to have. The crowd went crazy. They loved it! Eight short years later, the Anchor Bar was making thirteen and a half *tons* of chicken wings, in mild, medium, and spicy hot flavors, over the Christmas season alone. Numerous iterations of the story have appeared in publications ever since.[8]

In the early 1960s, John Young opened a restaurant called Wings and Things in Buffalo. His signature dish was breaded, whole wings tossed in Young's own mumbo sauce. Ten years later, Young moved to Illinois, and upon returning to Buffalo in another ten years, was surprised that (1) so many wing joints had set up shop in his absence, and (2) the Anchor Bar claimed to have invented the Buffalo wing they were serving. The Anchor Bar?? But it was Wings and Things that served the first wings! In fact, Young claimed Bellissimo actually ate *his* wings before "inventing" hers. Over the years, Young lobbied hard for the position of number one. Whether or not he got there depends on the account you are reading.[9]

Today's Wings: Wing Anatomy Lesson

Today, when we say "wings," what are we really eating? Chicken wings are literally broken into three parts. Drumettes, popular since the 1960s, look like tiny drumsticks. They offer an advantage to TV viewers watching, say, football games, as they can comfortably hold the drumette in one hand, eat the whole thing in a clean, smooth bite, and never have to look away from the screen. The second part of the wing, the wingette, is flat, thin, and especially tasty. No controversy there. As for the third part, that would be the small, pointy tip that generally goes the way of chicken wings of the past: people toss them. In fact, most people favor tip-less wings over whole ones, although some experts caution against it. They say the tips hold more flavor and have a delicious crunch to them.[10]

CHIPS AND DIP

> *Miss Emily Post says potato chips may be eaten with the fingers. Something tells us Miss Emily must have tried to spear one with a fork.* —News item about Emily Post, socialite and renowned etiquette authority, 1936[11]

Behold the Potato Chip

How did potato chips, the superstar of the dipping universe, originate? It's hard to say. No question, people had been frying sliced potatoes in oil, lard, or whatever else was available for ages. Recipes on the subject go back to newspapers in the early 1800s and make an appearance in such cookbooks as Mary Randolph's *Virginia House-Wife* in 1824. While they were crunchy and good, potato chips were, even more importantly, substantial (able to fill the stomach), affordable (potatoes grow happily in even rugged terrains), and indifferent to the condition of the potato (Speckled with eyes? Who cares. Fry them up.).

So, when did potato chips become *potato chips*? Sources everywhere tell us this happened: The year was 1852. The place, the Moon's Lake House Inn, Saratoga Springs, New York. The chef, George Crum, was preparing a classic meat and potatoes meal for his guests. Only difference from today—the meat would have been woodcock or partridge and the potatoes French fries. A customer complained that the French fries were too thick and sent them back.

Crum was aghast. The impertinence! How dare *anyone* criticize his fries. In retaliation, he cut the potato into insultingly thin wafers, then sent them from the kitchen curled and brittle. That, as you may have guessed, was the first potato chip. The person being served was not offended by the brittle bits—he was dazzled and delighted. In fact, he loved them so much that the proprietress, Harriet Moon, vowed to serve them every day. The diner was none other than the wealthy steamship owner Cornelius Vanderbilt.

So, true story? Not true? The answer: not true-ish. In the summer of 1852, when the said meal was served, Vanderbilt was off vacationing in Europe with his family. (Although, let it be known, for decades afterward the Vanderbilt family embraced the legacy that their descendent discovered the potato chip.) Proprietress Harriet Moon had yet to purchase the Lake House. And, it seems, Crum never exacted revenge on diners. However, he *was* a chef, and he *did* serve fried potatoes that were so delicious, they were called "Saratoga Chips." Only . . . back in July of 1849, the *New York Herald* reported from the Lake House that "Eliza, the cook," whose "potato frying reputation is one of the prominent matters of remark at Saratoga," was making potato chips. "Who would think," the *Herald* reporter wrote, "that simple potatoes could be made such a luxury!"[13]

In 1860, Crum opened his own restaurant, called Crum's House, where he served thinly sliced fried potatoes to clientele including Cornelius Vanderbilt.[14] Word spread, and Crum's potato chips swelled into an international sensation.

Whether he invented potato chips or not, you would think Crum could have patented the creation. Even if people were frying potatoes and, essentially, creating potato chips, he *did* popularize them. Only, at that time, people of color were not allowed to patent their inventions and so, Crum, who was half African American and half Native American, never did.[15]

POTATO CHIPS: THE HEALTH FOOD

Serve Lay's Potato Chip as the vegetable you don't have to cook . . . and even youngsters with finicky appetites will clean their plates. —Lay's ad, 1957[16]

By the late 1800s, Saratoga Chips were manufactured nationwide, from Kansas to Portland, Maine, where they were made fresh every day. By the 1920s, when industry was infusing old foods with new identities, potato chips became more than a sidekick to hamburgers. They were, remarkably enough, a health food.

So, why were potato chips considered a health food and not just a snappy fun food? That goes back to the potatoes themselves, long valued for their remarkable curative powers. In eighteenth-century Europe, for example, medical authorities believed potatoes' nutritional powers were strong enough to cure such ailments as leprosy.[17]

According to the Northern Plains Potato Growers Association, the average American eats around 4 pounds of chips a year, equaling 1.5 billion pounds of potato chips. Around 11.2 million pounds of chips are eaten on Super Bowl Sunday alone.[18]

By default, potato chips were endowed with the potato's powers. In 1927, one physician asserted that potato chips had high mineral content, high nutritive value, and were "capable of meeting the protein requirements of the body." Even better, potato chips could be "a substitute for meat, and when used with other vegetables and fats in the diet, can easily help to make a balanced meal." And, because they are rich in potash salt, potato chips can even replace cereals, which may create an acid stomach.[19] Even into the 1950s, potato chips were marketed as a healthy food alternative to vegetables.

But something else was at work where potato chips were concerned. They, and potatoes in general, were considered an aphrodisiac. In the 1930s, along came the aptly named Herman Lay, the man who transformed humble, albeit healthy, potato chips into a commercial powerhouse. Potato chips an aphrodisiac? Why deny it? Lay didn't deny it. Potato chips took off.[20]

Potatoes are native to the Peruvian-Bolivian Andes, where farmers cultivated them as early as 8,000 years ago. Throughout history, they have been used as a starch, much like grain-based flour; a sweetener, much like sugar; and, of course, a filling and delicious food.[21]

In the early days, potato chips were sold bulk and in tins, leaving the bottom layer broken and stale. For chips to truly succeed, they had to be packaged so people could buy them, intact, with a manageable shelf life. For that, we can thank Laura Clough Scudder, a prohibitionist, nurse, restaurant owner, and, above all, potato chip maker. She knew the problem. She found the solution. The perfect potato chip bag.

To get there, she asked her employees to iron wax paper sheets together at home, then fill them at the chip factory the next day. The result was the dawn of the airtight, protective bags we use today. Scudder literally sealed the deal through another food-saving concept: expiration dates. All this was wrapped in her marketing tagline: "Laura Scudder's Potato Chips, the Noisiest Chips in the World." Laura Scudder's chips are still around today.[22]

Laura Scudder's Creamed Chicken with Potato Chips

Like other food manufacturers, Laura Scudder put recipes in her advertising campaigns. Here's one for creamed chicken with potato chips. Old-fashioned. Well worth considering.

Prepare chicken in cream gravy with fresh peas. In small ramekins, place a layer of fresh potato chips. Fill with cream chicken and top with finely crushed chips. Place the ramekin in the oven to brown on top. Serve the ramekin in the center of the dinner plate and serve with crisp Mayflower potato chips. This is a delightful change from chicken on toast.[23]

HERMAN LAY AND OSCAR THE HAPPY POTATO

Lay's Potato Chips sharpen the appetite for foods important to a well-balanced diet . . . because Lay's Potato Chips are salted just right to delightfully accent the flavor of all the other foods you serve.—Lay's ad featuring Oscar the Happy Potato, 1957[24]

The beginning of the potato chip titans—the ones who dominate the potato chip industry today—started when Herman Lay became an on-the-road salesman for Barrett Food Products. Lay's trajectory was clear from early on. Born in 1909 in Charlotte, North Carolina, Lay opened his first ice cream stand at age ten. In 1932, he started working for Barrett Food Products. By year's end he had borrowed $100 to lease one of the company's warehouses and manufacture his own peanut butter cracker sandwiches and Lay's Tennessee Valley Popcorn, which was, essentially, French-fried popcorn.

Lay's chip rack, *Susan Benjamin, Courtesy True Treats*

In 1944, when Herman Lay started manufacturing Lay's Potato Chips under his own name, he enlisted Oscar the Happy Potato, the company's first spokesperson, to spread the word. It's true, Oscar was a mere sketch of a potato. But he was good enough to star in the first television ad for snack food on television, push Lay's ahead of the snack food pack, and return for years after he was first created.[25]

Oscar's messaging to moms was multifaceted. Naturally, he advised them, "When kiddies come home from school, give them Lay's Potato Chips in the red and blue bag." Should mom wonder *why* she should serve Lay's Potato Chips, Oscar was on hand to tell her Lay's chips were "easily digestible and highly nutritious."[26] Even better, he told mom this improbable nutritional tip: "Serve Lay's Potato Chips as the vegetable you don't have to cook."[27]

Like other "spokespersons" and real-life chip innovators, Oscar provided chip recipes and chip-related updates. In 1950, for example, he gave buyers the good news: "Now you'll notice something better-than-ever about Lay's Potato Chips—they're destarched, dextrinized . . . with extra starch removed." Good to know, all would agree. All the while Oscar reminded consumers with his wide potato smile that potato chips are "happy" food.[28]

But businesses cannot live by cartoon alone, and so, in 1963, Lay's advertisers came up with a blockbuster slogan: "Betcha can't eat just one."[29] It was compelling, frenetic, energetic, and endlessly repeatable, used and reused throughout the nation and other parts of the world. And, yes, consumers everywhere tested their wits to see if they could eat just one. It's unlikely any succeeded.

Small Potato Chip Companies Still in Business Today

Some of the original, small potato chip companies are still around today. Most have second- or third-hand owners, but even these newcomers aren't big business. Why not visit one near you, if you have the chance?

1908: Leominster Potato Chip Co., Leominster, MA (name later changed to Tri-Sum)

1910: Mikesell's Potato Chips, Dayton, OH

1919: Grippo's Potato Chips, Cincinnati, OH

1921: Wise Delicatessen Company, Berwick, PA

1921: Utz, Hanover, PA

1921: Magic Food Co., later Golden Flake, Birmingham, AL (now owned by Utz)

1926: Scudder's, Monterey Park, CA[30]

The story of Elmer Doolin's business more or less parallels Herman Lay's, until the two finally converged. In 1932, Doolin was operating an ice cream business. The business was struggling and Doolin needed an out. He found it by happenstance when he stopped by a San Antonio café where he bought a five-cent, plain package of corn chips. The chips were also known as *fritos*—a Spanish word for "fried"—which cooks flattened, seasoned, and fried.

The Sinister Frito Bandito

No question, the Frito Bandito was Mexican. Frito-Lay saw to that. No blond-haired kid, the Bandito was fully grown—albeit very short—with a sombrero, pitch-black greasy hair, a handlebar mustache, and a ready display of guns. His teeth were proportionally large—all the better to snivel at you—and his English highly nasal and flawed, as only a truly racist character could be. His theme song, riffed off the folk song "Cielito Lindo," was sinister, too: "Ay, ay, ay, ay! Oh, I am dee Frito Bandito. I like Fritos corn chips, I love them, I do. I want Fritos corn chips, I'll get them, from you. Ay, ay, ay, ay! Oh, I am dee Frito Bandito. Give me Fritos corn chips and I'll be your friend. The Frito Bandito you must not offend."

The American public seemed to enjoy the xenophobic ads, but the National Mexican-American Anti-Defamation Committee (NMAADC) felt differently and, in 1968, launched a protest against the ads. Frito-Lay was unrepentant, saying that 85 percent of Mexican Americans liked the Bandito. But, under continued pressure, the company gave him a friendlier countenance. After the assassination of Robert Kennedy, they even took away the Bandito's guns.

Eventually, radio stations started boycotting the ads, and after a multimillion-dollar lawsuit, the Frito Bandito went the way of the Frito Kid and disappeared. Fritos brand dipped into other ad campaigns, then, tired of it all, I suppose, took a fifty-year hiatus. In 2019, they finally launched an ad campaign, this one digital-only and broadcast during the Super Bowl featuring guys on couches, eating their chips.[31]

Turns out the café owner wanted to sell his operation and return to Mexico. Doolin seized the moment and bought the business, including the recipe, nineteen retail accounts, and an old handheld potato ricer, using money he borrowed from his mother. Then, he took to the road, selling his products from a Model T Ford. At night, Doolin made chips in his family's garage.

Doolin's corn chips took off with only a blip during World War II. The business rebounded, leaving him with revenues exceeding $27 million. A key to his success was licensing agreements for other companies to sell his products. And guess who was looking to expand their product line? That would be Lay's. Before you knew it, H. W. Lay & Company got an exclusive franchise to manufacture and distribute Fritos in the Southeast. And the two companies were almost one.

Lay's marketed "their" Fritos with gusto, adding an advisory should customers turn to other corn chips: "Eat Fritos, but remember there's only one Fritos made by Lay's." Hovering over the familiar-looking Fritos bag was Oscar the Happy *Potato*, which is odd, as you can imagine, since Fritos are made with corn. A year later, Frito introduced Chee-tos brand cheese-flavored snacks—an immediate hit—and embarked on a Lay-esque advertising campaign . . . only Oscar the Happy Potato was a blond-haired, friendly kind of guy named the Frito Kid in 1952. The Frito Kid was later replaced by the sinister Frito Bandito in 1967 and later the Muncha Bunch cowboys.

The Frito-Lay arrangement, profitable as it was, was more like friends with benefits than a lifelong union. So, two years after Doolin's death, the Frito Company merged with H. W. Lay and settled into a permanent arrangement as Frito-Lay, Inc. Four years later, in 1965, Frito-Lay merged with the Pepsi-Cola Company to become the behemoth chip-making enterprise it is today.[32]

The Underlying Factor That Drove the Chip's Success . . . Dip Dunks

The dips we know today didn't start as dips but as dunks. Basically, you *dunked* the vegetable, cracker, chip, or whatever you liked into whatever else you liked. You served these dunks *with dips* on a dunking "tray," which held a cup or small bowl with the dunk/dip.

Here are some that appeared in the *Woman's Home Companion Cook Book* in 1942:

Suggestions for Hot Dunking Trays

Hors d'Oeuvres: Codfish balls, hot seafood hors d'oeuvres, tuna-fish cones, cocktail sausages and frankfurters, corned-beef hash balls. Sauces: For fish and seafood hors d'oeuvres serve hot savory cocktail sauce or gourmet cocktail sauce or tartar sauce; for meat hors d'oeuvres, mustard cream sauce or hot savory cocktail sauce. Garnish the tray with crisp radish roses, carrot curls, celery curls, stuffed cucumbers, pickle fans, olives.

Suggestions for Cold Dunking Trays

Hors d'Oeuvres: Raw oysters arranged on cracked ice, cold cooked shrimp and lobster, raw-vegetable hors d'oeurvres, chicken rolls, dried-beef balls, gherkins in blankets, lettuce rolls, stuffed cucumbers, roast beef rolls. Sauces: Russian dressing or Thousand Island dressing, gourmet cocktail sauce or standard cocktail sauce, or tartar sauce . . .

Potato-Chip Scoop Tray

Fill a bowl with any soft savory cheese spread or with drained cottage cheese seasoned with salt, pepper and onion juice. Sprinkle with finely chopped parsley and paprika. Surround with crisp potato chips. The guests use the potato chips as scoops to dip into the spread. Crisp crackers may also be used.[33]

THE RISE OF DIPDOM

At the end of World War II, new dips appeared in multitudinous forms, using chips as a server. The art of dip-making was taught in home economics classes, and dips were recommended for bridge games, picnics, and parties and appeared in numerous guides, such as "Dipwiches," essentially French toast with fillings.[34] Dairy was at the heart of most dips in the 1950s, be it mayonnaise, sour cream, cream cheese, or the once-venerable cottage cheese, as is or strained.

From this confluence came the mid-twentieth-century California Dip, a cross between seventeenth-century French onion flavor and early nineteenth-century sour cream. No one knows exactly who invented California Dip—the story goes that a "homemaker" invented it, word spread, and other homemakers started making it, all in California. Regardless, the

Super Bowl onion dip, *Susan Benjamin, Courtesy True Treats*

Lipton Soup Company seized the moment and created its own California Dip, using its Lipton Onion Soup Mix. Lipton's arrival was fortuitous. The mix was convenient and women of the 1950s loved convenience. Instant soup mix? Perfect. Sour cream? Wonderful. Mixed together as a dip for social occasions? Fabulous! In short, one dip in a matter of seconds.

Soon, Lipton came up with an extensive advertising campaign with colorful ads in newspapers and magazines, soup-mix-centered cookbooks, and, in 1958, the French Onion Dip recipe on the soup mix box, where it still resides today.[35]

SALAD DRESSINGS WITHOUT THAT WORRISOME SALAD

French onion soup is not the only food that is one-part dinner food, one-part dip. Salad dressing, for example, took a leading role in dip history, especially the mayo-based Russian and French dressings. American-made Russian dressing is not remotely Russian, and American French dressing is closer to American Russian dressing than the French dressing in France, which is basically vinegar and oil. In fact, Russian dressing in Russia was based on the French "vinaigrette." Confused? Don't worry. Here's what you need to know: the French and Russian dressings we eat in the United States are purely American inventions.

If you're in the mood for Russian dressing, no matter how you use it, leave the bottles at the grocery store and try one of these old-time recipes:

Vegetable Salad with Russian Dressing, 1912

For this delicious salad, arrange on lettuce some string beans, asparagus, beets, and corn. Serve with Russian dressing, which is made by thinning a mayonnaise dressing with chili sauce, chopped parsley, onion, and green pepper.[36]

Russian Dressing, 1914

A very excellent recipe for "Russian Dressing" is as follows: Get a large bowl and mixer, then beat yolk of 3 eggs, 1 teaspoon of mustard and 1 of salt, a dash of paprika and $1/2$ cup vinegar. Mix up well and, while mixing, add 1 pinch olive oil and continue mixing until thick. Strain one-half bottle of chili sauce through a cloth and mix what remains with the dressing. Add some chopped chives and a dash of Worcestershire sauce and the dressing is complete.[37]

French and Russian aside, ranch dressing reigns among the top-performing Super Bowl dips. Unlike other dips, such as hummus and tzatziki, it did not originate in the Middle East or

> ### What is the *real* French dressing?
> French dressing is essentially a vinaigrette, containing olive oil and vinegar or lemon juice, or part lemon juice and part vinegar, and a dash of sugar, salt, and pepper or paprika, says Fanny Farmer in the influential *Boston Cooking-School Cook Book*.[38]

Mediterranean, it did not exist in the eighteenth or even nineteenth centuries, and it has never been held in high esteem by those in the elite food world.

The story goes that Steve Henson was living in Alaska with his wife Gayle in 1949. Before then, Henson "rode the rails" cross-country, taking odd jobs. Once in Alaska, he became a successful plumbing contractor. That's when he invented a dressing made with the classic base of mayonnaise and herbs and spices such as garlic, onion, pepper, and parsley, *and*, for a twist, buttermilk, to serve his hungry workers. Granted, it's hard to imagine work crews stopping to gather up forks, knives, and napkins and dive into a tasty, nicely dressed salad, but never mind.

At age thirty-five, the plumber-turned-chef was able to retire and head home to Nebraska and buy the Sweetwater Ranch, soon renamed "Hidden Valley Ranch." Once again, he was confronted with hungry crowds, only this time it was guests at the ranch, there to fish, ride, hike, and enjoy other outdoor activities then return to a home-cooked meal. And guess what dressing was on the salad?

Word spread, as so often happens in these stories, and Henson began selling make-your-own Hidden Valley Ranch dressing (a packet of dried herbs and spices) to the Cold Spring Tavern, then nearby store Kelley's Korner, then through a mail-order business established in his living room. By the late 1960s, he was filling orders for the dressing to all fifty states and more than thirty countries.

Hidden Valley Ranch soon added other dip packages, including a blue cheese dip option, a perfect segue into

The ever-eclectic ranch dressing, *Maryann Fisher, Courtesy True Treats*

the chicken wing dipping arena. But that was in the mid-1970s, a few years after the Henson story looped around to its most logical conclusion. Steve Henson, the onetime successful plumber, sold his business to Clorox.[40] Today, an online search for Hidden Valley yields over two million results.[41]

CHIPS AND DIPS: MEXICAN STYLE

Fritos aren't the only pseudo-Mexican chips on the market today. The variety is almost overwhelming, many owned by Frito-Lay with their Tostitos and Doritos, all very Mexican-ish. The dips that accompany them are likewise Mexican-ish, although some are truly of Mexican origin. Salsa is the most prominent, of course, in an array of styles made by an array of companies.

Salsa—What's in a Word?

For centuries, Americans have been embroiled in confusion about the true meaning of salsa. Is it a relish? A sauce? A chunky version of hot sauce? And, up until recently, as iterations reached the kitchens (and restaurants) of most Americans, the confusion has not been resolved. The funny thing is that, unlike other foods, salsa drew closer to its original use in Mexico as its popularity grew. Did I say *Mexico*? Actually, salsa originated in Mexico and the many nations of Central America.

EARLY SALSA—HERE'S WHAT WE DO KNOW

What Europeans of the sixteenth century knew about salsa came from Bernardino de Sahagún, a Spanish Franciscan friar and missionary who traveled to New Spain, aka Mexico, in 1529 when he was thirty years old. He spent the next fifty years there, chronicling the Aztecs' beliefs and lifestyles, all the while trying to change them. Among his writings, he detailed Aztec foodways, as in this excerpt from a translated edition:

> He sells foods, sauces, hot sauces, fried [food], olla-cooked, juices, sauces of juices, shredded [food] with chile, with squash seeds, with tomatoes, with smoke chile, with hot chile, with yellow chile, with mild red chile sauce, yellow chile sauce, sauce of smoked chile, heated sauce, he sells toasted beans, cooked beans, mushroom sauce, sauce of small squash, sauce of large tomatoes, sauce of ordinary tomatoes, sauce of various kinds of sour herbs, avocado sauce.

The large red tomatoes are today's red tomatoes, and the ordinary tomatoes are likely tomatillos. As for the chilies—these could be chipotle or smoked jalapeño with avocado sauce, essentially today's guacamole.[42]

Tomatoes, *Susan Benjamin, Courtesy True Treats*

The Secret of Excellent Mexican Food is largely due to the "salsa," the sauce of chili gravy.
—*South Bend Tribune*, 1926[44]

The steps to today's adoration of salsa took place one hot sauce at a time. Interestingly, the first hot sauce was bottled in Boston in 1807. From there, other hot sauces bubbled up, including the first Tabasco sauce, made by Edmund McIlhenny in the late 1860s. McIlhenny originally sold his aged Tabasco pepper sauce in 350 used cologne bottles. Everyone who tasted the sauce survived and apparently enjoyed it, edging salsa the dip toward its unique existence.[45]

By the late 1800s, salsa had started to reach the nomenclature of American foods. Even then, the recipes and ads had definitions so European Americans, the most financially solvent consumers, would know what they were buying. Some publications referred to salsa as pepper sauce (1908), as a sauce made after an Italian recipe (1929), and as "a relish. But none seemed to use "dip."

As the definition of salsa varied, its use continued to expand. Mrs. Robert Louis Stevenson contributed a recipe to the *Boston Globe* in 1893, made for "invalids." Called "Raw Beef and Salsa Sandwich," it was essentially a spicy paste with a dash of vinegar and oil atop raw meat hidden within folds of bread.[46] In 1925, one hodgepodge of a recipe was called "Tuna Mexicante"—a croquette made with canned tuna fish and salsa picante, described as a "well-made tomato sauce." In the late 1930s, companies were still trying to define the meaning of salsa, but in a utilitarian sense such as "Delicious with fish, steaks, Spanish rice, seafood cocktails, salad dressings, etc."

> Salsa as medicine? Originally salsa was thought to ward off fevers and other maladies and stimulate the digestive organs, especially the liver.[43]

In 1947, manufacturing lurched salsa into the future. One version was from Dave and Margaret Pace, who operated a small operation manufacturing syrups, salad dressings, and jellies in the back of their store in San Antonio. As with most rags-to-riches stories, they sold their products door-to-door. Eventually, Dave added picante sauce. By 1992, the top eight salsa manufacturers were Pace, Old El Paso, Frito-Lay, Chi-Chi's, La Victoria, Ortega, Herdez, and Newman's Own.[47]

SALSA INTO THE FUTURE—CREATIVE MEETS JOLTING

A barrage of creative and often jolting recipes using salsa appeared in recipe books and newspaper cooking sections in the 1950s. One was "Chicken with Fresh Tomato Salsa." Said a write-up in the *Oakland Tribune* in 1959: "Here's a new [recipe] that's popular with men.

> By 1991, salsa had surpassed ketchup as the best-selling condiment in the United States. Today, salsa and chips are the #1 favorite snack food during the Super Bowl.[48] In 2020, more than 218 million Americans purchased salsa, a number that was expected to increase to 224.64 million the following year. And that's only the store-bought kind![49]

Chicken with fresh tomato salsa, featuring the pleasing contrasts of hot and cold chicken, and a relish of fresh tomatoes, green chili, onion, celery or cabbage, and California wine." That's California wine in the *salsa*—not the glass. The author includes other uses of green chili salsa, including this interesting blend called "Green Chili Aspic Salsa": "Blend one package of lemon gelatin with $1^1/_2$ cups of hot water, add one can of green chili, and one can of all-American tomato sauce. Chill and serve on a bed of lettuce with mayonnaise on top."[50]

By the 1960s, salsa was sliding into existence as a dip, more a blend of Mexican and American food than anything Bernardino de Sahagún would have written about. One newspaper article, for example, recommended that readers make a "Salsa Dip" consisting of one can of thoroughly drained tomatoes, a pint of creamed cottage cheese with chives, and one can of chopped green chilies. The author recommended adding chili powder, salt, and pepper. Then, she introduced a remarkably sane yet novel twist for the time—that salsa (whatever it is) makes an excellent dip for corn chips.[51]

Most foods tend to separate from their roots as they become popular. Chicken wings, for example, lost the tip, which was one-third of its original self. Salsa, on the other hand, grew closer. By 1988, salsa was less about mixing in cottage cheese and more about being scooped up with tortilla chips or draped over an enchilada. Sometimes recipes listed salsa as an "Ethnic Favorite," but as more immigrants from Central America and Mexico settled into the United States, salsa became more of its original, and most natural, self.

In with the New: The Mysterious Chili con Carne

Everything about chili con carne generates some sort of controversy—the spelling of the name, the origin of the dish, the proper ingredients for a great recipe.—The Chili Pepper Encyclopedia, 1999[52]

No Mexican-esque food infiltrates the tables at Super Bowl games as much as chili. You know this. We all know this. But what is chili, exactly? That is an interesting question, and not so easy to answer. The theories abound, often more interesting than the chili itself.

Chili, of course, starts with the chili pepper, which is Mexican. In fact, chilies are so Mexican they were actually gathered and eaten in Mexico as far back as 7000 BC and were cultivated there before 3500 BC.[53] So why the confusion? For that, we must thank Christopher Columbus, the brave yet misguided bounty-seeking traveler we Americans love and, increasingly, loathe for his treatment of the native people he encountered.

One confusion arose after Columbus's first voyage. Upon discovering chilies, he called them "peppers" with as much enthusiasm as he called the native people "Indians." The mistake had more to do with wishful thinking than botanical analysis. Columbus was searching for the much-coveted *black pepper*, with its great monetary potential.[54] No matter what the name, the chili "pepper" spread like wildfire thanks to the efforts of explorers such as the Portuguese who, while busy ravishing the natives, loaded their chilies onto ships heading for the Portuguese colonies in Asia.

THE ORIGIN OF CHILI CON CARNE

Chili concocted outside of Texas is usually a weak, apologetic imitation of the real thing.
—US President Lyndon B. Johnson[55]

A detestable dish sold from Texas to New York City and erroneously described as Mexican.
—The Chili Pepper Encyclopedia, 1999[56]

Let's start with the chilies themselves. The difference between green chilies and red chilies is really confusing and we can't blame Columbus for this. So, here's how it goes: Green chili is chili that hasn't ripened enough to turn its mature color—red. That's it. What we do with green—or immature—chilies is stuff them, bringing us chiles rellenos (stuffed chilies). Or we add them to sauce, giving us green chili sauce. Or we grind them into a sauce that is simply green chili with spices. That's it. Unfortunately, we have recipes where food writers tell us: "The green chili group includes all green peppers that are hot, including 'Anaheim' (Capsicum annuum 'Anaheim'), 'Jalapeno' (Capsicum annuum 'Jalapeno') and 'Cayenne' (Capsicum annuum 'Cayenne')." The well-intended writer confuses us even more by saying that some chili peppers are "sweet." So, ignore it. "Sweet" peppers are peppers. "Green chili" is chili, not peppers. Red chili is green chili that has ripened on the vine and is spicier than it was when green.[57]

Chili con carne (aka Super Bowl chili) is a stew made with meat and usually onions, tomatoes, and/or beans cooked in a broth. It can contain red or green chilies, depending on when the chili was picked. In essence, it's the elderly uncle of the food family. He shows up at family events, such as Thanksgiving and maybe the odd Super Bowl, drinks whiskey but not too much, is reliable, amiable, and kind of rounds out the night. You don't see him much throughout the year, which is OK. As for intrigue, no intrigue. Or at least none that anyone has noticed.

Chili peppers for sale, Los Angeles, *Susan Benjamin, Courtesy True Treats*

The Otherworldly Origin Story of Chili con Carne

One story attributes the origin of chili con carne to Sister Mary of Agreda, a Spanish nun living in the early 1600s. It seems the sister, who never actually left the convent, had numerous out-of-body adventures. In one, she traveled across the Atlantic to preach Christianity to the inhabitants of Mexico, where the native people gave her a recipe for chili—chili peppers, meat (in this case venison), onions, and tomatoes—which her spirit dutifully wrote down and passed along to the masses. Another more in-body story says that Canary Islanders who immigrated to San Antonio used native chilies, wild onions, and various meats to create the first chili con carne.[58]

So, how did chili con carne originate? Many of us, recognizing the significance of the name—*chili con carne*—think the dish originated in Mexico, what with it being Spanish and all. That is no truer than thinking Fritos or Nacho Cheese Doritos are from Mexico (as it happens, nachos are a relatively recent American invention). Actually, the earliest sighting of chili con carne was made by J. C. Clopper, a Houston resident visiting San Antonio in 1828: "When the poor families of San Antonio have to lay their meat in the market, a very little is made to suffice for the family; it is generally cut into a kind of hash with nearly as many peppers as there are pieces of meat—this is all stewed together."[59]

The real burst in popularity, though, was in the 1880s with assistance from Captain W. C. Tobin. He stealthily transformed street food for the poor into chow for the military. Operating in Chicago, he made canned con carne, which was more like Spam than actual chili. Whatever it was, Tobin enlisted military generals, heads of the US Navy, and other officers to commend his products in ads.

Philip P. Wales, Surgeon General of the US Navy, proclaimed, "The food preparations known as "Chili con Carne" . . . holds the same rank as the best preparation of canned beef, while the fruit of the chili . . . confers valuable savory qualities upon the meat." The chili, he explains, was not only for the military, but also for people "prospecting, camping out, and soldiering in Texas, Indian Territory. . . . I have not found anything superior to this."[60]

From there, the ascent of chili con carne was swift. While still equated with the low-quality meat of the "poor," it steadily morphed into dishes for the middle class. By the early 1900s, chili con carne restaurants were opening in California, Tennessee, Illinois, and other parts of the Midwest. Festivals were held in Minnesota. Recipes were doled out to homemakers in newspapers and magazines. Through it all, a debate raged, albeit in a quiet, culinary way: should chili contain beans? Many had opinions, but the answer was never definitive. In other words—do what you want.

So, you'd think somewhere along the line *someone* may have realized that chili con carne is not Mexican. But no. In 1916, the syndicated Household Hint columnist gave readers in Muncie, Indiana, a recipe for "real Mexican and Spanish" chili con carne—actually for a dish called "Mexican Azado." A household advisor in Missouri enlightened readers about a favorite dish from our "neighbors to the South"—hot tamales covered with chili con carne. That same advisor also recommended *another* exciting Mexican dish—chili con carne with tomato soup over spaghetti or macaroni.[61]

Hormel, Super Bowl prep, *Susan Benjamin, Courtesy True Treats*

The Mexican-Texan confusion was helped along by canned chili con carne manufacturers. One was Gebhardt's, founded by Texan William Gebhardt in 1896. For decades, it advertised its chili con carne as being "truly Mexican in flavor as though it were served at your table in a famed café of Mexico City."[62]

Another long-term chili maker, Wolf Brand, was founded in 1895 by Lyman T. Davis, who rode his commercial success with the longtime tagline "Neighbor, how long has it been since you had a big, thick, steaming bowl of Wolf Brand Chili? Well, that's too long!" Hormel, yet another manufacturer of chili, was started by William Hormel in 1890. The company manufactured a star food and cousin to canned chili—the much loved and much loathed Spam. Like chili con carne, Spam got its big break with the military. In Spam's case, that was during World War II. Both Wolf Brand and Hormel are still around today. None of the founders were from Mexico or of Mexican descent.[63]

CHILI CON CARNE TODAY

> *Chili is a perfect Super Bowl food for many reasons. It's warm and hearty, which is perfect for February. It's filled with meat and cheese, making it just as American as football itself. And, it can serve as a legit meal among a sea of endless football snacks, so it's a smart thing to serve at any party.*—"17 Slow-Cooker Super Bowl Chili Recipes to Get You through the Big Game," 2019[64]

Today, food writers throw out as many chili con carne recipes as they once did salsa. Among the options—Vegetarian Pumpkin Quinoa Chili; Poblano Turkey Chili, served with tortilla chips and fresh avocado; Cream Cheese Chicken Chile; Buffalo Chicken Chili; and the very American gold-star chili concoction, Chili Mac, which is vegetarian. Says the author: "The meatless chili is hearty and healthy, so you'll definitely be energized through the game."[65]

Kids in the Kitchen: It's G-r-r-r-eat!

The story of how the cereal of old came to be the cereal of today is one of the strangest food stories around. It involves big names—Graham, Post, and Kellogg, plus Clara Barton, founder of the American Red Cross; Ellen White, founder of the Seventh-day Adventist Church; and, yes, Tony the Tiger. Like all good stories, it includes sex, insanity, and great fortunes. And—in the most bizarre twist of all—it includes how wholesome cereals became America's most popular fun food today.

IN THE BEGINNING . . . SYLVESTER GRAHAM

Sugary sweet cereals, *Maryann Fisher, Courtesy True Treats*

> *Dr. Bran, the philosopher of sawdust pudding.*—Name given to Sylvester Graham by a Northampton, Massachusetts, newspaper, 1830s[1]

Cereals started as hot cooked grains—whether popcorn, sorghum, or wheat—eaten with a splash of milk or whatever else was available. All that changed when Sylvester Graham entered the American food scene in the early 1800s. Born in 1794, he was the seventeenth child in a family of physicians and ministers. His father died young and his mother, likely weary from all those childbirths, went through bouts of insanity, leaving Graham to be raised primarily by relatives.

Undiminished by his rocky past, Graham grew up to be a fiery leader and the father of modern "health food." He espoused a fresh, wholesome, alcohol-free, meat-free, sugar-and-spice-free diet, consisting of whole grains, so whole they were barely chewable. Life, according to Graham, was to be lived on a strict schedule, including when to sleep (on a hard mattress), rise, and brush your teeth. He preached his viewpoints to vast numbers of followers so devoted they were called "Grahamites." Should detractors rise up, the fiery Graham didn't take

> Forty-three percent of US cereal consumers eat cereal as a snack at home. This does not include cereal bars, cereal cookies, and cereal snack bites.[2]

their objections in stride but called them names, accused them of devious intent, and, should these objections occur face to face, come close to what one reporter called "fists to cuffs."[3]

At the heart of Graham's vigor was his widely espoused viewpoints about sex. He was against it. Sex was a moral abomination. Bad for body and soul. Only appropriate for child-bearing purposes. But, in Graham's estimation, the lowest of the low of sexual deviation was masturbation. In his talks and such treatises as the well-known *On Self-Pollution* of 1834, he lectured that masturbation by the young led to blindness and early death.[4]

So, as you can imagine, Graham's original cracker was *not* the delightful cracker that we enjoy in our s'mores today. No, his cracker, invented in 1829, was made with his own "Graham Flour," which was not whole grain but "coarse grain," less sifted than the average whole-grain brands into pebble-like morsels. While grocers touted his flour as being "made from superior crashed [*sic*] wheat," Graham had another benefit in mind: it was a deterrent to the sex, mas-turbation included.[5]

Sylvester Graham died in 1851, a year before one of his most ardent followers was born. That would be John Harvey Kellogg. But first came James Caleb Jackson.

THE LIFE AND GREAT ACCOMPLISHMENTS OF JAMES CALEB JACKSON

Considered the father of dry breakfast cereal, James Caleb Jackson had a long, remarkable life. Born in 1811, he was a farmer and an avid abolitionist. In 1847, however, Jackson became too sick to continue his efforts and refocused, instead, on getting well. He did get well—in fact, he lived to be eighty-four, and started a spa to help others get well, too.

Called "Our Home on The Hillside," his Connecticut-based sanatorium welcomed patients including Clara Barton, who arrived exhausted from her years treating the injured during the Civil War. Another guest was Ellen White, founder of the Seventh-day Adventist Church. It was Ellen White who introduced Jackson's enclave to one of *her* followers and fellow sanato-rium proprietor, Dr. John Harvey Kellogg. More on him in a minute.

Jackson's treatments involved hydropathy, fresh air, exposure to the sun, and clean, whole-some, vegetarian-based eating, which included his own recipes. In 1863, he riffed off Gra-ham's early cracker, baking graham flour into brittle cakes, which he then crumbled and baked again. He named the invention "granula." It required no cooking and was eaten cold, making it a readily available no-cook breakfast cereal. Only one hiccup. The granula was *hard*—too hard to safely chew without a good twenty-minute soaking in milk or water. No matter, the granula caught on and was enjoyed by an increasingly wide range of people, including Jackson's many guests.[6]

Jackson died in 1895 in Dansville, New York. His obituary said, in part, that Dr. James Caleb Jackson was a philanthropist, friend of the oppressed, and upright man.[7] Then there was John Harvey Kellogg.

THE CORN FLAKES STORY: MADNESS, MONEY, AND SCREAMING SUCCESS

Use granula, the great health food. It has saved many a person's life.—Advertisement, 1883[8]

When John Harvey Kellogg entered the arena of sanatorium proprietor/cereal maker/moral trendsetter, James Caleb Jackson already had quite a following, both the man and his granula. The success of Jackson's granula was too much for Kellogg. So, he created his own cereal, made with ground oats, wheat, and corn, which he called (no surprise) "granula." Jackson sued Kellogg for the name and won. Kellogg, undaunted, changed the *u* to an *o* and called his cereal "granola."

Jackson influenced Kellogg on many other levels. There was Jackson's influence on Ellen White, a patient at his spa and founder of the Seventh-day Adventists, who, in turn, influenced Kellogg, an ardent member of her flock. Like Jackson, Kellogg was a vegetarian, disapproved of alcohol, and spoke widely about healthy eating. Still, on many fronts, Kellogg diverged sharply from Jackson in words and intent.

Unlike Jackson, an abolitionist, Kellogg was an extreme racist and outspoken zealot for eugenics. In Kellogg's opinion, the fate of humanity depended on allowing only high-level, literally card-carrying humans to procreate. Not surprisingly, Kellogg's view on sex was in league with Graham's, only more extreme, remarkable as that seems. Kellogg not only disparaged sex but advocated for tortuous devices to be inflicted on young boys to curb their erections and masturbatory temptations.[9]

Less horrendous was Kellogg's edible anti-sex/anti-masturbation treatments, such as Corn Flakes. The cereal was bland and void of culinary polish, much like Graham's crackers. Both men believed that spice was more than the spice of life—it was the fuel that ignited sexual tensions. No spice, no tension. But no torture either. Corn Flakes were the cure.

Oh, That Crazy Kellogg Clan

So, how did John Harvey Kellogg transform his Corn Flakes—a hard, dry sanatorium health food—into the popular cereal it would become? He didn't. That would be *Will* Kellogg, the beleaguered younger brother of John Harvey. Throughout their childhood, the older brother physically and emotionally beat the younger one, and humiliated, underpaid, and sabotaged him when they were adults working together at the sanatorium.

No matter—in this family feud, Will won. In his blood, Will was a businessman. A marketer. A strategist. It was Will who ran the sanatorium and helped perfect the Corn Flake recipe, a feat requiring innumerable trials. In what can only be called a eureka moment, Will saw the future and the future was *healthy* people—not just sick ones—enjoying Corn Flakes. Will left his brother and started his own company, the Battle Creek Toasted Corn Flake

Corn Flakes ad, 1910, *Life Magazine*

Company. He succeeded by doing something Dr. Kellogg despised: he added sugar.

Over the years, the brothers sued and countersued each other to own the Kellogg brand name. The matter went all the way to the Michigan Supreme Court. Harvey Kellogg insisted that he was the renowned doctor, the force behind the cereal. Will proclaimed he was the businessman who spent millions of dollars advertising the Kellogg brand. Will won.

Who stayed at Kellogg's sanatorium?

Patients included President William Howard Taft, Amelia Earhart, George Bernard Shaw, Henry Ford, and Thomas Edison.[10]

When Will Kellogg died, he was wealthy beyond imagination, dedicating a fortune to his philanthropic foundation, still around today. He had created Rice Krispies, All-Bran, and his own version of shredded wheat, as well as a company that would later spawn such cereals as Frosted Flakes, Sugar Pops, and Sugar Smacks. Harvey Kellogg also died a wealthy man. He had forty-six children, all adopted, with his wife Ella. When Harvey died, his fortune went to his own foundation, just like his brother's, although his was the Foundation for Race Betterment, dedicated to eugenics.[11]

The Last Word on Granula

The granula/granola story got even more complex at Kellogg's sanatorium. That chapter started with a patient who worked in the kitchen to defray the cost of his bill. The patient watched every step of every food-making process, then dutifully re-created them in his own budding business. His early cereal was similar to Jackson's and Kellogg's but with an entirely different name. Not granula. Not granola. His cereal was called "Grape Nuts," and the patient was future Kellogg competitor C. W. Post.

Post became a formidable competitor. By the early 1900s his company, the Postum Cereal Company, named for his breakfast beverage Postum, owned the largest processing plant of its kind with 2,500 employees and a net worth of $5 million. Later, his daughter Marjorie Merriweather Post took over the company and, in the 1920s, acquired Jell-O, Swans Down cake flour, Minute Tapioca, Baker's Chocolate, Log Cabin syrup, and Maxwell House coffee, and the company became known as General Foods. But by the 1920s, C. W. Post was long gone, having committed suicide in 1914 while recovering from appendix surgery.[12]

Corn Flakes: The Fun Food

Make no mistake, cereal did veer away from its health food past to take on sparkling colors, multitudinous sugars, and snappy shapes brought to you by cartoon spokespersons. But cereals, inexpensive and readily available as they were, also became *ingredients* in fun foods made at home from the dawn of the twentieth century. One is "Corn Flake Kisses," a homemade favorite since 1916. Here's what you do:

> *Two cups Corn Flakes; two egg whites; one cup granulated sugar; one teaspoon vanilla; one cupful coconut. Beat the whites of the eggs until stiff and dry; gradually add the sugar and beat continuously for two minutes, then add the other ingredients, stirring only long enough to mix thoroughly. Drop by teaspoons on oiled paper, and bake in a very moderate oven. This recipe may make about two and a half dozen kisses.[13]*

Among the infinite other Corn Flake recipes was this, from 1932:

About Kisses

You may be curious about the name "Kiss." Taken from Hershey's Chocolate Kisses, you might ask? Actually, the other way around. "Kiss," as defined in *Webster's Dictionary* of 1856, was a generic word for a small piece of confection. By the late 1800s, there were taffy *kisses*, cream *kisses*, fruit *kisses*, and on and on. Hershey's Kisses didn't appear until 1907—relatively late in the game. Milton Hershey didn't invent the concept of a candy kiss. He never claimed he did. But the Hershey Corporation spent years trying to claim the "Kiss" as its own nonetheless. Eventually, the company succeeded and owns the word today.[14]

GEMS MADE WITH CORN FLAKES

1 cup Corn Flakes

1 cup flour

$3/4$ cup milk

2 tablespoons syrup of molasses

$1/2$ teaspoon salt

1 tablespoon melted shortening

2 teaspoons baking powder

Sift the flour, baking powder and salt into a bowl, add the milk, syrup, or molasses and corn flakes [*sic*] and mix well. Brush gem irons with melted fat; fill three quarters full; sprinkle top with crushed corn flakes, place in hot oven; bake 10 minutes. They should be crisp.[15]

The diversion of Corn Flakes from a healthy food was probably enough to make Harvey Kellogg go apoplectic—but who knows? The excitement could have encouraged him to turn to sex.

PUFFED CEREAL . . .
THE START OF SOMETHING GREAT

The Eighth Wonder of the World.—Publicity line promoting the creation of Puffed Rice and Puffed Wheat, 1930

A dry method of swelling starch materials of all kinds to render them porous, thereby enhancing their nutritive value and rendering them more readily and completely digested.
—US Patent 707,892 for Dr. Alexander P. Anderson[16]

In the 1920s, Kellogg's created a cereal that would lead to one of the most popular cookies of the twentieth century. The cereal was Rice Krispies, and the cookie was variously called Rice Krispie Treat, Marshmallow Square, and Rice Krispie Square. But this wonder of twentieth-century delights started not with Kellogg but with botanist and researcher Dr. Alexander P. Anderson in 1901.

It was then that Anderson discovered a way to make grains, such as rice and wheat, explode into puffy digestible splendor. He did this, remarkably enough, with a self-styled "puffing gun." The result was promoted at the 1904 St. Louis World's Fair, complete with cannon-like cylinders that shot newly puffed rice into a giant cage, to the amazement of spectators. After the grains of rice had gone through their transformation, Anderson's assistants bagged them up and sold them to eager spectators for a nickel a pop. Altogether Anderson puffed over 20,000 pounds of rice and sold a quarter-million bags of cereal.

The public wasn't the only one impressed by the transformation. Quaker Oats offered Anderson a full-time position with their company, which he accepted. The company marketed the products we now know as "puffed rice" and "puffed wheat" cereal as "food shot from guns." Quaker Oats also launched a massive advertising campaign featuring Hollywood celebrities such as Shirley Temple (who enjoyed puffed wheat with peaches), Bette Davis, and Bing Crosby, ensuring puffed cereals found a place at the American table.[17]

From Puffed Cereal to Puffed Sweet

Like Kellogg's Corn Flakes, Quaker's Puffed Rice and Puffed Wheat became ingredients in numerous recipes showcased in newspapers, women's magazines, and anywhere else women could see them. One example was "Puffed Rice Brittle," circa 1916:

This is another wholesome candy relished by everyone—crisp the rice in the oven before using: One cupful of granulated sugar, one half cupful of water. Boil together five minutes; add two tablespoons of molasses, butter of a walnut, half a teaspoonful of salt. Boil until it hardens in cold water. Take from fire and stir in one half package puffed rice. Pour into buttered pans.[18]

The recipe slimmed down a bit, made easier and more congenial for the busy homemaker over the decades. In 1930, for example, food columnist Harriet Cooke introduced "Puffed Wheat Squares." She asked, "Do you find it hard to keep the children amused these days when vacation is no longer a novelty? If you do, then you will be pleased to set them to work making a batch of candy, for this will keep them amused for quite some time and, as well, will give you all real delight!" Here's the recipe:

PUFFED WHEAT SQUARES

   2 packages puffed wheat
   2 cups light molasses
   2–3 cups sugar
   3 tablespoons butter
   1 tablespoon vinegar

Heat the puffed wheat until crisp, stirring frequently. Heat the butter, molasses, and sugar over the fire until the sugar is dissolved. . . . Boil until it becomes brittle when tested in cold water. Add the vinegar and pour the syrup over the wheat. Stir until buttered well, then pour into a buttered pan and press it out to about an inch of thickness. When cool, cut into squares.[19]

Rice Krispies Meets the Campfire Girls

In 1927, Kellogg announced the arrival of its version of puffed rice—Rice Krispies, which it called "the talking cereal." The "talking" part comes from the rice itself, which Kellogg baked at high temperatures, causing the rice to expand and tiny air pockets to form inside. Add milk and pressure forms, forcing the air inside the grain to explode, making a "snap, crackle, pop" sound. Actually, these are *not* the sounds Rice Krispies make. They're the sounds the company's ad executives invented to sell the product. In reality, the rice just makes noise. No matter, in moments after hitting the milk, the sound—whatever it is—stops, the crispness wilts, and all in the cereal bowl is calm, quiet, and soggy.[20]

   All was well, except in the commercial cereal world, nothing is ever well enough. New products, new avenues for sales, are a must. So,

Rice Krispies, the talking cereal, 1933, *Wikimedia*

Kellogg created an R&D department, then called a "test kitchen," and hired Malitta Jensen and Mildred Ghrist Day to help run it. Among their many efforts, the pair made a version of "Puffed Rice Brittle," replacing Anderson's Puffed Rice with Kellogg's Rice Krispies. Unfortunately, the result was sticky, wet, and overall unappealing. So, the pair replaced the molasses with glue-like marshmallows to create a would-be sensation—Marshmallow Squares, later known as Rice Krispie Treats.

Here the story gets murky. What's known is that the Campfire Girls, like the Girl Scouts, had fundraisers. The Girl Scouts sold cookies. The Campfire Girls sold marshmallows, "Campfire Marshmallows." It seems they wanted to enliven their campaign with something heftier than marshmallows and contacted Kellogg for help. Fortunately, the recipe for Marshmallow Squares was on hand. But would the Campfire Girls want it? To find out, Kellogg sent Mildred Day to a Campfire Girl enclave in the Kansas City area, equipped with a giant mixer and huge baking trays. There she taught the mothers how to prepare the treat, which their daughters would then sell door-to-door.

Did the Campfire Girls' fundraising effort work out? Was it short-lived? Ads for Marshmallow Square fundraisers don't appear in magazine and newspaper archives. So, it seems, we will never really know. What we do know is that, since 1941, the recipe for Rice Krispie Treats has been on every box of Rice Krispies cereal.[21]

ORIGINAL RICE KRISPIE TREATS RECIPE, 1941

$1/3$ cup butter

$1/2$ pound Fluffi-i-est Marshmallows
   (a brand name)

$1/2$ teaspoon vanilla

1 ($5 1/2$ ounce) package Kellogg Rice Krispies

Melt butter and marshmallows in a double boiler. Add vanilla; beat well. Put Rice Krispies in a large buttered bowl and pour in the marshmallow mixture. Press into a shallow buttered pan. Cut into squares.

Yield: 16 $2 1/4$-inch squares (10 × 10-inch pan).

Note: Nut meats and coconut may be added.[22]

The many faces of Rice Krispie Treats, *Susan Benjamin, Courtesy True Treats*

THE ERA OF CEREAL MASCOTS: BEYOND BETTY CROCKER

The heavily sugared cereals drove the sanatoriums' health food into a breakfast dessert rich with economic possibilities. Cereal manufacturers had a plethora of strategies to make their economic dreams a reality: box top fundraisers, prizes tucked in the boxes, contests, comic books, sponsorship, recipes printed on the back of the cereal boxes, and, above all, mascots. No mere real-life movie star influencers, these mascots were one-of-a-kind creations. Birthed by advertising firms in the mid-1900s, they remain among us today, as ageless and indelible as another fictitious character, Betty Crocker, but with more imagination. Here's a few of them.

Your cereal mascots, *Susan Benjamin and Maryann Fisher, Courtesy True Treats*

1933

Name: Rice Krispies
Mascot: Snap, Crackle, Pop
Made by: Kellogg
First to: have cartoon characters recommend their brand[23]

Kellogg introduced its Rice Krispies mascots, originally called Mr. Snap! Mr. Crackle! and Mr. Pop! around 1933. Each represented the cereal's alleged "snap, crackle, pop," or, as radio ads put it, the way the cereal bits "merrily snap, crackle and pop in a bowl of milk." The company hired illustrator Vernon Grant to give each sound a human-ish personality, although *what* exactly these characters are wasn't, and still isn't, quite clear. Elves? Trolls? "Little fellows"? These days Kellogg's website dodges the question, calling them "the guys" or "the boys" and very occasionally "gnomes."[24]

At first, the characters were more or less amorphous, but as they self-actualized, so to speak, so did their advertising prowess. They initially starred in a Kellogg-produced film short around 1937 or 1938, tucked into other short films on the big screen. The audience didn't realize they were watching an ad until the end. The three were also featured in print ads, on swag, on Rice Krispies cereal boxes, and even in an ad with music sung by the Rolling Stones in 1963—a project the band no doubt regrets today.[25] The lyrics went: "Wake up in the morning, there's a Snap around the place, wake up in the morning, there's a Crackle in your face, wake up in the morning, there's a Pop that really says this is for you!" Not exactly "Wild Horses."[26]

Although roughly ninety years old, the trio lives among us today, still fit, with all their youthful abandon, although, let's be real, they have had face . . . make that body . . . lifts. They also make an appearance on the packaging of Kellogg's ready-made Rice Krispie Treats, which come in more varieties than even Snap, Crackle, or Pop could have imagined.

POW: THE EULOGY THAT NEVER WAS

It's only appropriate that we pay homage to Pow, the unlikely sibling of Snap, Crackle, and Pop. Pow appeared in two commercials in the 1950s, at a time when space-age images were proliferating in the world of advertising. Pow's name had nothing to do with the sound of the cereal, but the nutritional *pow*er of the grains. To underscore the point, Kellogg dressed Pow not in elfin/gnome/boy's attire, but a *spacesuit*. Sadly, Pow vanished without a trace soon after he was created.[27]

1952

Name: Frosted Flakes
Mascot: Tony the Tiger
Made by: Kellogg
First to: give a voice to the mascot

In the 1950s, children, many offspring of returning World War II GIs, were demanding nutritious breakfasts. Actually, that's what advertisers said. Really kids just wanted to eat something for breakfast that they liked. As for the mothers who fed them? On TV shows such as *Leave It to Beaver* and *The Donna Reed Show*, actress-mothers were serving up bacon, eggs, and toast with, yes, orange juice before moving on to the magic of vacuum cleaning. Plenty of real-life mothers were doing just that, but many just wanted to get the morning routine over with: breakfast on the table and kids out the door. Cold cereal was the answer.

Enter Sugar Frosted Flakes, i.e., corn flakes wrapped in sugar. To convince mothers to buy Frosted Flakes, Kellogg hired the advertising agency Leo Burnett, the force behind the cigarette-smoking cowboy, the Marlboro Man, and the Jolly Green Giant with his canned peas and beans (ho-ho-ho). Tony the Tiger's message was unambiguous and reassuring—Sugar Frosted Flakes were tasty, fun, and even *healthy*. Who knew? For mothers of growing kids, Tony also assuaged their guilt for serving breakfast not from a frying pan, but a box.

Like the American children who enjoyed his cereal, Tony grew up. He started life walking on all fours, as tigers do, then stood upright, *then* got extremely fit and muscular as the nation started veering toward health foods. Tony's real power, though, was not his physique but his voice—the first cereal mascot to have one. For fifty years, that was brought to you by singer Thurl Ravenscroft, who proclaimed, "They're g-r-r-r-eat!!!!"

If Ravenscroft's voice sounds familiar, you also heard it in "You're a Mean One, Mr. Grinch" of *Dr. Seuss' How the Grinch Stole Christmas!* He also sang with such old-time notables as Bing Crosby and Rosemary Clooney and more recently did voice work for Disney's *The Haunted Mansion*, *Country Bear Jamboree*, *Pirates of the Caribbean*, and more.[28]

Frosted Flakes, the Ingredient

Frosted Flakes, like its precursor, Corn Flakes, has been an ingredient in recipes since its inception. As if the sugar from Frosted Flakes weren't enough, it mainly appears in recipes for candy and desserts. Maybe for that extra crunch.

SUGAR FROSTED FLAKES LOLLIPOPS, 1957

3 cups Sugar Frosted Flakes

1 quart vanilla ice cream

3 wooden skewers

Crush Sugar Frosted Flakes slightly. Shape ice cream into balls. Roll quickly in crushed cereal. Insert a wood skewer in each ball for a handle. Put into freezer to harden. Do not leave in freezer for more than two hours.[29]

KIDDIE-SIZE COOKIES, 1959

Ever try making cookies kiddie-size? Sugar Frosted Flakes is a star ingredient, contributing both flavor and texture, and the cookie is chewy, slightly coconut flavored, and requires only 12 minutes baking time.

$1^1/_4$ cups sifted flour

1 teaspoon baking powder

$^1/_2$ teaspoon salt

$^1/_2$ cup butter or margarine

$^1/_2$ cup granulated sugar

$^1/_2$ cup brown sugar

1 egg

1 teaspoon vanilla

1 teaspoon coconut flavor

$1^1/_2$ cups Sugar Frosted Flakes

Sift together flour, baking powder, and salt. Blend butter and sugars; add egg and flavoring and beat well. Sift in dry ingredients with Sugar Frosted Flakes. Drop by teaspoons onto greased baking sheets. Bake in moderate oven (375 degrees F) about 12 minutes.

Yield: $2^1/_2$ dozen cookies about $2^1/_2$ inches in diameter.[30]

1954

Name: Trix

Mascot: Rabbit

Maker: General Mills

First to: contain fruit-flavored cereal, have a mascot who was an antihero

Fact: Trix is actually a flavored version of another General Mills cereal—Kix. Name aside, Kix is all about healthy eating. From the start, Trix was all about *dessert*. Make that breakfast dessert, crunchy, fun, and rich in flavor, 46 percent of it coming from sugar. Never to miss an opportunity, General Mills parleyed the high sugar content into an advantage, telling consumers, "No [additional] sugar was needed." But sugar is sugar and any cereal, however liberated from its former health-crazed self, needed something else. And Trix had it![31] Bright, energy-inspiring colors, which the company proclaimed were "gay little sugared corn puffs in a happy mixture of colors—red, yellow, orange. . . . The most *exciting* thing that ever happened to breakfast cereal." Later, General Mills added blue, green, and purple to the assortment, taking "exciting" one step further.

But the sugar, the colors, even the shapes were not enough to launch Trix into success. That required a nameless rabbit dedicated to conjuring schemes for getting Trix away from the kids and all to himself. The Trix rabbit owes its existence to Joe Harris, creator of the legendary cartoon character Underdog and the "Rocky and Bullwinkle" series. Harris also wrote the now-infamous line: "Silly rabbit, Trix are for kids."[32] The line, by the way, came before the rabbit had been created.

The Trix rabbit changed through time, looking first like a papier-mâché rabbit, then a stuffed animal rabbit, and, finally, a cartoon rabbit. He even appeared as a hand puppet who introduced General Mills–sponsored kid shows such as *The Adventures of Rocky and Bullwinkle and Friends* and *Captain Kangaroo*.[33] But all this begs the question—why a *rabbit*? A tiger, like

> ## The Strange Relationship between Betty Crocker and Trix
>
> General Mills' other made-up mascot, Betty Crocker, was a trusted advisor and friend because, unlike the Trix rabbit, people believed she was real. In a co-mingling campaign of cartoon and actress, animal and human, the nonexistent Betty Crocker endorsed Trix, and so much more! Here's what she says: "Trix really does bring gaiety to your breakfast. And it is a wonderful way to give children the nutrients they need. I hope you'll try TRIX soon."[35]
>
> Should that have been legal?

Tony the Tiger, we get it. Tigers are strong and exotic with plenty of theatric potential. But rabbits? In the end, it wasn't rabbits but this particular rabbit who was fun, or at least fodder for fun, such as a magic show's magician pulling a rabbit out of his hat.

The Trix rabbit and, indeed, Trix cereal were successful not because they were healthy but in spite of the fact they weren't. As the rabbit himself told young audiences, "I'm a rabbit, and rabbits are supposed to like carrots. But I hate carrots. I like Trix."[34]

Today, Trix is ranked twenty-fourth in the top fifty cereals Americans love to eat.[36]

1963

Name: Cap'n Crunch
Mascot: Cap'n Crunch
Made by: Quaker Oats
First to: have cereal name and mascot be the same, mascot has a biography

Never in the history of cereal—or probably any advertising—was there anything like Cap'n Crunch. For time immemorial, food makers have known crunchiness can enhance our experience of certain foods. To double-check, Quaker Oats surveyed kids about their cereal preferences. Lo and behold, kids love crunchy cereal . . . until it gets soggy. So, Quaker Oats set out on a mission: to create a cereal that was the crunchiest, the longest. The result was Cap'n Crunch.

Texture done, the cereal needed a flavor. The woman to do it was Pamela Low, a flavorist with the firm Arthur D. Little, who brought us the flavors of Almond Joy and Mounds candy bars. Low tossed food science aside, focusing instead on a dish her grandmother made—rice topped with butter and brown sugar sauce. She coated the crunchy nuggets with the rice-pudding-like topping and a new cereal was born.[37]

Next step: tell people about it. While the possibilities of advertising and marketing were wide open, competition was fierce. Quaker Oats needed more than advertising—they needed a campaign. Jay Ward, the genius behind such cartoon figures such as Dudley Do-Right (of the Royal Canadian Mounted Police), Peabody and Sherman, and George of the Jungle, was the guy to do it. Unfortunately, when Quaker Oats called, all of Ward's staff was on vacation except for one guy—Allan Burns.

Quaker Oats instructed Ward and Burns to do the following: (1) use the word "crunch" and (2) use a tagline that says: "It stays crunchy in milk." That's it. No further guidance involved. The company did send an early sample of the cereal, which, according to Burns, "just about ripped your mouth to shreds," adding that the cereal would stay crunchy even in hydrochloric acid.[38]

Crunchy or deadly, Ward and Burns pulled it off, creating a universe inhabited by a seafaring captain whose name doubled as the cereal's name. Cap'n Crunch, the mascot. Cap'n Crunch, the cereal. It just worked. Burns even gave the captain a family tree and bio. About ten years later, he created another compelling character whose name was the name of a *show*—the *Mary Tyler Moore Show* starring Mary Tyler Moore.

> ## Crunchiness: The Ultimate Taste Sensation
> Crunchiness affects our experience of food in hidden but powerful ways. A good crunch tells us on a subliminal level that the food is fresh and, by default, safe to eat. And, crunchiness broadens our eating experience: we *hear* it when we bite into crunchy food, and even as we chew it. Crunchiness is so important, makers of chips, crackers, and other crunchy-fun foods make their *packaging* noisier, more crunch-like, so you're in crunch-heaven even before you eat.[39]

THE LIFE AND TIMES OF CAP'N CRUNCH

Based on a fictional Royal Navy officer, Captain Horatio Hornblower, Cap'n Crunch was born in 1387. His father, Sven Crunch, navigated the first Viking vessel ever. The crew had a Columbus-like journey: they arrived in New England but intended to land in the French Riviera. They were so disappointed, they sailed away on the vessel, leaving Sven stranded. He ultimately married Gidget Running Star, a local Native American girl, and together they bore Horatio Magellan Crunch. As a youngster, Crunch considered American school too limiting, so went to England for a better education. As luck would have it, he was kidnapped by pirates who taught him the ways of the sea.

The story was fascinating, funny, but way too complex for a cereal mascot. So, a few years later, the company whittled down the story to this: Cap'n Crunch was born on the Oz-like Crunch Island, located in a sea of milk. It had talking trees, crazy creatures, and, at the center, Mount Crunchmore, made entirely of cereal. Don't worry. This story is no cliffhanger. Here's how it ends: Crunch grew up to become captain of the SS *Guppy*, on which he traveled with four kids (to win over the cereal-loving youth market) named, in alphabetical order, Alfie, Brunhilde, Carlyle, and Dave, and Seadog, the loyal companion. Cap'n Crunch was about 4 feet, 11 inches and weighed 102 pounds. As for his hobbies, sailing and dueling.[40]

Quaker spent nearly two and a half years developing the cereal and roughly $5 million launching it. They created a cartoon series, small comic books stuffed in the box as a gift, advertisements, sponsorships, and giveaways such as rings, trading cards, Seadog's bosun whistle, and more. The payback was impressive: Cap'n Crunch became one of the most beloved and longest-running cereal spokesmen.

Only one Crunch-esque event triggered scandal, something that even Ward could not have thought up. A faux newsflash went out that the beloved and trusted Cap'n Crunch is *not* really a captain. His uniform has only three gold stripes on the cuffs—that of a lower-ranking commander. A true captain would have four. Papers everywhere reported on the finding, one blogger even weighing in describing the "captain" as a traitor to the United States.[41]

Today, Cap'n Crunch has his own cereal empire, including Donut Crunch, Donut Crunch Snack Packs, Choco Donuts, Blueberry Pancake Crunch, and Peanut Butter Crunch, plus a line of Cap'n Crunch toys, "action figures," a Cap'n Crunch PEZ dispenser, and a bevy of Cap'n Crunch cereal snack bars called "Treats," such as Strawberry Shortcake and even (get this, Kellogg!) Crunchy Marshmallow Treats. And let's not forget Cap'n Crunch Cookies, with high lunch box potential. Says one ad targeting moms, "Score an A in lunchmanship with these big, gooey, chocolate chip cookies. Your youngster will love em."[42] Closing note: An "A" for honesty also goes out to General Mills, which didn't, even once, claim that the cookies were healthy, nutritious, or anything besides fun.

1964

Name: Lucky Charms
Mascot: Lucky the Leprechaun, aka Lucky
Made by: General Mills
First to: be made from a candy

In the early 1960s, in Minneapolis, Minnesota, home to the Mall of America, Mary Tyler Moore, Jesse Ventura, and the Artist Formerly Known as Prince, came a star of its own, Lucky the Leprechaun. Lucky's very existence rested on the controversial circus peanut and an event that occurred, yes, right there, not only in Minnesota but at the General Mills campus, on the street named for another made-up mascot, Betty Crocker Drive. It was there that General Mills managers instructed their product developers to come up with a new cereal using either the company-made Wheaties or Cheerios. The cereal had to be unique, marketable, and kids had to love it.

Hard at work, product developer John Holahan got an idea. He took some of his favorite candies, Brach's Circus Peanuts, chopped them into pieces, and put them into a bowl of Cheerios. Eureka! They were amazing. Or anyway, kids would think they were amazing.[42] Whatever they were, the company gave them shapes, colors, and an abbreviated name, going from "marshmallow bits" to "marbits," which may sound scientific but are really just marshmallows—a bit hard, a bit gritty on the teeth.

So how did the scientific-ish marbits transform into "charms"? Evidently, one of General Mills' advertising consultants mentioned something about charm bracelets, possibly in passing. "Why not call them charms?" the GM execs asked. Marshmallow charms that were "magically delicious," or something to that effect? The charms were also magically morphing into newer and newer iterations such as Blue Diamonds, Swirled Whales, and tiny little Eiffel Towers.

The changes brought an uptick in sales, regardless of how removed they were from Lucky the Leprechaun, who was more Irish than French and more old-timey than swirled.[43]

Regardless of the charm's color, shape, or national origin, Lucky the Leprechaun was on a mission to get Lucky Charm cereal all for himself, much like the Trix rabbit. Unlike rabbits, though, leprechauns are tricksters, but not likable tricksters. They have long ears, more pointed than floppy. They can be nasty. Edgy. And cold. As for Lucky, he was also greedy. And he wouldn't share.

So, in 1975, General Mills decided that Lucky had to magically disappear. In his place was Waldo the Wizard, a middle-aged, chubby wizard who wore a green suit and bow tie, much like an usher at an old-time movie theater. Waldo was friendly, greeted the kids in an appropriate fashion, and was always ready to share his Lucky Charms. Waldo even had a sense of wordplay, muttering that Lucky Charms were "ibble-debibble-delicious." Not exactly "magically delicious," but it did inspire the phrase "bibbidi-bobbidi-boo" in a song from Disney's *Cinderella*.

Within a year, Waldo the Wizard was out and Lucky the Leprechaun back in. The story goes that General Mills just couldn't get past losing the millions of dollars they devoted to giving Lucky a happy and profitable future. So, they transformed Lucky into a nicer guy, more accommodating and kid-friendly. Even his name changed. It started as Sir Charms, became the formal L. C. Leprechaun, and is now Lucky. Which he is.[44]

About Circus Peanuts

These strange candies were made in the late 1800s for circuses, which, at the time, may have included up to twenty elephants. Full-page newspaper ads proclaimed: "The circus is coming!" Followed by: "Get your circus peanuts now!" No one actually claimed to invent the circus peanut but it's still around, on candy store shelves, in supermarket aisles, and in boxes of Lucky Charms.[45]

What's Grillin'? Hamburgers, Hot Dogs, Plenty to Eat

For many Americans, cookouts and barbecues are indistinguishable. They're both about meat, the odd cooked vegetable, and men. That's because cookouts and barbecues are presented to us, the general public, as the one act of cooking every man is willing to do. It's got flame, flesh, and daring, right? That perspective, regardless of how warped, leaves out an even more important point: cookouts and barbecues are different. Let's start with barbecues.

THE ORIGINS OF BARBECUE

Origin Story #1

Experts say that barbecuing originated somewhere in the Paleolithic era when humans first used outdoor fire to prepare meat. This method is obvious—they didn't have stoves. What were the options? But this culinary shift was a defining moment in human development. Freed from the vast energy and time required to chew raw foods, early humans spent that energy developing their brains, leaving us with the cognitive abilities of today.[1]

Numerous forces, such as climate, food sources, and migratory practices, shaped how these fires were started and harnessed over time. In North America, Native Americans used an array of methods for cooking their foods. To start fires, many used sticks that they rubbed together, often with the help of a wood- or stone-based drill. Others hit stones together, which created sparks that ignited dry materials into fire. Some nomadic tribes stored the hot coals in a hollowed-out buffalo horn, moose antler, or other vessel, which they carried to the next destination as an ancient fire starter.

Once the fire was lit, they cooked food in a surprisingly similar way to what we do today. Some used sticks to pierce and cook their food, hot dog and marshmallow style. Others wrapped food in leaves and tucked it into the heat of hot ash or coals, a method called "ash cooking." Today, the leaves are replaced by tinfoil. The most influential of all cooking methods, though, were pits dug into the earth and lined with animal hide, fur removed. The food was placed in the hide; covered with hot coals, another hide, leaves, and other substances; and remained in the pit until the food was cooked.[2]

Origin Story #2

For barbecue, we owe thanks to the Spanish conquistadors, not exactly a wholesome bunch, who took to the sea to pillage other people's riches and bring them to the motherland, which was busily engaged in the Inquisition. During their journey, they found the inhabitants drying meat in the sun to lengthen its shelf life, a process also used by the Native Americans on the continent. For the North Americans, this process ended up with pemmican—dried meat, mixed with animal fat and berries, a version now sold, more or less, as "jerky."

Jules Caribbean BBQ, Leesburg, Virginia, *Susan Benjamin, Courtesy True Treats*

For the native people of the Caribbean, this practice, unfortunately, attracted bugs. To keep the bugs away, the natives, under the observant eye of the conquistadors, built small smoky fires. They placed the meat on racks, which helped dry the meat, keep the bugs away, and provide an additional layer of preservative. The process was called *barbacoa*, which some believe is the origin of the word "barbecue." The Spanish delivered this method to North America, where it eventually transformed into the modern barbecue.

Who *Really* Started the Barbecue Tradition?

The answer to who started barbecues is ultimately "yes." Yes, the Native Americans set a standard of all a barbecue should be: reliable, repeatable, with a long cooking process rendering flavorful and digestible meats. But, yes, it was the British colonists who delivered the meats we so enjoy at barbecues today—namely cows and pigs. The British also introduced the technique of layering sauce onto the meat while it was cooking. Their predilection for tart foods meant these sauces were frequently vinegar-based. Other immigrants brought their own sauces. In South Carolina, for example, French and German immigrants introduced mustard-based sauces.[3]

Of the meats, pigs were a favorite of the South. Unlike cattle, which required room to graze, pigs were inexpensive and resilient, often left to forage for themselves. Animals were typically cooked uncut, the "whole hog" as it were—no barbecued ribs sectioned out for the taking, as today. The meat was lean and tough—barbecuing made it tender. This was significant to enslaved workers and others with few options. The process turned virtually inedible meats into substantive foods.

Barbecues started transforming into the social event of today in the late 1700s and moved with locomotive speed in the decades thereafter. The gatherings went from festive social events, such as July Fourth gatherings, to community get-togethers. Politicians, including George Washington, used barbecues to woo voters with the promise of sumptuous meats with alcohol trimmings, a tactic called "treating." During the Civil War, groups hosted barbecues to rally support for the troops.[4]

Barbecues also doubled as fundraising events, more like Mardi Gras than backyard gatherings with the neighbors. According to one newspaper report, one such event in 1900 was a fundraiser sponsored by the A.M.E. Zion Church. Allegedly attended by 5,000 African Americans, the barbecue involved fourteen hogs, eight sheep, two calves, four four-quarters of beef, several dozen good-sized fish, a wagonload of bread, forty gallons of ice cream, and soda water in "unlimited quantities and beer in similar proportions."

Great detail was given as to the process of cooking the meat. First, men dug the barbecue pit, two feet deep, twenty feet long, and three feet wide. The holes were filled with red-hot embers and ash, a coating of charcoal, then "long lengths of iron pipe that were laid over the holes." The meats were treated with vinegar, cayenne pepper, black pepper, salt, and spices and left to sit in the heat, turned from side to side at intervals.

A smattering of guests started arriving, then progressed to everyone from laborers to servants to businesspeople as day rolled into night. Inside the dining pavilion, "a score of waiters dashed madly to and fro in their efforts to supply the demand for barbequed delicacies." Meanwhile, the dancing pavilion was "so crowded that dancers seemed to bump into each other every glide, but that was no cause for worry. The bands fairly outdid themselves in their efforts to entertain." The barbecue ended at dawn.

The account is obviously exaggerated, but then the media at the time had no allegiance to accuracy or truth. What we can believe is reports that everyone left happy and the A.M.E. Zion Church raised $1,000.[5]

The African-American Influence

Throughout the history of barbecuing in the southern United States, enslaved African Americans were assigned the job of chopping wood, digging trenches, starting and monitoring fires, cooking meat, and otherwise making barbecues possible, an exhausting and hazardous job. During those years, enslaved workers developed their own sauces, spices, and other seasonings—not to mention barbecuing techniques.[6]

After the Civil War, these African-American specialists were sought out nationwide to prepare barbecues for an eager public. They entered towns and cities, created a barbecue event enjoyed by many, got paid a respectable amount, and left. Some stayed around and opened restaurants. Others lingered to sell spices and sauces that locals could take home. In the 1900s, as large numbers of African Americans left the South to find decent jobs and better living conditions up North, they brought barbecues with them. Many went to large cities, where they did not have the space to prepare whole animals. So, they cut the animals into manageable pieces, bringing us, for example, barbecued ribs.[7]

GRILLING: COMPANY'S HERE! IN A HURRY

Grilling . . . it's a man's art and a job that the gals will gladly relinquish, for a woman never looks her best working over a hot fire and a man never looks better.—Ogden Standard-Examiner, 1961[8]

The history of grilling is the history of men. This could be due to the semi-rigorous aspect of grilling, what with the fire, the coals, and so on. But grilling had a unique part in American history where men were at the forefront, which in this case was the literal front during World War II.[9]

Before then, grilling was part of the assembly of campsites—a ready-made barbecue pit without the bother. More than a setup for fishermen and hunters, it was part of the American way of life. Around the turn of the century, many Americans moved into the badlands of cities, in pursuit of factory and other industrial jobs. The captivity of indoor work led to a hunger for the great outdoors and recreational sports like baseball and football, as well as bicycling and, of course, camping.

The budding automobile industry made escape easier and destinations farther. Some people even attempted cross-country trips where camping was not only an alternative but the *only* alternative as few hotels, restaurants, and, certainly, rest stops were available.[10] These travelers needed to cook but didn't have the desire or wherewithal to dig barbecue pits. The ready-made grill was there to help them.

Enter the Grill

The early grills were essentially wire frames, some with legs, that stood directly over the fire. In 1909, Sackett's Camp Broiler described its premier grill as "a broiler with a level standard for coffee pot and skillets." Only one problem: the legs on the grill didn't lock into place. The grill, and everything on it, wobbled and spilled, especially on wet or rocky ground. Learning a lesson from Sackett's, other outdoor grill-makers provided not only a flat surface for cooking but camp stools for sitting, with wobble-reducing reinforced legs.[11]

By the 1920s, companies went even further, providing campers with full-fledged oil cookstoves. Already used in full-size kitchens, these smaller versions were easy to carry and relatively lightweight. To help things along, Henry Ford "invented" fire starters, what we now know as "briquettes"—essentially a version of what Native Americans were using all along. By the 1930s, Ford also produced the Ford Picnic Kit, a carry-as-you-go kit with a grill with charcoal briquettes that fit neatly into the automobile.

The big break for grills, however, came during World War II when the War Department enlisted the Coleman Company to design the five-pound pocket stove. The stove was much like the already existing oil cookstove but even lighter, more reliable, and easy to use with any kind of oil. After the war, the pocket stove became popular among the general public just as another shift in outdoor cooking was looming.[12]

Out of the City and into the Grill

After World War II, Americans experienced newfound prosperity, enabling millions to move out of the working class and into the middle class, with all the trimmings. Out of the city they went and into suburbs, houses duly appointed with lawns, decks, and, above all, patio space for a grill. And there, appropriately dressed husbands and wives served cocktails, wine, and beer as steaks lay on the grill, gently sizzling. And thus began the American cookout. And central to its success was the Weber grill.

Until Weber, people at home may have used the oil cookstove or constructed their own grills following directions from cookbooks and magazines. These early versions had no covers, exposing the would-be dinners to wind, rain, and debris. Weber took care of all that with a lid that sheltered the food and held in heat, regardless. Other companies were on hand to offer ever-new ideas. General Electric in 1960 announced its new electric grill for indoor and outdoor cooking "without the muss and fuss of charcoal,"[13] which sort of misses the point of a cookout in the first place.

Another change was afoot in the backyards of America. When the GIs returned from war, many women left the workplace and returned to housekeeping full-time. In the kitchen, they were responsible for the full lineup of meals. They also washed dishes, bought food, and ensured a decent meal with a well-appointed table setting was ready when dad came home from work.

Not that all women embraced the new lineup of responsibilities. And for them, especially, cookouts were a boon. Food preparation was mercifully in the domain of men. Naturally, men required *manly* paraphernalia—women's options would never do. Underscoring the point, in 1961 food writer Melanie De Proft advised hosts to purchase manly asbestos or well-padded gloves (aka oven mitts); long-handled hand tools (otherwise described as spatulas, forks, and so on); sharp knives (of course); and aprons, oversized and worthy of firefighters, which she says are "big enough to keep grease splatters and soot away from your favorite sports clothes."[14]

By the 1960s, cookouts were seamlessly entrenched in the American experience. The grill was what got them there.

WHAT'S GRILLIN'? HAMBURGERS, OF COURSE

The hamburger is the single most popular food item consumed in the United States, with Americans eating billions of them each year.—Oxford Encyclopedia of Food and Drink in America, 2004[15]

Beyond all measures, hamburgers are popular. They're so popular that they have a steady and undiminished presence in cookouts, fast-food digs, and American culture. Think Wimpy, the popular sidekick in Popeye cartoons. Popeye had spinach, Wimpy had hamburgers. The amazing thing was spinach made Popeye strong, hamburgers made Wimpy fat. As much as Popeye appealed to the hero in us when we were kids, Wimpy appealed to the inner hedonist, if not the inner slob. Which only proves hamburgers are so loveable that even a cartoon antihero can't diminish their worth.

Hamburger: The Name/The Burger

The question "Who invented hamburgers?" requires attention, but who invented the *name* "hamburger" does not. The German seaport city of Hamburg was a renowned exporter of high-quality beef from cows grazing on Germany's beatific mountainous meadows. When German immigrants arrived in the United States in the mid-1800s, fleeing political upheavals at home, they brought the reputation of Hamburg's good meats with them. In fact, many earned their livelihoods by opening restaurants in large cities like Chicago and New York. American

Burger list on food truck, Los Angeles, *Susan Benjamin, Courtesy True Treats*

chefs, ever on the lookout for new means of attracting diners, began offering "Hamburg-style" meats, Hamburg steaks, and Hamburg sandwiches.[16]

Another name for the hamburger was "Salisbury steak," which comes to us with its own backstory. In the mid-1800s, chopped, chipped, ground, or otherwise refined raw beef was prescribed as a remedy for digestive problems. In 1867, New York doctor James H. Salisbury stepped in to suggest that cooked patties might be just as good. The idea caught on, bringing us the "Salisbury steak," made with the hallmark brown gravy some restaurants still serve today. Handily enough, the first commercial meat grinders appeared at that time, making Salisbury's ground meat readily available and instantly popular. As for Salisbury, he endorsed one called the American Chopper.[17]

Early Hamburger Sightings

It's fair to say hamburgers are encoded in our culinary DNA. Since early history, humans chopped and cut meat—the essence of hamburgers. Through the centuries, hamburger-like foods appeared in occasional cookbooks, when cookbooks were produced only occasionally. One, Apicius, a collection of almost 500 recipes enjoyed by ancient Romans in the fourth century, explains how to make a hamburger-like patty mixed with pine kernels, black and green peppercorns, and white wine. Jump a few centuries to 1747 and food author Hannah Glasse described "Hamburgh [sic] Sausage" in her book The Art of Cookery, Made Plain and Easy. This hamburgh/sausage was made from minced meat mixed with nutmeg, cloves, black pepper, garlic, and salt and served with toast.[18]

Yet another recipe appeared in Mrs. Lincoln's Boston Cook Book in 1884, written by the influential Boston food expert and teacher Mrs. D. A. Lincoln. Her inclusion of hamburger was both a statement about the rising popularity of hamburgers and a recommendation that readers should make it. The recipe for "Hamburgh Steak" went as follows:

> Hamburgh Steak.—Pound a slice of round steak enough to break the fibre. Fry two or three onions, minced fine, in butter until slightly browned. Spread the onions over the meat, fold the ends of the meat together, and pound again, to keep the onions in the middle. Broil two or three minutes. Spread with butter, salt and pepper.[19]

As for who propelled hamburgers to the top of the American food chain, no one knows for sure—but plenty claim to know where. A German restaurant opened at Philadelphia's illustrious Centennial Exposition in 1876, serving Hamburg steaks to thousands of customers. Many believe this event created a demand for hamburgers, which, as it happens, were soon found in non-German restaurants and cookbooks thereafter.

Less-illustrious gatherings, at the state or local level, also purport to be the launching point of hamburgers. Folks in New Haven, Connecticut, insist that Louis Lassen was the first to popularize hamburgers, which he sold from his pushcart in 1900. Charlie Nagreen was said to have sold the first true hamburger (whatever that means) at a fair in Seymour, Wisconsin, in 1885.

Go to Akron, Ohio, and you discover that it was actually Frank Menches who introduced hamburgers at the Summit County Fair. Legend has it, he also invented the ice cream cone.

The who and where of hamburgers aside, an undeniable factor in their popularity has to do with work. Factory workers needed something quick, cheap, and filling to eat. To answer that call, food carts with coffee and small edibles waited at the ready outside. Later, when these carts became rigged with gas grills, "hamburger steaks" showed up on their menus. Rather than have their customers hold the food in their hands, which was awkward, vendors placed the patty between two slices of bread. And the hamburger *sandwich* was born.[20]

The Near Demise of the Hamburger and a Heroic Intervention

While the hamburger's timing in the food world was just about perfect, it couldn't have been worse. Starting in the early 1900s, an alarm bell was sounding about adulterated foods in general and meats in particular. And even *more* particularly ground meat. Countless investigations were launched and picked up by newspapers nationwide. "Commission Finds Much Impure Hamburger Steak" one 1909 headline read. "Practice of Adulteration with Sodium Sulfate Prevalent—Gives Aged Meat Fresh Appearance—Violates State Law."[21] Household columnists cautioned women to buy their own fresh meat and grind it in the safety of their own kitchens.

The pièce de résistance came in 1906, when Upton Sinclair published his seminal work *The Jungle*, exposing the horrors of meat production plants to an already disgusted public. Ground beef, he told America, contained undesirable organs and high volumes of animal fat, and was typically ground when it was just about to spoil. The Great American Hamburger seemed doomed.[22]

Who Would Want to Eat *That*?

So, who would want to eat hamburgers? Everyone, thanks to the efforts of Billy Ingram and his partner and fry cook, Walter Anderson. With undaunted focus and marketing prowess, they delivered a new and altogether better burger in the 1920s. It was made in sanitary conditions. It used first-rate beef. And it was ready when you wanted it at their regal-sounding, pre-fast-food restaurant, the White Castle.

It was at the White Castle that the nation's first flat patty on a bun emerged. And clean? Ingram boasted his restaurants were spotlessly clean and even whitewashed the exterior to prove it. The fixtures were made of gleaming stainless steel. And he ground fresh, wholesome beef in the restaurant window right in front of his customers. The chain started around 1921 and by 1929 had spread across the Midwest and was firmly entrenched in New York.[23]

By the 1930s, ground meat was back as an American food, if only because it was inexpensive and readily available during the Great Depression. The hamburger had risen again as the workingman's food, laying the groundwork for grilled burgers at home. Besides, if White Castle made it and Wimpy loved it, how could people at home resist? In the postwar 1950s, when grills heated with a flick of a match, they didn't.

THE LOVE, HATE, LOVE OF AMERICAN HOT DOGS

Hot dogs. We love to eat them. In fact, a recent survey stated that 80% of Americans think hot dogs taste great or fantastic. But also, we love to hate them. —"History of the Hot Dog," 2022[24]

Hot dogs have a lot in common with hamburgers. Both are connected to Germany. Both arrived in the United States with German-speaking immigrants. Both have murky histories—no one knows for sure where they came from or who invented them. Questions arise. Maybe hot dogs are related to sausages. But are they sausages? And, as with hamburgers, plenty of people have ideas.

Americans eat twenty *billion* hot dogs every year, which equals seventy hot dogs per person, served in 95 percent of American homes.[25] That's a lot.

Hot Dogs at the Start

Where did hot dogs originate? That depends on where you're asking. Folks in Frankfurt will say the answer is obvious. They were invented in 1487 in Frankfurt—why else call them Frankfurters? Others say Johann Georghehner invented hot dogs in Coburg, Germany—not Frankfurt—in the late 1600s. Georghehner, a butcher, *then* traveled to Frankfurt to promote his new food. Those in Vienna (and Chicago for reasons we'll disclose momentarily) believe hot dogs descended from Vienna. What all these early hot dogs had in common: they were sausages.

In Chicago, hot dog lovers don't deal with such trivial matters as the European past. The correct question is where did the *American* hot dog get its start? Why, where else? Chicago. And where did these hot dogs make their debut? The Columbian Exhibition, or, as it's more often called, the Chicago World's Fair of 1893. There two Austro-Hungarian sausage makers, Emil Reichel and Samuel Ladany, sold their Vienna Beef hot dogs. They were so-named because Vienna's (not Frankfurt's or Coburg's) sausages, and, by default, hot dogs, were the best in the world. The hot dogs were such a smash that Reichel and Ladany opened a Vienna Beef store, then started distributing their meats to restaurants by the late 1800s. The Vienna Beef company is still around today.[26]

What Is a Chicago-Style Hot Dog?

The Chicago-style hot dog was invented during the Great Depression when hot dogs were considered viable, if not measly, meals. To give the hot dogs heft, vendors added inexpensive condiments and vegetables. The bulky, albeit airy, result was called the "Depression Sandwich." Today, Chicago-style hot dogs are enjoyed at sports events, festivals, and restaurants. You can also make them at home. But the rules are strict. Very strict. One ingredient gone amiss, and it's not a Chicago-style hot dog. (BTW: You can eat it anyway.)

First, cook the hot dog. Steaming is preferred. If boiling is necessary, do it on low heat.

Steam a poppy seed bun until it's warm. It has to be poppy seed. Otherwise, it's not a Chicago-style hot dog.

Add the following toppings in the following order exactly: mustard, relish, onion, tomato, pickle, peppers, and celery salt. The tomato wedges must be tucked between the hot dog and top of bun on one side, and the pickles should be between the hot dog and bottom of bun on the other side. No infractions. See above.

Don't even think about adding ketchup. Ever. In fact, stop thinking about it now.

Enjoy.

As life would have it, lots of iterations of the Chicago hot dog theme run rampant in Chicago, even to this day. Possibly especially to this day. For the most part, they all taste good and are well worth a try.[27]

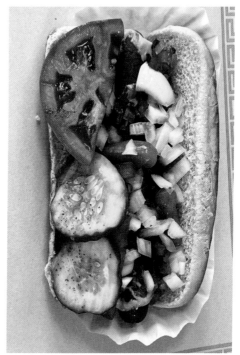

Dan enjoying grilled sausage at the beach, *Susan Benjamin, Courtesy True Treats*

Chicago-style hot dog, Chicago, Illinois, *Susan Benjamin, Courtesy True Treats*

Hot Dog: The Name

No one knows for sure, but the name "hot dog" was not necessarily complimentary. Food advocates on the hunt for adulterated foods flagged hot dogs as a top concern. They were right at the time. Manufacturers added sawdust, formaldehyde, and other fillers to the mix. The "dog" in the name, however, most definitely didn't signify man's best friend. Another possible reason: German immigrants kept hot-dog-looking dachshunds as pets. The coincidence led to legions of jokes, many centered on the ingredients within the casings. Said one of them: "Oh Hagenbeck, oh Hagenbeck, how can you be so mean to grind up all those doggies in your hot dog machine."[28]

Hot Dogs: The Industry

Hot dogs are practically impossible to make at home, unlike hamburgers, which simply require a meat grinder. And so, hot dogs depended on industry for their existence. One of the most famous is the Oscar Mayer Wiener. The hot dog operation was started by Oscar Mayer, a Bavarian immigrant who came to the United States at fourteen years of age in 1873. He started in Detroit and then moved to Chicago, where he worked in the meatpacking industry. In 1883, Oscar and his brothers Max and Gottfried, a sausage maker and ham cutter, respectively, opened a store that would become the marketing powerhouse that lives on today.

1880s: Sold packaged bacon, liverwurst, and bockwurst with the Oscar Mayer name on it—becoming the first branded meat manufacturer in the country.

1880s: Called their product *not* hot dogs, like everyone else, but wieners.

Early 1900s: Engaged in a never-ending advertising campaign, starting with newspapers.

1929: Added the signature yellow band (think: mustard) on all their products—still there today.

1936: Introduced the Wienermobile, a hot-dog-shaped car, coming to a location near you!

1963: Released a catchy and humorous jingle called "The Oscar Mayer Wiener Song." Impossible to miss or forget.

1965: Launched their first TV commercial.

1973: Released another catchy jingle, "My Bologna Has a First Name."[29]

The Oscar Mayer Wiener Song

The song, actually a jingle, reached an estimated forty-nine million families, was aired in nineteen countries, and was featured on a Hallmark card. The creator, Richard Trentlage, an Illinois-based jingle-writer, entered his jingle in an Oscar Mayer contest in 1962. It took him only one hour to write. The company took a year to select it. Trentlage became a millionaire. The company today is worth billions.

VERSE 1: Sung by a kid:
Oh, I wish I were an Oscar Mayer Wiener,
That is what I'd truly like to be-ee-ee.
'Cause if I were an Oscar Mayer Wiener,
Everyone would be in love with me.

VERSE 2: Sung by another kid:
Oh, I'm glad I'm not an Oscar Mayer Wiener,
That is what I'd truly hate to be,
'Cause if I were an Oscar Mayer Wiener,
There would soon be nothing left of me.[30]

When Oscar Mayer passed in 1955 at ninety-five years old, the company's annual sales were more than $150 million. And his legacy lived on. When health concerns related to bologna put a dent in sales, the company created the ever-successful, well-branded and -marketed Lunchables.[31]

AND ALL THE TRIMMINGS . . .

Condiments are no mere extras where cookouts are concerned. They are the very reason hot dogs and hamburgers are the principal players at American cookouts. That's because hamburgers and hot dogs are essentially bland, even with the charcoal flavor from the grill. The bold mustard, rich ketchup, and zesty relish, from pickled cukes to coleslaw, make the cookout menu work. Coleslaw a condiment? The standard lineup of condiments is expansive.

Condiments may seem like uncomplicated add-ons, but they actually have a highly contentious, even *sexy*, past.

Coleslaw, *Susan Benjamin, Courtesy True Treats*

Controversial Condiments

Condiments the Most Harmful of Any Part of the Daily Diet.—Newspaper article byline, 1897[32]

In the past, condiments covered a broad range of food, including butter, jam, molasses, and sugar; spices ranging from salt and pepper to Native Americans' cayenne pepper, ginger, and sassafras; and, of course, mustard, pickles, and other standards. They all started innocently enough. Native Americans used many of them as medicines and tasty additions to food, as did middle- and upper-class colonists who valued salt, which they used as a seasoning and preservative, above all.

In the nineteenth century, condiments hit a rocky road that lasted for over a hundred years. One culprit was the "purity" movement. By purity we don't mean the twentieth-century concern about adulterants. We're talking sex and an even greater tyranny, lust. One such purist was

Spices, the heart of condiments, with fruit, *Susan Benjamin, Courtesy True Treats*

Sylvester Graham, inventor of the graham cracker, which was, at the time, hard, unseasoned, and most definitely tasteless. He asserted that condiments were "highly exciting and exhausting," that they "over-stimulated the senses," and should be avoided along with "tea and coffee, tobacco, opium, and all alcoholic portables."[33, 34]

Welcome Back, Condiments

Immediately after World War I, when money was tight and food marginal, condiments brought welcome flavor to foods. In 1928, one journalist expressed the feeling of the time: "Over the last few years we have looked at old fashioned condiments with something of contempt . . . today we have an appreciation for them." While Americans were still forced to eat cheap, tough meat, condiments were there to tenderize and flavor them.[35]

Others were concerned for health-related purposes. One newspaper commentator claimed, "It may be well to consider what not to eat and the so-called condiments are perhaps the most harmful that enter into the daily diet." They are "strong stimulants," so powerful that "the nerves of sensibility become benumbed . . . and no longer offer remonstrance against harmful substances until the individual breaks down with some chronic disorder of the liver, kidneys, or some other important vital organ."[36]

Some disagreed, leaning far to the opposite side of the condiment analysis. In 1877, one food writer proclaimed that condiments are "valuable elements in our daily food . . . without which we may suffer from vomiting and diarrhea."[37]

The Truth about Ketchup

The ketchup that we slather on hamburgers started as a pungent fermented fish paste made from fish entrails and soybeans. The combination was made in China, quite possibly more than two millennia ago. It had no tomatoes. No smooth texture. Only the name was similar—*ge-thcup* or *koe-cheup*—which may explain the name "ketchup" of today. And, unlike today's ketchup, the salty paste was durable, able to hold up over a long journey at sea. It withstood the rigors of the spice trade, ending up in Indonesia and the Philippines. There, British traders discovered it, adopted it, and brought it home in the early 1700s. The English embraced ketchup, then immediately changed it into something else.

Fish went out but oysters, mussels, mushrooms, walnuts, lemons, celery, fruits, and other combinations were in. Some recipes were simple—mushroom ketchup, for example. Others more mystifying. One recipe contained one hundred oysters, three pints of white wine, and lemon peels spiked with mace and cloves. These concoctions were either boiled down or salted and left to sit until they were appropriately fermented. And then eaten and, yes, enjoyed.[38]

BBQ makers: ketchup, mustard, and relish, *Susan Benjamin and Maryann Fisher, Courtesy True Treats*

KETCHUP GOES TO PHILLY

Across the ocean, Americans didn't have ketchup, and tomato ketchup was the last thing they expected to eat. Gardeners valued tomatoes for their beauty, planting them as an ornament, but not as a food. Most Americans of the time believed tomatoes were poisonous. Why? Maybe because the acid from tomatoes caused lead on pewter plates to leach into the food, creating lead poisoning. Maybe because tomatoes resembled another, unnamed, toxic plant. Or maybe because the deadly nightshade was its cousin.[39]

Whatever the reason, Philadelphia scientist James Mease was not convinced. In 1812, he developed a recipe for the ketchup we know today. Mease's tomatoes were more than safe, they were considered an aphrodisiac. In fact, tomatoes were dubbed "Love Fruit" and their finished form as ketchup—thick, rich as tomato sauce, and delicious—was convincing. Only problem: ketchup spoiled easily. To ensure its longevity, food-makers needed to add chemicals such as coal tar, which, as you can imagine, was off-putting. Ketchup remained a condiment outlier.[40]

Two events moved tomatoes in a more culinary direction. One was the Civil War. While tomatoes didn't do well on pewter plates, they grew quickly, were easy to pick, and excelled storage-wise in cans processed for the Union Army.[41]

In 1876, another Pennsylvanian found an even better solution to the spoilage problem, bringing ketchup to the tables, and cookouts, of Americans everywhere. The man was Henry J. Heinz, who got his start in the condiment industry by selling horseradish based on his mother's homemade recipe. His idea was to use ripe tomatoes, whose natural pectin created a nice, bright color while acting as a preservative. Then he helped it along with vinegar to further enhance the shelf life, and sugar to offset the vinegar flavor. To top it off, he added a variety of spices.

Heinz is famous for its "57 varieties." But the reason for the "57" had less to do with the variety and more to do with the numbers five and seven. They were Heinz's wife's favorites. At the time, the company's products were at sixty-plus.[43]

The Versatile Tomato

Tomatoes are more versatile than most of us realize. People enjoyed fresh pineapple salad on rings of tomato jelly, potato salad in tomato jelly, tomato mayonnaise, and another dish from 1931 that's quick, easy, and not at all alarming—"Frapped Tomatoes." You might like to try it for yourself:

Remove paper from one 8-oz can of tomato sauce and immerse in a mixture of ice and salt for four hours. Remove top from can and slide out frozen mold. Slice thin and lay in beds of shredded lettuce. Serve with meat course. May pour the tomato sauce in refrigerator trays if desired and freeze that way.[44]

What literally sealed the deal for Heinz, though, came in 1890 when the company introduced the iconic ketchup bottle. Easy to carry, pour, and seal, plus made of glass so the customer could see exactly what they were getting. And that was a good thing.

Heinz Ketchup still lives on in the refrigerators of 97 percent of American homes today—with and without sugar. All told, Americans today buy ten billion ounces of ketchup a year.[42]

Mustard: Greeks, Jesus, and Hot Dan the Mustard Man

The mustard plant is likely the first crop ever cultivated. It has had a long and prestigious life—ancient Indian and Sumerian texts mention mustard as a spice and medicine. In northern Greece people enjoyed mustard as early as 2000 BC. The classic Greeks and Romans blended ground-up mustard seeds with unfermented grape juice to alleviate just about every ailment imaginable. Bump ahead in time and you find numerous versions of mustard from numerous nations—yellow, spicy brown, English, Chinese, German, and, of course, the creamy Dijon from France. In 1634, mustard from Dijon was declared the *only* true French mustard.[45]

MUSTARD IN THE USA: HOME RUNS AND HOT DOGS

Mustard was made in early America, but these efforts could hardly compete with Jeremiah Colman's of England. Colman began making mustard flour in 1814 and by 1830 was shipping it around the world and prepared mustard to the United States and Canada. The big break for American-made mustard came when twenty-one-year-old Robert Timothy French started working for a spice merchant in New York City. By the late 1800s, French owned a flour mill and bakery and had relocated to Rochester, New York. Among his products—mustard and turmeric.[46]

All went well, and the spice-selling business was successful. But the real, almost-literal home run was when the R. T. French Company made a new "cream salad mustard" consisting of the ever-popular mustard made garishly bright yellow with turmeric. The company showcased its creation at the St. Louis World's Fair, where it was displayed atop one of America's favorite new foods—the hot dog.[47]

Hot dogs and with them mustard became a "hit" at baseball stadiums. By 1915, the French's mustard–baseball–hot dog connection was so strong the company adopted a pennant as its

French's Mustard ad, *Ladies Home Journal*, 1928, *Wikimedia*

logo—still there today. By then French's mustard was outselling all its competitors combined. Rather than rest on its laurels, the company continued to advertise throughout the 1920s. But Colman's Mustard was never far behind. In 1926, Reckitt and Colman—the successor to Colman's Mustard of England—bought French's brand and they became one.[48]

THE FEMININE SIDE TO FRENCH'S

While mustard was a guy's thing—in a baseball kind of way—it had another life in women's domain. This is not sexism speaking but advertising, and mustard companies targeted women at home with such zeal, it's as if they didn't know the male demographic existed.

Articles in women's sections of newspapers and magazines proclaimed the virtues of mustard as a healer of everything—digestive issues, the effects of poisonous mushrooms, and as a bath to relieve colds and chills. They raised mustard to biblical proportions, connecting women's use of mustard in home-cooked meals to purveyors of what is just and right. French's advertisers had a more functional approach, positioning mustard as a useful and easy-to-use ingredient in delicious recipes. Should you want to try one, French's introduced this exciting new recipe called "Tomato Surprise!" in the *Baltimore Sun* in 1924:

> *Peel and cut center out of several large, firm tomatoes. Put them in a cool place. Dice some boiled tongue and sour pickles. Mix with French's mustard and fill center of tomatoes. Make a dressing after the recipe on French's mustard bottle and put a tablespoon on top of each tomato. Serve on lettuce leaves.*[49]

Should your food mission be a healthful lunch for the kids, why not try "Cheese and Nut Sandwich Filling"? Here's what you do:

> *Use equal parts of cheese and pecan nut meats. Mix the cheese with finely chopped nuts. Add: one-third teaspoon of salt; enough sweet cream to soften the mixture; two tablespoons of French's mustard. French's pepper to taste. Mix together thoroughly and spread on a slice of buttered bread.*[50]

Mustard Made in Heaven

Mustard was so good it was literally biblical. At least that's what advertisers had to say, telling readers that mustard was sold by peddlers in Solomon's time and, should they doubt the importance, that Christ likened Heaven to the mustard seed. But realistic writers did give purpose to the biblical claim. One food writer in 1916 explained: "Although the Bible only mentions mustard as symbolizing rapid growth, early writers were warm in praise of it as a relish."[51]

In the 1940s, advertisers were helped along by "Hot Dan the Mustard Man," the mustard equivalent of Tony the Tiger or Betty Crocker. He had helpful tips for homemakers, such as making a lunch no husband would refuse: "Egg salad sandwich with French's mustard added to the mayonnaise. So smooth and creamy it blends perfectly." Dan also had a cheerful way of rhyming. "His lunch-box food should be nutritious—also make it taste delicious. Use French's mustard smooth and bright—for FLAVOR that's exactly right."[52] Dan's life only lasted until the 1950s, following the brief but poignant trajectory of so many cartoon spokespersons.

Today, French's is owned by another spice company that started in 1889—McCormick.[53]

Mayonnaise: The Story

For a moment, let's overlook the fact that a version of mayonnaise, made with oil and eggs, was probably eaten by ancient Romans and Egyptians. Yet, as with so many foods, food aficionados say the birth of mayonnaise was in *France*. The French origin story is unlikely—or, at least, somewhat likely. But, if nothing else, it makes for good reading. Here it is:

Mayonnaise was invented at a victory banquet after France had captured Mahón, a city in Minorca, just off the coast of Spain. At the time, sauces were made of egg and cream but, as the story goes, the cream at this celebration had run out. So, the chef used olive oil instead. His creation was a success. He named it *mahónnaise* in honor of the other success on the battlefront.

A nice, tidy story but . . . one that's triggered consternation and debate for decades. One food commentator pointed out Mahón was hardly a hub of haute cuisine. Why name it for Mahón? Never. Instead, call it *bayonnaise* after Bayonne, a French town famous for its succulent hams. Others insist the name came from the French *manier*, meaning "to handle," or an old French word for yolk, *moyeu*. In the 1920s, the Spanish weighed in; one renowned chef even drafted a pamphlet proclaiming that the real name is *salsa mahonesa*.[54]

MAYO AT THE START

Who *invented* mayonnaise is one thing, but who put it on the culinary map is another. That would be the great French chef, founder of haute cuisine, *and* inventor of hot soufflé, Marie-Antoine Carême. It seems he lightened the existing mayonnaise by blending vegetable oil and egg yolks into an emulsion. His recipe became famous throughout the world, helped along by his own notoriety and high-level connections. Carême was known as "The King of Chefs and the Chef of Kings," as he worked for Napoleon, the Rothschilds, Prince Talleyrand, and Tsar Alexander, among others.

MAYO GOES TO THE USA

It took Americans to bump mayonnaise off its royal pedestal and make it the people's condiment. Granted, mayonnaise appeared in American cookbooks for the well-to-do and influential, starting in the early 1800s, and was served at restaurants such as the illustrious

Delmonico's in New York. There patrons could enjoy such dishes as chicken or lobster drenched in mayonnaise.

About seventy years later, numerous factors conspired to pitch mayo onto the populist front. First was the price. Originally, mayonnaise was made with expensive olive oil. But the price of olive oil dropped, and with it the price of mayo, making it affordable for all. Second was improved modes of transportation, trucks bringing veggies from California and Florida to the tables of colder climates in the North. Veggies meant salads, salads meant dressings, and dressings meant mayo. Third was versatility. Mayonnaise was equally at home in garden party Jell-O molds and as a replacement for butter on sandwiches.

By the late nineteenth century, home cooks were making mayonnaise in their kitchens, blending oil with vinegar and eggs. In 1923, President Calvin Coolidge gave mayo a boost, saying his Aunt Mary's homemade mayonnaise was his favorite food.[55]

MAYO ON THE SHELVES

In the 1920s, mayonnaise makers started bottling their selections for grocery store shelves. Richard Hellmann, a German immigrant, was the first to do so. He started by selling from his New York deli and within a decade dominated the market. The time was right—refrigeration extended the shelf life of mayonnaise. As more and more mayonnaise makers crowded the food field—600 by the mid-1900s—Hellmann maintained the lead. The reason for his success was his ongoing ingenuity. Hellmann continually invested in new modes of production. By the end of the 1920s, he could produce three tons of mayonnaise an hour.

Then there was marketing. Everything Hellmann did was geared to sell. By 1912, for example, his mayonnaise was in clear-glass screw-top jars for easy opening and closing, and to showcase the purity of the creamy white contents. Each had a wide mouth, perfect for a good-sized spoon, and was reusable for home canning. Need a new rubber ring? Hellmann could accommodate for a penny each.

Should you question the integrity of the product within, Hellmann's had a blue ribbon on the label, suggesting that *very jar* just won first prize at a competition—or it should have. By 1922, the product was known as "Hellmann's Blue-Ribbon Mayonnaise." And should you forget about Hellmann's? The company created legions of recipe books with titles such as *That Amazing Ingredient: Mayonnaise!* Definitely tempting.[56]

A decade or so later, mayonnaise went from being a luxury item for the rich to being a staple at the workingman's table and, soon, the backyard grill.

THE REAL SECRET BEHIND THE REAL MAYONNAISE

In the end, the real success of mayonnaise is all about mayonnaise. It has just enough flavor to be recognizable but not so much it drowns out other ingredients. In essence, mayonnaise is the perfect helper food, doing the job discreetly, then stepping aside while others get the credit. The versatility of products with a mayo-helper is jaw-dropping.

Two salad recipes from 1911 demonstrate the point nicely. There's the Devonshire Salad with soft yet firm curds of cottage cheese, served with salt, black pepper, and cayenne pepper on a bed of mayonnaise-draped lettuce. The other, Veal Salad, was a prize-winning recipe, reports the *Baltimore Sun*. It contains one-part boiled veal and one-part boiled pork, mixed with a bunch of tender white celery and a small onion, all chopped and mixed together with mayonnaise.[58] Should you be a more lettuce and cukes kind of person, you'll appreciate the substantive role mayonnaise plays in Thousand Island, French, and Roquefort dressings.[59]

As for homemade mayonnaise, ditto that the varieties seem just about endless. Among these are ginger mayonnaise, orange marmalade mayonnaise, stewed tomato mayonnaise, horseradish mayonnaise, anchovy mayonnaise, and fluffy mayonnaise made with extra eggs, beaten dry. The recipes are so easy, anyone can make them. Just mix, mix, mix whatever you like with mayonnaise. While the quantities of each may vary, in the end, the amount is "to taste."

Fairs, Festivals, and Movie Screens
ALL ABOUT POPCORN, AN AMERICAN ORIGINAL

Popcorn is close to miraculous. As one reporter put it in 1883, "The corn in its natural state scarcely covered the bottom of the popper, but now a beautiful metamorphosis takes place. Every little yellow grain grows Crack! Crack! And is instantly transformed into something which resembles nothing so much as a white blossom. The cracking noise becomes louder—the foamy, white mass in the popper swells with every undulating move of the box—and in another minute where there was nothing but a handful of yellow grain there is a great armful of soft, flossy, snow-white corn. With a graceful jerk, the contents are emptied into a bin."[1]

Today, the ubiquitous popcorn appears at just about every occasion from bar mitzvah parties to car dealership lobbies. So, how did popcorn become America's fun food darling? And what kept it from being an honored food such as breakfast cereal? The answer is all about us.

Popcorn: An American Necessity

Popcorn can hardly be called a luxury, it is so very much like one of the essential necessities of life. —Boston Globe, May 2, 1874[2]

Popcorn is ours: it's been American since before there was an America. And while the saying might go "It's as American as apple pie," neither apples nor pies are native to North America. Popcorn, on the other hand, started in the culinary terrain of Native Americans how many years ago? An 80,000-year-old corn pollen fossil, discovered 200 feet below nearby Mexico City, was similar to the corn pollen of today. And, as it happens, the first use of corn was for popping.

That being said, the oldest ears of popcorn in North America were found in a New Mexican bat cave. They ranged from being smaller than a penny to about two inches and were about 5,600 years old. A 1,000-year-old kernel of popcorn appeared in another cave, this time in Utah, which had been inhabited by the forerunners of Pueblo Indians. And, in 1612, Iroquois were popping corn in the Great Lakes region, according to a French explorer who witnessed the fact.

Strangely enough, aside from some colonial dips into popcorn as a breakfast cereal (eaten with cream or milk), popcorn took off relatively late on the American food scene; in fact, it wasn't even *mentioned* in farm papers or seed catalogs, no less advertisements in general stores, until around 1880. Then it went from relative nonexistence to a smash hit. It was such a hit that it appeared at just about every festive occasion, and gave levity to aspects of day-to-day living just by being ... popcorn.[3]

Popcorn also appeared in more sedentary goings-on as well. While Americans had long used cornmeal, cornstarch, and the great confuser corn syrup, they also used popcorn, but not for the reasons you'd expect. Regardless, popcorn never actually entered the nomenclature of American mealtime. This fact is a pity, actually, seeing that popcorn is delicious, with mouth-feel, not to mention fiber, and whatever else you'd want from food you like to eat.

The Other Popcorn: The Recipes of Day-to-Day Living

Some of the alternate uses of popcorn have been around for centuries, but never center stage. They're fun, healthy, versatile, and a real treat. And yes—you *can* use pre-popped popcorn!

POPCORN SANDWICHES

This lunchtime popcorn delight is perfect for kids and grown-ups who want to add fun to function midday. *Even better*, bring them on a picnic or excursion that's guaranteed fun. This recipe is from 1915—you can definitely change the filling: Put the popped corn through a food chopper and make a paste of it mixed with cream cheese or peanut butter. Spread this paste between thin slices of bread. Tip: Forget the paste and chopper—it's too much work. Just chop up popcorn and mix it in the peanut butter or cream cheese for a satisfying crunch. Don't be shy—add raisins, tiny marshmallows, even chocolate chips to the mix, as the spirit moves you.[4]

POPCORN CEREAL

Do not scoff at this! It's *wonderful*—just like oatmeal but with more texture. The cereal recipe goes like this: Pop the corn, run it through a food chopper, and add four cups of the popcorn to two cups of boiling water. Then cook until thickened. They say the cereal will come up fluffy, something like oatmeal that isn't over-wet or underdone. What's left over you can slice and fry for next morning's breakfast.[5] Tip: This is really good with butter, salt, and sugar. Eat while hot. Another option: Add milk and a sweetener to popped corn, as taste requires. Stir. Enjoy.

Popcorn cereal in a bowl, *Maryann Fisher, Courtesy True Treats*

POPCORN AS GARNISH

Simple, but true! Esteemed master chef Louis P. De Gouy of the acclaimed New York Waldorf-Astoria (1930s to 1950s) recommended popcorn as a garnish for salad and soup. For soup, he explains, "Serve the soup in heated soup plates, each plate garnished with a little popcorn, lightly toasted."[6]

Popcorn: The Egalitarian Food

Popcorn had a lot going for it as fun food, but two things stood above the rest. First, it was portable. It required little more than a bag—no dishes, spoons, or even napkins involved. Unlike ice cream, it didn't melt, and unlike chocolate, it wasn't messy. Second, popcorn was cheap to make commercially or at home—requiring only popcorn kernels, a little oil for the pan, and easy-to-afford flavorings such as salt. Popcorn showed up in all sorts of places, even on trains where vendors hocked it to passengers.

Even the act of *buying* popcorn had a festive edge. One newspaper in 1883 described a popcorn vendor as a "fantastically attired individual with a broad, brass sign of 'popcorn' on his cap, a trumpet in reserve and two enormous bags flung over his shoulder." As for the happy vendor, he said, "I sell these bags out in a few hours. Each holds hundreds of quarts, each done up one quart to a paper bag. To whom? Everybody. Every class that rides on these trains eats corn. Rich men and poor men, merchants, lawyers, doctors—though some of them don't approve of it, they eat it all the same—clerks down to laborers going home from a hard day's toll. . . . No, I ain't getting rich out of it but I'm making a living, and a good one."[7]

In the first part of the twentieth century, popcorn became a standard at fairs, movie theaters, festivals, and other gatherings. And the seed of that particular distinction was planted at the World's Fairs. Not that popcorn was invented and introduced at the World's Fairs—it wasn't—but it did reach a broad audience and reaped lots of publicity.

PHILADELPHIA CENTENNIAL EXHIBIT

The Philadelphia Centennial Exhibit opened on May 10, 1876—on the one-hundredth anniversary of the signing of the Declaration of Independence and just over a decade after the Civil War. While the federal government approved the event, it didn't fund it, so planners doubled as fundraisers. No matter. On opening day, over 100,000 people flooded into the event, welcomed in an address by President Ulysses S. Grant.

So, it makes sense that popcorn, a native child of North America long before the USA was a wrinkle on a page of parchment paper, would be a hit. The conduit for its presence was I. L. Baker, who paid either $3,000 or $8,000, depending on the source, for exclusive rights to all popcorn concession stands throughout the event. He set up "curious

Old-fashioned popcorn, *Susan Benjamin, Courtesy True Treats*

and attractive gas furnaces" around the exhibit with an impressive display in Machinery Hall, where men and women roasted popcorn over a gas furnace and formed them into popcorn balls, a popcorn favorite.[8]

As for the varieties, they may have included rice popcorn, pearl white popcorn, and branching popcorn, according to a reporter covering the event.[9] The display "was crowded all day and thus showed the attractiveness of the exhibitors' peculiar wares and machinery."[10] The popcorn sold for five cents, including a newcomer to the popcorn world—"sugared popcorn."

CHARLES CRETORS AND THE COLUMBIAN EXHIBITION

If modern popcorn was conceived in Philly, it was born at the Columbian Exhibition in Chicago. Also known as the Chicago World's Fair, the event opened in 1893 to celebrate the 400th anniversary of Christopher Columbus's journey to the "new world"—a year late, owing to one mishap after another. Still, the fact that the fair opened at all was something of a miracle: Chicago had just recovered from a disastrous fire, and another, smaller fire threatened to destroy the midway of the Chicago World's Fair . . . twice.

In spite of all odds, there it was, the buildings grand and white, giving the event yet another name—the White City. The buildings were also temporary, and after the World's Fair ended, they caught on fire yet again, only this time the flames were deliberate.

Among the many features of the fair were the dazzling lights of the first Ferris wheel and an impressive German chocolate-making machine—the inspiration for Milton Hershey to leave caramel and start making chocolate (he actually bought the machine after the fair ended). It was also the birth of a new era of popcorn-making, which brings us to Charles Cretors.

An entrepreneur and innovator from Lebanon, Ohio, Charles Cretors transformed popcorn. When he started his career, popcorn makers were pouring melted butter and salt on the freshly popped corn. Only problem: Some batches were soggy. Some were dry. Some were a combination of the above. But Cretors had an idea—why not pop the corn *in* the butter and salt mix so every piece is nicely coated and the result deliciously predictable?

Even more impressive was Cretors's mechanical prowess. He invented a steam-powered popcorn machine able to heat and shake the corn automatically. Once the corn was fully popped, the vendor had only to release a wire that opened the kettle's lid and dumped fresh popcorn into a bin below. No more snatching popcorn out of the fire. No more shaking a popper until the kernels popped. The machine did it all. But it did even more: Exhaust from the machine's steam engine was piped into a pan to keep the popcorn continually warm. And warm popcorn emanates a compelling popcorn smell, luring in all who passed. Should they miss or otherwise ignore the smell, the steam activated a small shrill whistle to catch their attention. All this was housed in a fetching popcorn wagon—as festive and eye-catching as the popcorn itself.

Cretors had fine-tuned his machine and was ready to display it just in time for the Chicago World's Fair. It was an event unto itself: in addition to popping corn, the machine could roast twelve pounds of peanuts and twenty pounds of coffee, bake chestnuts, and even roast peanuts and popcorn simultaneously.[12] Cretors's hope was to sell these machines to businesses, while making money by selling the popcorn as well.

A few days went by, but sales were lackluster. So Cretors came up with yet another daring, albeit uncomplicated, idea: give the popcorn away for free. He did and word spread about this wonderful popcorn, which, according to his sign, was a "New Taste Sensation . . . Popcorn Popped in Butter . . . a New Revolutionary Method." As demand increased, so did his price, making him a more-than-decent profit.[13] Cretors's success inspired other popcorn enthusiasts to make their own versions of the machine, his influence still present wherever popcorn pops.

Popcorn at the Movies

Popcorn was a snack food favorite before most people had ever seen a movie. Most entertainment was live, featuring stars or lesser-known traveling troupes who performed on stage, from elaborate opera houses to impromptu stages set up at the edge of corn fields. That changed when nickelodeons appeared in 1905. These early movie theaters continuously ran one- and two-reel films, each lasting anywhere from fifteen minutes to an hour. As they were silent films, sound came from a piano in the theater and words appeared on the screen—typically a short sentence or cluster of exclamations. Within five years, there were 10,000 nickelodeons and the movie industry was off![14]

While movies became exponentially popular over the years, they were definitely popcorn-less, at least on the surface. Movie-house owners aimed to portray their theaters as grand, exquisitely appointed entertainment palaces, and food was out of the question. Spills could happen. Pieces drop. No matter: candy stores and other venues set up close by, and vendors sold their popcorn close to the theater doors. Some vendors even walked up and down the aisles, in ballpark fashion, selling salted and buttered bags to those in the audience.

But it was the Great Depression that truly brought popcorn into the theaters. Money was scarce, and ticket sales were not enough to keep the theaters running. Some theater owners actually brought in candy, which they sold from candy dispensers, but popcorn, with its compelling smell, lively pop, and affordable price, was the real money-maker. Popcorn continued to ride the wave of popularity through the sugar shortages of World War II when candy and other treats were unavailable.

One of the first movies ever, *The Kiss*, took all of eighteen seconds, where viewers watched actors John Rice and May Irwin kiss. It was a short, hesitant kiss but scandalous nonetheless.[15]

After the war, movie-theater owners saw yet another decline in popularity. It wasn't the economy that stood in their way, but television. Concession stands were, once again, there to rescue them. It wasn't just popcorn that filled their shelves, but an array of candy, hot dogs, and bubbling sodas. Concern that the treats might spill was partly mitigated by drive-ins—if something spilled, the customer had to pick it up.[16]

BRING ON THE CANDY!

Sugar shortages aside, movie-theater owners featured a variety of candies meant to reflect their brand and entice sales. Some were upscale truffles and other sumptuous delights. For the most part, though, quick, available, and neatly packaged treats won out. Like popcorn, candies weren't made for theatergoers, but they were tasty, manageable, cheap, and suited the concession stand well.

Some, like Goobers, aka chocolate-covered peanuts, and their cousin, Raisinets, had been a favorite among bridge players for decades. First made in the late 1800s, the pieces were small and tidy enough to eat with the fingers of one hand while holding the cards in the other. And, as women became increasingly diet-obsessed, the size was not intimidating.

Others, such as licorice, played a role onscreen and off. Off-screen, licorice makers were duking it out brand-to-brand: Twizzlers, started in the mid-1800s, were up against the 1920s newcomer, American Licorice. To get ahead, the American Licorice Company later made the first non-black licorice—and a concession stand favorite—Red Vines.[17]

The American Licorice Company also won the *onscreen* battle with the movie *The Gold Rush*. Comic silent-screen actor Charlie Chaplin played a little tramp seeking his fortune during the gold rush. His fortunes were few (actually none), so he was forced to boil and eat his boot, eating the laces like spaghetti. The footwear was actually black licorice and the laces, today's licorice laces. Just to be on the safe side, the American Licorice Company made two sets, and the rest, as the saying goes, was history.[18]

What Exactly Is Licorice?

Licorice is an extract from the licorice plant, native to temperate parts of western North America. It was used as a medicine, spice, and candy. In fact, kids chewed licorice roots bought in candy stores in the 1800s and early 1900s. Licorice was also an essential part of tobacco production—so much so that post–Civil War Southerners hoped to boost their economy by growing licorice crops. The idea, dependent on government funding, never took off.[19]

Where Am I ? Fair, Festival, Carnival . . . What's Up??

The difference between a fair and a festival? A carnival and an amusement park? An amusement park and a theme park? And *Disney*? Where does Disney fit? The names seem like a blur, but no worries. There *is* a difference between them. That may not matter if you're having fun . . . but it's always good to know.

Fairs: Community-based events rich in local culture, foods, and entertainment. These are not traveling shows but can include traveling carnivals on the grounds. Who can say no to a sparkly Ferris wheel?

Festivals: Just like fairs, festivals are local and often homespun, typically with a cultural or religious orientation. They can double as fundraising events.

Carnivals: Carnivals may go back to the Romans, but these days are more equated with Roman Catholics and the pre-Lent festivities such as Mardi Gras. Traveling carnivals provide rides and games, set up in local parking lots or embedded in other events.

Amusement parks: Immobile and dependable, amusement parks offer the usual lineup of attractions and cotton candy–type festive foods. But they're also regional, some of the best alongside boardwalks such as New York's Coney Island—behold clams and calamari!

Theme parks: Theme parks are amusement parks with more branding. Disney is a great example: the rides, entertainment, and festive foods run from classic to new but are all about the Disney brand. Brought to you, of course, by Mickey Mouse.

Circuses: Old-world traveling circuses with their trapeze acts, animals, and clowns amaze, engage, and leave. The abuse of animals that were part of the circus attraction diminished their popularity. Today, circuses are reappearing—animal free.

Sausage stand, West Virginia State Fair, *Susan Benjamin, Courtesy True Treats*

BBQ, Berkeley Springs, West Virginia, Food Truck Festival, *Susan Benjamin, Courtesy True Treats*

Boardwalk? Circus? Amusement park? Who knows?, *Susan Benjamin, Courtesy True Treats*

THE ULTIMATE FESTIVE FOODS

Cotton Candy

Cotton candy is a favorite at festive events, if only because the feather-light strands defy the boundaries of normal food. The thinking, in terms of cotton candy history, is that a dentist invented it in the late 1800s. That is partially true. The partial part dates back about 600 years when pastry chefs in Venice created spun sugar that put today's cotton candy to shame. They would take the sugary strands while warm and through human ingenuity and tools such as broom handles, weave them into shapes—even entire scenes.[20]

Cotton candy remained a festive, hand-spun treat until industrialization came along to liberate it. Enter dentist William Morrison. He and his friend, candymaker John C. Wharton, developed a cotton candy machine that enabled confectioners to bypass the hand-spinning and let a machine do the work instead. Cotton candy was then called "fairy floss," possibly for a light and breezy fabric popular at the time.

Naturally, Morrison and Wharton showcased their cotton candy at the St. Louis World's Fair of 1904. The event attracted twenty million people over seven months—Morrison and Wharton sold more than 68,000 servings of cotton candy to many of them. In the 1920s another dentist, Josef Lascaux, changed the candy's name to another fabric, giving us the "cotton candy" of today.[21]

Doughnuts, Oily Cakes, and Funnel Cakes

Then the company sat round the large round table to their tea, while a plentiful supply of fire-cakes and dough-nuts furnished out the repast.—Boston Times, January 30, 1808[24]

Doughnuts are not just a fun food, they're a many-things food that have been enjoyed just about everywhere, just

---

Feeling guilty about loving cotton candy? Don't. Your average cotton candy has 105 calories and no sodium, fat, or cholesterol, and only 26 grams of sugar— less than a funnel cake or caramel apple.[22]

Still feeling guilty about loving cotton candy? Really. Don't. It may save your life. Turns out researchers at New York– Presbyterian Hospital and Cornell University noticed that the size and arrangement of cotton candy filaments mimicked our capillary systems. Researchers are now using the cotton candy model to create synthetic flesh that could supply blood to damaged tissue. Or as the website Futurist put it: "Cotton Candy May be the Key to Creating Artificial Organs."[23]

Everyone loves doughnuts, everywhere, *Susan Benjamin, Courtesy True Treats*

Doughnut making behind Plexiglas, Eastern Shore, Maryland, *Susan Benjamin, Courtesy True Treats*

about all the time. They make an easy transition from household to theme park, from a kid's treat to a worker's breakfast food with coffee.

An early version of the doughnut was brought to North America by Dutch immigrants. *Olykoeks*, or "oily cakes," as the name implies, were fried in oil. Once settled in their new home, the Dutch saw the light, or at least one light, trading their oil for the more popular and available lard.[25] Unfortunately, the inside of the doughnut didn't cook as quickly as the outside, leaving them with a well-done exterior and undercooked interior. So, the enterprising Dutch stuffed the balls with fruits, nuts, and other fillings that did not require cooking.[26]

In 1809, Washington Irving described these doughnuts as a party dish. The parties, he said, "were generally confined to the higher classes, or noblesse . . . that is to say, such as kept their own cows and drove their own wagons. . . . Sometimes the table was graced with immense apple pies, or saucers full of preserved peaches and pears; but it was always sure to boast an enormous dish of balls of sweetened dough, fried in hog's fat, and called doughnuts, or olykoeks—a delicious kind of cake, at present scarce known in this city, except in genuine Dutch families."[27]

Among other early doughnuts were sopaipillas, a name derived from *sopaipa*, the Spanish word for a honey cake that is *served* with honey. There were also fritters that descended from the Romans and beignets, which evolved from the fritters and are now enjoyed by the French.

The strangest part of doughnut history occurred in the late 1800s when rumors circulated that doughnut shapes were entwined with sorcery. Said one reporter, hags "made images of men, women and children which they heated over a gentle fire, tormenting the neighbors these images represented."[28]

Jelly doughnuts were brought by Germans, and doughnuts with a hole were allegedly created by an American sea captain, Hansen Gregory, in 1847. The hole allowed the surface area of the doughnut to expand so it could cook through and through. No messy fillings—just quick and clean. In the interests of full disclosure, some believe angels bestowed the doughnut hole idea in one of Gregory's dreams.[29]

The turning point came in World War I when doughnuts, like their culinary cousins, pies, were considered a taste of America in the trenches. Hand-delivered by volunteer "doughnut girls," they were so significant that Great War soldiers (ironically called "doughboys") clamored for more when they returned home. Lucky for them, Adolph Levitt, a Jewish refugee from czarist Russia, was on hand to invent a doughnut machine in 1920 that could churn out eighty dozen identical doughnuts an hour. These were then dusted with sugar, often to an audience of customers, who were mesmerized by both the process and the result.

Throughout this time, doughnuts were a jewel at festive occasions, enjoyed by Christians during Carnival leading up to Lent. Jews serve fresh jelly doughnuts at Hanukkah parties, a tradition that started in Poland in the 1600s and carried over to the United States. But doughnuts were also an everyday guide to good living, even when good living was hard to find. During the Depression, doughnuts were available and affordable.[30] When immigrants arrived at Ellis Island, the Salvation Army greeted them with a blanket and a doughnut.[31]

Doughnuts were more than fun and filling—they were romantic, in the classic sense of the word. As one poem in 1838 put it:

> When round the old table in pleasure were seated,
> The bright rosy children and parents so bland,
> While smoking before them their glad eyes were greeted,
> With the pile of huge doughnuts, the pride of the land,
> The New England Doughnut—
> The rich smoking Doughnut—
> The brown twisted Doughnut, the pride of the land.[32]

Whatever the reason, why not make these truly old-fashioned doughnuts at home? The recipe is exactly the same.

Dough Nuts, 1828

3 pounds sifted flour.

1 pound of powdered sugar.

Three quarters of a pound of butter.

Four eggs.

Half a large tea-cup full of best brewer's yeast.

A pint and a half of milk.

A tea-spoonful of powdered cinnamon.

A grated nutmeg.

A table-spoonful of rose-water.

Cut up the butter in the flour. Add the sugar, spice, and rose-water. Beat the eggs very light, and pour them into the mixture. Add the yeast (half a tea-cup, or two wine-glasses full) and then stir in the milk by degrees, so as to make it a soft dough. Cover it and set it to rise. When quite light, cut it in diamonds with a jagging-iron, or a sharp knife, and fry them in lard. Grate loaf sugar over them when done.[33]

Or try Albert's Favorite Doughnuts from 1877, submitted to *Buckeye Cookery and Practical Housekeeping* by Mrs. A. F. Ziegler: "One pint sour milk, one cup sugar, two eggs, one tea-spoon soda, half cup lard, nutmeg to flavor; mix to a moderately stiff dough, roll to half inch in thickness, cut in rings or twists, drop into boiling lard, and fry to a light brown."[34]

FUNNEL CAKES: A FESTIVE FAVORITE

Funnel cakes, a favorite treat at fairs and festivals, are an easy-to-make member of the dough-nut family. They originated in northern Europe, likely during the Middle Ages, but arrived in the United States in the 1800s. They were originally celebratory foods for German immigrants known as the "Pennsylvania Dutch." Here's a funnel cake recipe from 1935 you might want to try:

> *Mix 1 pint of sweet milk, 2 eggs well beaten (yolks and whites together), enough flour to make a thin batter, $^1/_2$ teaspoonful baking powder, $^1/_4$ teaspoonful salt. Mix in a pan thoroughly. Place enough lard in a pan to cover the bottom. Let it get quite hot before cooking the batter. Now put the batter through a funnel into the hot lard, beginning at center of pan, and turning the stream around in a gradual enlarging circle, being careful not to touch the sides of the other dough. Fry a light brown and serve hot with any tart jelly.*[35]

Maryann loves funnel cake, *Susan Benjamin, Courtesy True Treats*

Corn Dogs

Corn dogs are a mystery. When were they invented? Who invented them? And how did they end up in fairs, festivals, and other amusements? While many origin stories fly, the most likely starts in the 1940s, when vaudeville performers Neil and Carl Fletcher decided to sell a new creation they called "corny dogs" at the Texas State Fair in 1942. The Fletchers apparently didn't know that Pronto Pup, a small fountain shop in Portland, Oregon, was selling a cornmeal-battered and deep-fried hot dog on a stick in 1941.

Then there's Ed Waldmire, who was visiting Muskogee, Oklahoma, also around 1941, when he tried his first corn dog. Believe it or not, the story gets complicated from here. Waldmire told his friend Don Strand about the little-known corn dog. Strand told his dad, who was a baker. For reasons unknown, Waldmire, Strand, and possibly Strand's dad worked for years to perfect the corn dog recipe, which culminated in the opening of the Cozy Dog Drive-In and the beginning of corn dogs (so they say) in 1946.

So, take your pick. Who invented corn dogs? Whatever you decide, you're probably wrong because newspapers were loaded with ads for corn dogs as far back as 1940. The *Palm Beach Post*, for example, proclaimed that it was introducing its very own "Corn Dog Sandwich," which seems to have been doing quite well in New Orleans, where "more than 70,000 corndogs were sold in a period of three weeks."[36]

Don't get too excited, though, because that very year the San Angelo, Texas, *Evening Standard* proclaimed, "Demand Has Been So Great the Corn Dog Has Puppies . . . Over 500 Sold on Sunday." The corn dog is "the newest, tastiest sandwich you've ever seen."[37] Same year, different newspaper: this time the *Tallahassee Democrat* headlines a story proclaiming the "American Hot Dog Puts on New Dress." That dress, of course, being cornmeal.

You might be thinking that the story of the corn dog, whoever created it, begins somewhere in the South. Only . . . the *Tallahassee Democrat* tells us its origin story of corn dogs, saying, "The Corn Dog started its coast-to-coast trek in the New England states and made its way Westward, dropping back to the home of its ingredients' origin, the deep South, then out West." So, it seems, the corn dog actually originated in New England, then headed south where "the corn dog makes its debut . . . nestled in a delicious cradle of good old fashion Southern Cornbread."[38]

One last thing: Articles about the ever-delightful, if not *magical*, corn dogs never mentioned they were being sold at fairs, festivals, amusement parks, or other such gatherings—the places where we most enjoy them now.[39]

What's New? Turkey Legs, Deep-Fried Oreos, and What Else?

Most festivals these days are home to what would otherwise be seen as an anomaly of nature: turkey legs. They're big. They're brazen. And they beg to be clutched in a likewise giant fist while being eaten. So, it should come as no surprise that turkey legs are popular at Renaissance

Fairs, where reenactors gorge, as it were, medieval style. Only turkey legs weren't actually eaten in the medieval period, which was between the fifth and late fifteenth centuries. Lots of time. No turkey legs.

At this point, you might guess turkey legs aren't actually turkeys' legs. Or, worse, they are turkey legs pumped up with toxic gas of some sort. How else could they weigh one and a half pounds—more than a French poodle puppy? No worries. Those turkey legs really are from turkeys, but unlike the more genteel legs at the supermarket, they are from male turkeys. The leg encompasses the thigh and drumstick and, as they're all dark meat, they're relatively inexpensive.[40]

So, how did turkey legs find their way into American food folly? The answer would be the corporation behind the nation's number-one theme park: Disney.

Turkey legs, Frederick County Fair, Maryland, *Susan Benjamin, Courtesy True Treats*

Turkey legs weren't particularly relevant to any of Disney's themes—Mickey, Donald, the whole gang, were never seen eating them—but they *were* something you could write home about. When they first appeared in the 1980s, they were sold at Magic Kingdom's Frontierland next to a retail display of coonskin caps. They were almost as much a hit—and brand—as the Little Mermaid. So, Disney welcomed turkey legs into its magical fold. Between Disney's four parks in Orlando and two in Anaheim, people are buying two-million-plus legs every year.

While Disney productions such as *The Little Mermaid* can be copyrighted, turkey legs cannot, and other theme parks including Universal Studios, Dollywood, and SeaWorld have included them in their fun foods lineup. Today, vendors at fairs large and small sit outside in the warm, festive air selling turkey legs to those strolling past them.[41]

Disney World plastered images of turkey legs and funny sayings about them all over T-shirts and boxers. At one point, they even created turkey leg air fresheners. In the past, Disney's Main Street Confectionery whipped up turkey leg Rice Krispie Treats.[42]

Fried Green Tomatoes and What Else?

Before there were deep-fried Oreos at carnivals, fairs, and festivals, there were deep-fried vegetables. There were deep-fried onion rings, of course, from the 1930s, and deep-fried pickle chips, which landed in the 1960s. Depending on the region, these were accompanied by deep-fried broccoli, string beans, and mushrooms. Other, more local, specialties such as fried green tomatoes made an appearance, too.

Most of us consider fried green tomatoes a Southern dish, but that has more to do with *Fried Green Tomatoes at the Whistle Stop Cafe*, a book written by Fannie Flagg in 1991. The setting was a small Alabama restaurant whose specialty was, indeed, fried green tomatoes. Only fried green tomatoes were actually a Midwestern and even Northern dish, possibly brought to the United States by Jewish immigrants in the late 1800s.[43]

Deep-fried vegetables continue to have a presence at carnivals, fairs, and festivals. They're as glaring and delightful as the cotton candy, funnel cakes, and deep-fried Oreo cookies and Twinkies—all of which makes us grateful for the deep-fried-any-kind-vegetables roughage.

Fried Green Tomatoes—a Recipe
From Chicago's newspaper *Daily Inter Ocean* via *Smithsonian Magazine*:
"Cut a thin slice from top and bottom [of an unripe tomato] and throw them away, then cut the remainder in slices, roll in flour, sprinkle with pepper and salt, and fry brown in butter."[44]

Going Local: Oysters, Lobsters, and Fried Calamari

The more locally situated the event, the more diverse and culturally significant the foods. An all-but-perfect example is Coney Island, New York. One-part boardwalk, one-part amusement park, and one-part local town, Coney Island is technically part of Brooklyn, but it's more like a different planet.

Once the seaside home of the Native American Lenape, it morphed into a three-and-a-half-mile amusement park/boardwalk with rides, exhibitions, restaurants, souvenir shops, and, of course, concession stands starting in the late 1800s. Yes, they have ice cream. Cotton candy. Freshly baked cookies. But they also have such regional favorites as fried shrimp, fried clams, fried calamari, lobster rolls, and an ocean-side delight that dates back to forever: oysters.

AND SPEAKING OF CONEY ISLAND: ALL ABOUT NATHAN'S

The story of Nathan's and Coney Island hot dogs started in 1867 with Charles Feltman. Considered the inventor of the elongated hot dog bun, Feltman began selling what he called "Coney Island Red Hots" from a pushcart in the Coney Island dunes. These hot dogs were a rather small but significant building block to the illustrious Ocean Pavilion that Feltman went on to develop.

Known as the largest restaurant in the world, the "Pavilion" was said to have served up to 10,000 guests at once. That number jumped in the 1920s, as the New York subway system opened its doors on Coney Island, bringing in five million visitors a year. The Pavilion encompassed a full city block with nine restaurants, a beer garden, outdoor movie theater, hotel, and amusement park, without losing sight of its hot dog past, selling up to 40,000 Red Hots *a day*.[45]

In 1915, during the Ocean Pavilion's ascension, the company hired Nathan Handwerker, a Polish bun-cutter. The industrious youth saved money by more or less living on Feltman's hot dogs for about a year. Then he quit the job and opened a competing restaurant next door.

Nathan's Hot Dogs, Coney Island, *Susan Benjamin, Courtesy True Treats*

Yes, Handwerker had nerve, but he also had marketing smarts. His restaurant had literal bells and whistles that sounded like a fire engine siren to lure people in. While Feltman was charging ten cents for his hot dogs, Handwerker charged a nickel. Rumor has it that Nathan even hired college students to eat his hot dogs outside, dressed in white coats, giving the impression that his dogs were so reputable and hygienic that even doctors would stop by to eat them.

By the Depression, Nathan's hot dogs were known throughout the United States. In 1939, when President Franklin Roosevelt hosted the British King and Queen at a picnic in Hyde Park, First Lady Eleanor Roosevelt put grilled hot dogs on the menu. An audacious but fair representation of life in the United States.[46]

As for Feltman's, they went out of business but have now returned. Their website tells their story as being "The Start, End, and Revival of the Original, *Original* Hot Dog," which you got to love. Only thing—Feltman's new business isn't the raucous, fun-loving venue of the past. It's "one of the fastest-growing natural food companies in the U.S.," whose hot dogs are sold in 3,400 grocery stores across the country. "Just as Charles would have liked it," they say. Well, OK then.[47]

Ice Cream: Pop, Bowl, and Sandwich

Good Ice Cream Is a Distinctive Food—Satisfies the Taste and Builds the Body.—Seale-Lilly Ice Cream ad, 1923[1]

THE DELIGHT AND DIFFICULTY OF ICE CREAM

Historically speaking, ice cream had been one of the most difficult fun foods—probably *any* food—to make. It was a balancing act between having deeply frozen ice or really cold water on a grand scale. The ice itself needed to be harvested, which meant cutting, storing, and delivering it from freezing cold mountaintops, often for great distances. It also must be mixed with salt . . . but for scientific, rather than culinary, reasons.

The problem is that ice water freezes if the temperature gets lower than thirty-two degrees Fahrenheit. Add salt and the freezing point can drop to six degrees below zero, making the smooth, cold ice cream we enjoy possible, without it regressing to, say, popsicle status. This particular chemical equation was discovered by the ancient Chinese, recorded in India in the fourth century, and described from a technical perspective by Arab medical historian Ibn Abu Usaybi (AD 1230–1270), complete with a breakdown of various kinds of salts.

How Chinese ice cream got to Europe is yet another mystery. Many fingers point to the explorer Marco Polo, who was said to discover ice cream in China, which he brought back to Europe. Only problem: Marco Polo never actually went to China. But, if he had, he may have tasted a mixture like the one enjoyed by King Tang of Shang.[2]

For a minute, though, let's say that Marco Polo *did* bring ice cream to Europe. Who, then, brought ice cream from Europe to America? As you probably guessed, there are lots of theories. Some say the colonists from Scotland. Others, Quakers from England. And still others, an Italian named Giovanni Bosio, who left his home in Genoa to open the first American ice cream parlor—a gelateria—in New York in 1770.[4]

> The first known ice cream can be traced back to King Tang (AD 618–697) of Shang, who enjoyed a chilled milk-based early ice cream. He loved the dish so much, legend has it, he devoted ninety-four ice-men to make it. Here's what you do: Heat and ferment buffalo, cow, and goat milk. Add flour for thickening and camphor for flavoring. Yes, camphor. That's it. Chill to the point of freezing. Enjoy.[3]

While not exactly ice *cream*, Native Americans in cold climates did pour maple and other syrups over snow to create the equivalent of European sorbets and sherbets. Europeans followed their example for generations. These "ice creams" are the earliest version of today's snow cones and other ices, frequently sold from trucks.

ICE CREAM COMES TO AMERICA

The truth is that Giovanni Bosio did open a gelateria in New York in 1770. But was he the first to do so? Other ice cream makers were around at the time. Philip Lenzi, a London confectioner living in New York, opened a confectionery that sold ice cream around 1774. The shop's name is unknown and possibly nonexistent, as specialty shops often went by the proprietor's name and trade. Philip Lenzi, Confectioner—the man and the shop—advertised in the *New York Gazette* of May 12, 1777. Ice cream is, indeed, mentioned at the end.

> *Philip Lenzi, Confectioner from London, Having removed from Dock-street to Hanover-Square, No. 517. Takes this method to return his sincere thanks to all his friends and customers for their past favours, and hopes for a continuance, and will have in this present season, a very great variety of the best sweetmeats; preserves marmalades, jellies, &c. in brandy, and very reasonable rate as the times will permit, for read money only; and every thing of the said branch will be executed to all perfection as in the first shops in London. Said Lenzi will, in the ensuing season, give a very good price for the very best sort of fruit, such as strawberries, gooseberries, cherries, raspberries, peaches, pine apples, green gages, apricots, &c. & c. May be had almost every day, ice cream; likewise ice for refreshing wine, &c. N.B.*[5]

Around that time, colonists also enjoyed homemade ice cream, especially when they had in-house laborers to make it. In a journal entry of 1786, George Washington described the first stage of the ice-cream-making process at Mount Vernon—gathering ice from the Potomac. He wrote: "Renewed my Ice operation today, employing as many hands as I conveniently could in getting it from the Maryland shore, carting and pounding it."

Once delivered, the ice was stored in a dry well or icehouse until spring. That's when cows started producing milk and cream, and chefs and enslaved workers in Martha Washington's kitchen got busy making ice cream. Their recipe, aka "receipt," came from a popular cookbook of the time, *The Art of Cookery Made Plain and Easy*, written by Hannah Glasse, a friend of the Washington family. The result: a slushy, creamy treat served in white French porcelain cups, an ounce or two of the mixture in each.[6]

Ice cream balls, *Susan Benjamin, Courtesy True Treats*

As for the ice cream flavors? From the start, ice cream was flavored with fruit, sugar, and honey. Other iterations were chocolate and coffee, as well as vanilla, enjoyed and made famous by Thomas Jefferson. Other flavors are equally familiar—raspberry, coconut, caramel, and lemon—while others are not, such as oyster. Yes, oyster ice cream, which tasted more like frozen oyster stew than anything you'd want to eat on a cone.[8]

Who Really "Invented" American Ice Cream?

Obviously, Thomas Jefferson didn't sit around making ice cream. Neither did Martha Washington or such fans as Dolley Madison or, for that matter, any of their close relations or friends, with some exceptions. Ice cream was made primarily by African Americans, many enslaved, such as James Hemings, Jefferson's half-brother-in-law and enslaved chef. Dolley Madison's strawberry ice cream was said to be made by "Aunt Sallie Shadd," who made ice cream in the 1810s and 1820s.[9] Aunt Sallie Shade wasn't actually a relative. "Aunt" and "Uncle" were the surnames given to African Americans of the eighteenth and nineteenth centuries, as they weren't entitled to use "Miss," "Mrs.," or "Mr."

Another African-American contributor to the ice cream world was Philadelphia-based Augustus Jackson. Like many successful people, his influence was so great it stretched beyond recognition. Into the mid-twentieth century, he was considered the inventor of modern-day ice cream. Said one publication: "Augustus Jackson was the first to make America's favorite frozen confection—ice cream—according to the records in the possession of citizens living in the City of Brotherly Love."[10]

What Jackson *did* do was leave his job as a cook in the White House in the early 1820s and open a confectionery and catering business in Philadelphia. There he made custards, which he cooled on a cake of ice, then froze in a tin bucket, completely covered with ice. The result was an influential and much-loved ice cream dish that made Jackson a wealthy man.[11] Other local African-American confectioners and caterers continued his tradition, including his daughter.

Ice and Innovations

As the ancient Chinese knew so well, harvesting ice was difficult and dangerous. To make the harvest easier, communities often came together to get the job done. Together they also created better icehouses and other storage areas. Thanks to these efforts, it is said that in 1808 customers enjoyed ice cream in the steamy streets of New Orleans, made with ice plucked from the Ohio River in winter, shipped down the Mississippi, and put into storage there. Availability of ice aside, *making* ice cream was still difficult. But—a solution was afoot.

The problem: The process of making ice cream was, ultimately, exhausting. This fact is no better illustrated than in Lettice Bryan's book of 1839, *The Kentucky Housewife*. Here's what you do:

1. Place a pot full of ice cream mixture into a tub.
2. Add five inches of ice and coarse salt, in equal portions to the exterior of the tub.
3. Insulate the pot by placing a carpet over the top.
4. Rotate the pot back and forth by hand for two hours, while pausing to scrape the frozen cream off the sides of the pot with a long spoon.
5. Spoon the resulting ice cream into molds.
6. Place molds into a tub filled with fresh ice and salt for another two to three hours. Serve.[12]

The solution: Ice cream makers everywhere owe New Jersey native Nancy Johnson a round of thanks for inventing the first portable ice cream freezer/maker. The device, which she patented in 1843 as an "artificial freezer," was essentially a tall wooden tub with an internal cylinder and external crank. To operate, just add an ice cream mix containing that ancient combination of salt and ice. Then turn the crank and keep cranking, as the concoction is stirred and scraped within the tub until, eventually, it is ice cream. Difficult? Yes. But at least the artificial freezer did *some* of the work.

Johnson's device was so influential that between 1848 and 1873 at least sixty-nine ice cream freezers were patented. By then Johnson had sold the rights to her machine for $200. Her artificial freezer was the basis of modern ice cream production.

As for harvesting ice? The first of many artificial ice plants opened in 1865. Still, Americans continued harvesting ice the old-fashioned way until 1886, when it peaked at a harvest of twenty-five million tons.[13]

INTRODUCING ICE CREAM, LOTS OF ICE CREAM

I Scream, You Scream, We All Scream for Ice Cream.—Popular song published in 1927

By the early twentieth century, new, exciting ice cream styles emerged as Americans invented more complex machinery to make the ice cream, and more reliable transportation to get it to ice cream lovers who practically screamed for it.

I Scream, You Scream, We All Scream for Ice Cream

A "novelty song" is a type of song that is written to be fun, often set in exotic locations. This one was composed in 1927 by Howard Johnson, Billy Moll, and Robert A. King. The song later became a jazz standard.

Lyrics to "I Scream, You Scream," 1927
Wikimedia

Oh!

I scream, you scream, we all scream for ice cream!

In the land of ice and snows

Up among the Eskimos,

There's a college known as Ogiwawa!

You should hear those college boys,

Gee, they make an awful noise

When they sing an Eskimo tra-la-la!

They've got a leader, big cheer leader,

Oh, what a guy!

He's got a frozen face just like an Eskimo Pie!

When he says, "Come on, let's go!"

Though it's forty-five below,

This is what the Eskimos all holler:

I scream, you scream, we all scream for ice cream!

Rah! Rah! Rah!

Tuesdays, Mondays, we all scream for sundaes,

Sis-boom-bah!

Boola-boola, sarsaparoolla,

If you got chocolate, we'll take vanoola!

I scream, you scream, we all scream for ice cream!

Rah! Rah! Rah!

I scream, you scream, we all scream for ice cream!

Rah! Rah! Rah!

Frosts and malts that are peppered and salted,

Sis-boom-bah!

Oh, spumoni, oh, cartoni,

And confidentially, we'll take baloney,

I scream, you scream, we all scream for ice cream!

Rah! Rah! Rah!

Rah! Rah! Rah! Rah! Rah![14]

> **Where were these ice creams enjoyed? In ice cream parlors, yes, but also luncheonettes, restaurants, and, most especially, pharmacies with "soda dispensers" or "soda fountains."**

Baked Alaska

In 1802, Thomas Jefferson served a descendent of today's Baked Alaska made with ice cream in a pastry shell. Here's what George Washington, a guest at the party, had to say about it in a letter:

> On Tuesday I wrote that I was going to dine with the President [Jefferson]. The party was easy and sociable, as all these parties are. Among other things ice-creams were produced in the form of balls of the frozen material enclosed in covers of warm pastry, exhibiting a curious contrast, as if the ice had just been taken from the oven.[15]

However, the Baked Alaska we know today was made in 1867 by Charles Ranhofer, the renowned chef at Delmonico's restaurant in New York City. As for the name? To commemorate the United States' acquisition of Alaska in 1868 from Russia. Other iterations of the Baked Alaska theme, and names that went with them, sprang up over the years, including the "Omelet," as eggs were often added to the shell, "Surprise Omelet, Alaska," "Alaska Baked," "Frozen Dainties," and "Alaska, Florida," so named by Ranhofer in 1894. *Fountain Magazine* described Baked Alaska this way in 1925:

> A solidly frozen brick of ice cream which has been wrapped in a thick meringue of powdered sugar and egg whites whipped thoroughly and then placed in a very hot oven until the meringue browns. The cream will not melt if the oven is hot enough. A typical hotel dainty, which cannot be served economically at either luncheonette or soda fountain.[16]

Ice Cream Cakes

Still trendy today, ice cream cakes, like Baked Alaska, evolved from Renaissance-era trifles made with cream and biscuits. They took hold in Victorian England and, by default, in the United States in a variety of guises, often placed in fancy molds starting in the late 1800s.[17]

Sorbet

Sorbet originated in Italy in the 1600s. In the mid-1800s, it became a favorite of the very rich who enjoyed it at elaborate dinner parties. More than just a side dish or light dessert, sorbet was a coping mechanism to get diners through the vastly rich and overly abundant number of courses. The delicate sorbet, served in petite quantities between courses, offered a respite from eating, cleansed the palate, prepared the stomach for ever more food, and replaced the then-unpopular mid-meal liquor or cordial with a cool, icy treat. Today, a smattering of restaurants hoping to impart a fine-dining experience serve sorbet between courses. Diners, with no knowledge of the tradition, are typically surprised.[18]

America's oldest ice cream brand is based in Philadelphia. Bassetts Ice Cream began operating in 1861, opened its first shop in 1885, and moved into the city's iconic Reading Terminal Market when it opened in 1892. It's been serving up scoops in that location ever since.

Sundaes

Sundaes were invented sometime in the late 1800s, although no one knows exactly when. Most likely they just morphed into existence as people started adding fruits, nuts, creams, and syrups to their ice cream. As for the name, it may have been related to the blue laws that some states or counties applied forbidding alcohol, ice cream, and other foods on Sunday. Or the name may have actually encouraged people to buy sundaes on Sundays. Or, as some say, it was originally an "ice cream Friday," but people liked "Sundae" better.[19]

Why sundaes were so popular is a different matter. W. O. Rigby, one of the great confectionery experts of the early 1900s, says the following about soda fountains where sundaes were served: "The mixture of ice creams, and the arrangements of fancy dishes not only furnishes the soda dispenser an outlet for his ideas, but they produce a big revenue." He adds, "It is suggested that a china or silver cup be used. Wafers, mints, and other tidbits are very nice to serve along with the ice cream. A small glass of ice water should always be served with each order."[20]

SHOW this Pineapple Sundae in the windows, at the fountains and in the parlors of your dealers and see your gallonage grow. These Four Color Process Reproductions make other people feel just like you feel now, hungry for ice cream.

And the cost of keeping them constantly displayed is surprisingly small.

FREDERICK C. MATHEWS COMPANY
"SERVANTS TO THE DAIRY INDUSTRY"
685 MULLETT STREET   DETROIT, MICHIGAN

This four-page insert was produced complete by the Frederick C. Mathews Company

Exemplary sundae in ice cream trade journal, 1905
Digitized by Google

In other words, sundaes were:

- innovative, allowing shop owners to indulge their creative impulses;
- profitable, as the ingredients were inexpensive and easy to upscale with toppings; and
- expansive, so there was always something for everyone.

And speaking of something for everyone, sundae makers went to town, creating dishes that defied explanation, but, quite clearly, people bought them anyway. The lineup may have included Oriental Nut Sundae, Almond Bisque Sundae, Cantaloupe Sundae, and Mallow Mint Nut Sundae or such nondescript options as Lovers Delight, Best Yet Sundae, Knoxville Girl's Desire, and Gold Dust Twins. Sound delicious? We may never know.

HOW ABOUT THAT CHERRY ON TOP?

The ever-ubiquitous maraschino cherry has gone through hard times where its reputation was concerned. With all the flash of a Victorian showgirl, maraschino cherries showed up in the United States around the turn of the century. The cherry, native to Croatia, was soaked in maraschino liqueur, a spirit derived from the pits, stems, leaves, and flesh of the cherry.[21] They found an immediate home in a variety of desserts, salads, side dishes, alcoholic drinks, and, of course, sundaes. In fact, one maraschino-laden sundae concocted in 1907 was actually called the "Whole Maraschino Sundae."[22]

The maraschino–ice cream union ended in 1912 when the cherries were banned from sundaes. It seems "pure food advocates" were against it. The group was composed of private and government-based advocates on a mission to rid the American diet of all "impurities." The problem with the maraschino cherries wasn't artificial color and flavorings, which were aplenty at the time, but alcohol. Laws were passed and the cherries could still float carefree in cocktails, but not on ice cream.

As one cherry supporter put it in 1912, "The seductive maraschino cherry, stolen from the cocktail, can no longer nestle snugly amid the creamy content of luscious confection. . . . The pure food authorities and the internal revenue officials have placed their ban upon it." In other words, maraschino cherries with their (albeit minuscule) alcohol content were a bad influence on other, purer foods and those who ate them.[23]

Once Prohibition hit full force in the 1920s, the alcohol-linked maraschino cherries were doomed. Fortunately, they were kept from total annihilation by Oregon Agricultural College professor Ernest H. Wiegand, who developed a process to make the cherries ever-more color-ful and alcohol-free.[24] Maraschino cherries resumed their place atop sundaes and other dishes they once occupied in the past; minced in fruit cocktail; floating in gelatin-based salads with pickles, pineapple, and stuffed olives; and, starting in 1903, wedged between sherry-soaked macaroons and dense whipped cream in the illustrious dessert French Charlotte.[25]

> Formaldehyde in cherries? Today, Americans enjoy maraschino cherries with trepidation due to reports that the cherries are processed with formaldehyde. Turns out, that horrifying fact is actually fiction, the result of one magazine writer who confused "formaldehyde" with "benzaldehyde," an extract used to make maraschino cherries.[26]

Ice Cream Sandwiches

Expecting guests? With no time to bake pie or cake or make a fancy dessert? Ice Cream Sandwiches will solve your harried-hostess problem.—Philadelphia Inquirer, August 27, 1948 [27]

Ice cream sandwiches found their way onto the American fun foods landscape in two ways. One was commercial, primarily sold by "hokeypokey men," otherwise known as pushcart vendors, around the turn of the century in New York. These sandwiches were considered novelties at a penny apiece and were pretty egalitarian in nature—enjoyed equally by the working class and those who were well-to-do. Ice cream sandwiches showed up in soda fountains and confectioneries, with such specialties as ice cream made with maple syrup.

Endless varieties of ice cream sandwiches, *Maryann Fisher, Courtesy True Treats*

But the most creative versions were made at home and definitely *not* for people on the go. They were real sit-down desserts with a touch of elegance. The ice cream in the ice cream sandwich was typically vanilla, maybe chocolate, or even both. They were generally slabs, purchased from ice cream manufacturers, so they fit neatly in the "sandwich." The outer portions of the sandwich, the layers hugging the ice cream, may have been delicate sponge cake cut in thin slices, any variety of cakes topped with nuts and chocolate sauce, or ginger cookies or waffles.

Columnist Josephine Gibson advised in 1947: "Serve ice cream sandwiches in fancy dress." By this she meant ice cream in meringue shells, ice cream in puff pastry shells, ice cream atop chocolate wafers, or ice cream tarts. Whatever the arrangement, it might entail a chocolate or butterscotch sauce or any fruit or berry that may be in season. [28] By the mid-1900s, ice cream sandwiches were enjoyed with almost as much delight and seriousness as pumpkin pie.

THE AMERICAN ICE CREAM SANDWICH ORIGIN STORY

How ice cream sandwiches came into existence is anyone's guess. But plenty of people are willing to tell us. Pennsylvania's *Daily Republican* carried a great story in 1906 that's well worth believing, even if it leaves pieces out. It's about an immigrant—nation of origin not stated, name not stated, and reasons for his immigration not stated either. This immigrant had a pushcart from which he sold *something* on the East Side of Manhattan.

He managed to make enough money selling whatever it was to return for a visit home. On the return trip, where he traveled in steerage by the way, the vendor stopped in London. There he saw an "ice cream man." That's when it occurred to our nameless vendor that he too could sell ice cream sandwiches. So, he spent all his money buying wafers and, at some point when he got home, ice cream (we must assume). Then he got to work, pushing a cart in New York City and calling out "Ice Cream Sandwiches!"

The response was *amazing*. After the first week, a dozen men were working for him and many more awaited the chance. To keep his supply up, he imported wafers from England. According to the author, "All that summer there hardly was a vessel coming to New York from London that did not bring its quota of ice cream sandwich wafers."

The next year, American biscuit makers got wise and became ice cream sandwich men using their own biscuits. But our ice cream sandwich man was indifferent. He was so successful, he had retired, with a house in town and a country place on Long Island.

True? Not true? You decide.[29]

What to Use for Your Homemade Ice Cream Sandwiches

Over the years, the sandwich part of ice cream sandwiches varied depending on who was making it. Don't be shy about using whatever cakes or cookies you like. As for the ice cream—vanilla and chocolate were standard, but, again, use what you like. Someone somewhere was likely doing the same.

Waffles
Oatmeal cookies
Molasses cookies
Ginger snaps
Sponge cake
Vanilla cake
Chocolate chip cookies
Biscuits
Puff pastry
Piecrust (with the ice cream uncovered)
Whatever cake you have at home at the time

Since their humble beginnings—whatever it was—ice cream sandwiches have become pure Americana. Today, ice cream sandwiches are the second-best-selling ice cream novelty in America. And, boy, do Americans love them: forty-eight ice cream sandwiches are eaten on average every *second*. Place these ice cream sandwiches end to end and they would circle the earth three and a half times. And, while almost half of all ice cream sandwiches are eaten on the Eastern Seaboard, it is such a symbol of Americana that it's even sold at the Smithsonian Institute in Washington, DC. [30]

Banana Splits

Modern soda fountain concoctions contain everything except the liquid—that cooling draught the Banana Split looks like a shore dinner.—Idaho Statesman, August 4, 1912[31]

It's impossible to relay the story of ice cream without mentioning the banana split. The seed of this festive creation was planted in the late 1800s when bananas were still considered deliciously exotic. Banana ice cream and sherbet were popular, and early versions of banana splits were making an appearance. One was this recipe, from 1897, then called "Bananas a la Crème." "This is an entirely new dessert, most refreshing and delicious," the author said. And she was right! Here's what you do:

> *Take six entirely ripe bananas and put them in the refrigerator until they are cold. Just a few minutes before dinner, peel, and split them in halves, then lay them lengthwise in an oblong glass dish. Squeeze over the bananas the juice of two large oranges. Stand the dish in the refrigerator while you prepare the cream. Put a pint of rich cream in a bowl. Add two heaping tablespoons of powdered sugar and half a spoonful of salt. Crush a dozen ripe strawberries and pour their juice into the cream. Whip the cream until it is stiff and pour it over the bananas. Keep the dish in the refrigerator until it's ready to serve. Then ornament the top of the cream, which should be a delicate shade of pink, with a few slices of banana alternated with slices of strawberries.[32]*

Within ten years, banana splits were widely available, festooned with nuts, fruits, maraschino cherries, and even maple syrup. The glory of the banana split, however, is that it is recipe-less. Add what you want, do what you want. One banana split of 1915, in Pennsylvania, consisted of split bananas resting on sponge cake, with a grated tablespoon of pineapple, a dusting of sugar, and a dollop, more or less, of whipped cream.[33] Another, more recent banana split skipped the ice cream and was served as cupcakes instead. In the 1960s, the Verifine ice cream company skipped the extras and made their very own, all-in-one, banana split ice cream. The taste, said the company in one ad, is "simply super—from the first tingling taste to the last luscious spoonful."[34]

The banana we know and love is actually a mutant strain of a fruit found in Jamaica called plantain. The sweet banana was imported from the Caribbean to New Orleans, Boston, and New York—and what a treat! So honored they were eaten on a plate with a knife, fork, and napkin on the lap. In 1876, sweet bananas were introduced at the Philadelphia Centennial Exposition, where visitors willingly paid 10 cents to buy one. Eventually bananas showed up everywhere, especially at the center of a new treat sensation, made in 1930: Twinkies.

But all this begs the question—"Who invented the banana split?" Some point to David Strickler, a twenty-three-year-old pharmacy apprentice in Latrobe, Westmoreland County, Pennsylvania. In 1904, inspired by a soda jerk he saw in Atlantic City, Strickler placed three scoops of ice cream on a split banana; topped it with chocolate syrup, marshmallow, nuts, whipped cream, and a cherry; and sold it for a dime. Word spread and the dessert took off—it even got its own bowl.[35]

But wait! Folks in Wilmington, Ohio, claim restaurant owner Ernest R. Hazard created the banana split back in 1907 as a way to draw younger customers into his restaurant. The name "banana split" wasn't as popular as the dish itself, but no matter.[36] The city of Boston, Massachusetts, was also a contender with their claim. The *Soda Fountain Magazine* declared that Stinson Thomas debuted the first-ever banana split at a conference in Boston in 1905, a year after Strickler.[37]

Thank You, Prohibition!

Ice cream sales soared as Prohibition boomed in, giving the newly sober citizens a chance to relax with a nonalcoholic substitute. One journalist reported in 1922 that people took to whetting their thirst with ice cream: every man, woman, and child ate an average of three gallons of the delicacy a year. Another said in 1922 that soda fountain sales rose to $1 billion in one year due to ice cream sales.[38] After the end of Prohibition, and sugar shortages during World War II, that number sharply dropped.

So, who really invented the banana split? Strickler, Hazard, or Thomas? Or was it someone else, someone whose identity is lost in the annals of time? Not to push the point too far, but maybe lots of someones? And was this first banana split really the prototype for the ones today? The answer to all this, and so much more, is "yes."

Popsicles—True or False?

In the mid to late 1800s, Americans started putting sticks into fun foods. Lollipops, for example, were actually hard candy on a stick, and fruit-flavored ice on a stick was called "frozen ice" or "frozen sucker." One Oklahoma newspaper article in 1924 proclaimed, "Frozen suckers are a real innovation. Simply a delicious piece of sherbet in most any desired flavor, stuck on a stick like a candy sucker."[39] And in 1925, Van's Lunch Room in Illinois promoted its ice, Pop-Cicle, of unidentified substance but so good "kids will want a dozen more!"[40] Most companies stuck with fruit flavors with their own spin. Lafayette Ice Cream Company in Indiana proclaimed it made the best frozen suckers with "Kist" fruit flavors. "Kist" was actually a flavor manufacturer based in Chicago, whose name gave it the aura of a rarified product no one could resist.[41]

According to NPR, the *New York Times*, and many other sources (all with iterations on the theme), popsicles were invented in (roughly) 1905 when eleven-year-old Frank Epperson of San Francisco accidentally left a glass of lemonade out overnight. The batch froze with the spoon (or wooden stick) upright in the cup. Frank had an epiphany—why not turn the spoon into a stick that could become a holder for the frozen ice? He called the result an "Epsicle." In 1923, his kids convinced him to rename the treat "Popsicle," as in "Pop's 'Sicle."

It's a great story but, at the very most, Epperson invented one version of the Popsicle. That's important because we *do* know Epperson applied for a patent, which was granted in 1924, so the Popsicle really was all his. Only, one problem: he couldn't afford to manufacture it. So, reluctantly he sold the rights to his creation to the Joe Lowe Co. The new owners pitched the Popsicle to stardom, even in the Great Depression. At that time, sweets vendors had long been selling their treats for a nickel each. The Depression-era Popsicle had *two* pieces side by side, giving the impression you were getting two for the price of one.

As for Frank Epperson, he regretted selling his Popsicle for the rest of his life. Except—maybe he shouldn't have had regrets. Lowe and the many companies who owned the rights to Popsicles after him were embroiled in one expensive legal battle after another . . . not to mention relentless battles to maintain market share. With the expense and the headaches, Epperson was probably better off leaving his (possible) creation to someone else.[42]

Don't Forget Fudgsicles, Creamsicles, and Dixie Cups

Creamsicles. A Frozen Treat. 5-Cents.—Entire advertisement for Creamsicles in the *Montana Standard*, 1938.[43]

Iterations of the Popsicle theme have been around for over a hundred years. What they have in common with Frank Epperson's creation is the stick and the root of the name. In 1923, A&P put ice cream cabinets in 1,500 of its grocery stores, bringing ready-to-eat ice cream into the American kitchen. Two, Fudgsicles and Creamsicles, were held by sticks, and a third (among others) was an evolutionary cup.

FUDGSICLES

Invented in the 1920s, Fudgsicles started as chocolate fudge ice cream dipped in chocolate. Later they got a stick. Throughout the 1930s and '40s, iterations of Fudgsicles popped up everywhere, from the Polar company, which advertised widely in newspapers in Florida,[44] to small-town dairies in the Midwest. The treat took on various names, including "Fudgies," depending on who made them.

CREAMSICLES

The Creamsicle is a sidekick of the Fudgsicle, with less notoriety or stature. This frozen treat on a stick is made of vanilla ice cream with orange-flavored ice on top. The two were often advertised together, such as one ad in 1950 targeting kids. This particular ad involved an incentive promising a "free" quill pen for kids who sent in ten wrappers *plus ten cents*. The ten cents may seem like a lot for kids, especially for a free gift, especially one unrelated to ice cream. But this particular "quill" pen was a "historical feather pen brought up to date with a ball point." Even better, it's the "same style as used by Great American Presidents and Statesmen when signing the Declaration of Independence."[45]

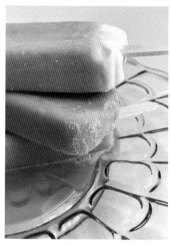

Ice-cold Creamsicles, *Maryann Fisher, Courtesy True Treats*

DIXIE CUPS

As cute and lovely as Dixie Cups seem, they were also, quite literally, lifesavers. The story begins with Lawrence Luellen of Boston, who invented the first paper cup in 1908. The cup would replace the "tin dippers" found alongside free water stands, or "public water vessels," located in public buildings, railroad stations, and schools. Legions of thirsty men, women, and children drank from the communal dippers, which no one bothered washing, essentially a happy home for germs of all varieties and an effective spreader of death and disease. If that wasn't bad enough, ice cream vendors would sell a small cup of ice cream to kids who would literally lick it clean and hand it back, where it was refilled and handed to the next in line.

Dixie Cups were different. They were not made to last. As *Smithsonian Magazine* put it, the life of a Dixie Cup entailed "Drink. Toss. Repeat." Tin dippers out. Disposable cups in. Death and disease gone. Then in 1923, the company started making hygienic two-and-a-half-inch ice cream cups that sold, like other candies and ice creams of the time, for a nickel, ushering in "Eat. Lick. Toss." A boon for everyone.[46]

Last word: The Dixie Cup model of "Drink. Toss. Repeat." was the first of an avalanche of disposable items—and environmental liabilities—such as pens, razors, and water bottles.

Welcome the Ice Cream Man!

Making ice cream is one thing. Selling it from your shop is another. Taking your shop to the street? That's all about ice cream trucks. Not that the idea of selling ice cream streetside was new. Pushcarts and the hokeypokey men who pushed them had been around since the nineteenth century. But ice cream trucks were a cleaner, more reliable source of delights than the pushcart, constantly under scrutiny from the pure foods advocates.

It's no irony that the ice cream truck was inspired by an ancient medicinal belief. But it is surprising that the creator was humble Harry Burt who, in 1893, had opened a penny candy store in Youngstown, Ohio. From candy store to soda fountain to grill then restaurant, Harry Burt's empire, albeit a small empire, grew. But Burt's next efforts, literally and figuratively, went in a new direction.[47]

In the 1920s, as confectioners were announcing their new innovative products (often the same product at the same time), Burt came up with one of his own-ish. His creation was a chocolate-covered ice cream slab, much like his closest competitor's I-Scream Bar, aka the Eskimo Pie. But, unlike his competitors', Burt's creation—in fact, his entire business—was relentlessly reassuring, wrapped inside and out around the concepts of health and cleanliness. The name of his business was "Good Humor," which may have referred to the ha-ha kind of humor but also to the *humors*, the parts of the body the ancients believed dictated our health. His ice cream treat, the Good Humor Ice Cream Sucker, was on a stick, which Burt referred to as "a new clean convenient way to eat ice cream."

The name and the ice cream were a pure food advocate's dream come true, outdone only by Burt's newfangled pushcart—the refrigerated ice cream truck. No mere sales vehicles, these too were all about hygiene, a sparkling white kind of hygiene. His trucks were spotlessly white. The drivers, in white uniforms, bowed to women and saluted men. They wore gloves. White gloves. And should you miss the dazzling white of his fleet—twelve to start with—you wouldn't miss the bell, originally constructed from bobsled bells at Burt's home. So reassuring were the

> Like all good innovators, Harry Burt wanted to protect his product and, more to the point, the rights to the machinery that produced it. So, he applied for a patent. For three years Burt waited for word of his patent application, but none was forthcoming. So, he headed to DC with a five-gallon pail of ice cream bars that he handed out to patent officers. The patent was approved.[49]

men in their white trucks with their white superhero uniforms, they became an American icon, appearing in comic books, children's books, and radio shows.[48]

But the Good Humor man did confront real-life trouble. In 1929, when Good Humor opened a plant in Chicago, the mob demanded $5,000 in protection money, the equivalent of $70,000 today. Burt refused, and the mob destroyed part of his fleet. No matter. The business kept rolling.[49]

Today, Good Humor–Breyers is one of the largest branded ice cream producers in the nation. The trucks, always glimmering white, are no longer among us. But the memory lives on in the food trucks that evolved from Burt's idea, selling everything from grilled cheese sandwiches to kebabs and, of course, plenty of ice cream.[50]

Soft Serve

Soft serve is unquestionably a favorite American treat, as well it should be. The texture is divine; the flavor, inoffensive; and the possibilities—whether in banana splits or chocolate-coated atop a cone—practically endless. In other words, soft serve is old-fashioned "deliciousness," which is odd because it's actually quite corporate.

Dairy Queen and Carvel both claimed to have invented soft serve in the 1930s, when Prohibition was boosting ice cream sales. The texture was stabilized by whipping extra air into the blend, making soft serve predictable and dependable. Other ice cream manufacturers caught on. Eventually, soft serve found a home in ice cream trucks, ice cream stores, restaurants, clam shacks, and, most especially, beachside ice cream stands.[51]

Soft serve, Gloucester, Massachusetts, *Susan Benjamin, Courtesy True Treats*

Dairy Queen sign, *Wikimedia*

Ice cream became an edible morale booster during World War II. Each military branch tried to outdo the others in the quality and quantity of the ice cream they gave the troops. In 1945, the first "floating ice cream parlor" set sail, so to speak, to sailors in the western Pacific. When the war ended, America celebrated victory with ice cream, consuming over twenty quarts of it per person in 1946.[52]

ICE CREAM: THE STORES

By the 1960s, most people were getting ice cream in the freezer section of the grocery store and not at ice cream stores. No question, ice cream did well at amusement parks, fairs, and especially boardwalks, where it was, and still is, the quintessential treat to eat. Still, three companies, all starting as storefronts, made an indelible mark on the ice creams of today, no matter where we get them.

Howard Johnson's

What you need to know: Howard Johnson brought ice cream to the nation as the first restaurant chain on the first interstate in the 1950s. His signature ice cream came in twenty-eight flavors. The secret to his success: the ice cream was rich in butterfat.

The original Howard Johnson's twenty-eight flavors of ice cream were banana, black raspberry, burgundy cherry, butter pecan, buttercrunch, butterscotch, caramel fudge, chocolate, chocolate chip, coconut, coffee, frozen pudding, fruit salad, fudge ripple, lemon stick, macaroon, maple walnut, mocha chip, orange-pineapple, peach, peanut brittle, pecan brittle, peppermint stick, pineapple, pistachio, strawberry, strawberry ripple, and vanilla.[53]

Here's what happened: Howard Johnson was born in 1885 in Wollaston, Massachusetts, a beachside section of Quincy, near Boston. He dropped out of school at age fourteen to apprentice in a drugstore, then left to fight in World War I. After returning, he opened his own drugstore and soda fountain, featuring rich and delicious ice cream, made with extra butterfat. His ice cream was a hit with nearby beachgoers.

Johnson soon added more ice cream shops then, unable to resist the lure of expansion, added Howard Johnson's the restaurant, Howard Johnson's the hotel, and Howard Johnson's the best (and only) place to stop at the rise of interstates in the 1950s. Howard Johnson's restaurants, with their improbable orange roof, were also one of the first franchises, offering travelers a hefty menu promising quality, such as their "assured best quality of meats" in 1939.[54] Eventually, "Howard Johnson's" was shortened to the spunkier, more marketable "HoJos." The company shut down in 1971. Above all, Howard Johnson's was known, loved, and now remembered for its twenty-eight flavors.[55]

Baskin-Robbins

What you need to know: Baskin-Robbins introduced extreme ice cream flavors to the American palate. The business was started by two men, brothers-in-law, whose mission was to create outrageously unique flavors. They advertised thirty-one varieties, upping HoJos by three. In reality, over the years they made roughly 1,300 varieties of ice cream. The number "31" was the idea of their advertising firm, just because it sounded good.

Here's what happened: Irvine Robbins's father was in the ice cream business. His brother-in-law, Burt Baskin, was also in ice cream. In 1948, the two businesses merged to form Baskin-Robbins—the order of names determined by a coin flip. Their brand, and mission, was to find new and exciting ice cream phenomena that they sold in the garish interiors of their shops. Some selections were so extreme they never made it to the retail store, such as bagels and lox ice cream and ketchup ice cream. Others are standards today—think pink bubble gum ice cream and pecan praline. So outrageous were these flavors, customers were reluctant to try them. So, the company created tiny, bright pink spoons to give samples to their customers. It wasn't until 2014 that Baskin-Robbins started selling in grocery stores.[56]

Häagen-Dazs

What you need to know: The story of Häagen-Dazs is the story of the American dream, American business, and American ice cream. Häagen-Dazs was started in 1960 by two Jewish immigrants. The business was competitive and well-branded, renowned for its richer, higher-quality ice cream. The secret of their sumptuous ice cream? Extra butterfat. Talk to HoJos about that.

Here's what happened: Reuben Mattus was born in Belarus in 1912 or 1913. His early years were impacted by World War I coupled with a typhus outbreak, leaving him forced, at four years old, to pick through garbage for food. Eventually his uncle Sam, who lived stateside, sent him a ticket to Ellis Island. Once in New York, Reuben met his neighbor, a young Rose Vesel, whose family had endured similar dire conditions. Eventually Rose and Reuben married and in 1959 opened Häagen-Dazs. Why "Häagen-Dazs"? Actually, the name is meaningless. But it *sounds* Danish, in honor of Denmark's exemplary treatment of Jews during World War II. As for the umlaut: not Danish, but it looked good and gave the ice cream a worldly, superior, if not exotic, touch. Originally, they only sold chocolate, coffee, and vanilla flavors, although the company has expanded its repertoire ever since.[57]

Ice Cream Stores Today

Howard Johnson's last restaurant closed in 2022 after a bumpy road full of controversies and depleting profits.[58] Baskin-Robbins has changed hands numerous times and is now owned by another Massachusetts start-up: Dunkin' Brands, maker of Dunkin' Donuts.[59] As for Häagen-Dazs, the Mattuses sold the company to Pillsbury for $70 million in 1983. One of their new products was pecan praline, the flavor invented by Baskin-Robbins. Today, Häagen-Dazs makes an array of flavors and varieties, including frozen yogurt, sorbet, and ice cream bars. The brand is currently sold in fifty countries worldwide.[60]

More Than a Spoonful: Soda and Candy

Candy has always been something we love, hate, and love to hate. We love eating it, which we experience through guilt. We give it as a gift of love and, traditionally, a gateway to sex. These mixed emotions have been fodder for candy marketers while a secret lure for consumers. A candy store in Venice Beach, California, reflected the feeling with a graffiti-looking window front and bright, garishly colored candies behind it.

CANDY FOR HEALTH AND DELIGHT

As improbable as it seems, candy got its start in pharmacies, aka apothecaries. One example is Turkish delight, a confection practically everyone knows about but few have tried—or even seen. The sweet was first made around AD 900 as a medicine for sore throats. It later became the origin of the jellybean.

If you think about it, most flavors in today's candy reflect a medicinal past: mint, lemon, licorice, chocolate, vanilla—name it. Sugar, the most controversial food around, was considered medicinal, used to ease sore throats, cure stomach ailments, and even take on the plague. So significant was sugar to medicine that from the thirteenth through eighteenth centuries, the expression "like an apothecary without sugar" referred to a dire situation.[1] Today, we eat way too much sugar. But the reality is, our bodies need it. If we don't have enough sugar, we die.

Over the decades, candy moved away from its medicinal roots to become a fun food. Here are some of the most influential candies—and their stories.

The Nutty Sugarplum, circa Seventeenth Century

Most people know about sugarplums from *The Nutcracker*'s immortal "Dance of the Sugar Plum Fairy." But just about no one knows what a sugarplum is. To explain, let's start with what it isn't. It isn't a fruit. But it is a seed or nut with a sugar coating, such as a Jordan almond. As

> ### Candy: The Hidden Symbols
> The value of sweets has always gone beyond taste and purpose. They played a huge part in the symbols that punctuated rituals and gave shape to important events. Almond-based candies are one of them. In the ancient Middle East and Mediterranean, the almond tree was the first tree to flower in spring. So, almonds became a symbol of good beginnings. And that is why, thousands of years later, we eat Jordan almonds at weddings and almond-rich marzipan at Easter.[2]

Candy store window, Venice Beach, California, *Susan Benjamin, Courtesy True Treats*

for the word *plum*—that means "good." Good sugars. Simple as they seem, sugarplums were made by highly skilled craftsmen who apprenticed for years, absorbing the nuances of a trade that makes Julia Child look like a scullery maid in comparison.

The process began with the confectioner coating seeds or nuts with gum arabic, putting them in a "balancing pan" suspended over a large, low fire, and rolling them in sugar syrup. To keep the coating even and the sugar from crystallizing, the confectioners had to keep the seeds and nuts in constant motion, stirring with one hand and moving the pan with the other *while* controlling the temperature of the heat by controlling the intensity of fire.

Next, the confectioner set the newly formed sugarplums aside to dry for a day or two, then began the process *again*, stirring and moving, adding layer upon layer over a period of weeks.[3] In the last stage, the sugar coating smooth as glass, they often added a flourish of color: mulberry juice or cochineal for red, indigo stone for blue, spinach for green, and saffron for yellow.[4]

Given the labor and cost involved, sugarplums were a symbol of good taste and refinement, available to the wealthy few. They were enjoyed as a digestive after a large meal, a breath freshener, and an exclusive treat.[5]

Sugarplums: Late Nineteenth-Century Candy for the People

The sugarplums of yesterday became a favorite kids' candy in the late 1800s. So, how did this metamorphosis take place? It's like asking how the Greek god Hercules became a Disney character. It took a long time, but it happened. The apex was during the Industrial Revolution when confectioners replaced the balancing pan with a rotating drum that circulated the seeds and nuts in sugar syrup, creating a smooth shell with relative ease.

At some point, candymakers replaced the seed or nut with a sugar crystal, rolling hundreds of layers of sugar syrup over a nucleus of sugar, until the sugarplum was the size of a large, very round grape. Add some coloring, a little marketing, and you have the Gobstopper, aka Jaw Buster, aka Jawbreaker. Unlike their predecessors, these sweets were enjoyed by everyone, especially kids. Today, jawbreakers

Sugarplums in glass, *Susan Benjamin, Courtesy True Treats*

seem to come and go in a variety of sizes, some frighteningly large. Think tennis ball size.

The word "sugarplum" does refer to a specific kind of candy. But in the nineteenth and much of the twentieth centuries, it also referred to candies in general. The process of sugar-coating newer candies from the late 1800s, such as jellybeans and Good & Plenty, is called "panning."

Stained Glass: The Hidden World of the Most Gorgeous Candy

Stained glass candy has many names—stain glass, broken glass, hardtack—but all represent a shimmering beautiful candy. Unlike sugarplums, they required little in the way of process, were made at home, and were inexpensive to make. Stained glass was (and still is) popular in rural areas such as Appalachia, especially at Christmas.

Essentially, they poured a sugar-water mix into a pan and added coloring, flavoring, maybe nuts, a few petals, whatever struck their fancy. The sugar, meanwhile, could have been cane, corn syrup, sorghum molasses, or any combination of the above. They may have cooked it over a fire or in an oven—either way, when it hardened, they smacked it into pieces of glimmering, glasslike shards. Originally, stained glass may have contained medicine as well.[6]

Stained glass candy, *Susan Benjamin, Courtesy True Treats*

The First American Commercial Candy Company

The story of the first commercial candy company is altogether different from what most people think. There were no weary settlers stumbling off the boat to find religious freedom and finding enterprise in the process. No savvy businessmen or legal wrangling (that came later). This story starts in 1800 when Mrs. Mary Spencer and her young son, Thomas, were shipwrecked in Salem, Massachusetts, after sailing over from England. Mary was destitute, having lost all her worldly possessions in the wreck. The town's women felt bad for her and, likely learning she was an excellent cook, raised money to buy her a barrel of sugar. Mary used the sugar to make what she called the "Gibralter," named for a British style of confection that tastes much like an after-dinner mint but with substantial heft.[7]

That done, Mrs. Spencer sat on the steps of a church in Salem, selling her candy from a pail. She made so much money, she bought a horse and buggy and sold her candy from town to town. At this time, women couldn't vote, rarely owned property, and certainly weren't entrepreneurs. Undeterred, in 1806, Mary bought a house in Salem, where she opened the first commercial candy store on the first floor and lived above it with her son.

Later, her son Thomas became a soapbox abolitionist, who literally stood on a soapbox on a busy Salem street railing against slavery. As for Mary, the buggy she used to transport her candy had a secret compartment, known as a "false bottom." As she went from town to town selling the nation's first commercial candy, she secretly transported escaped slaves to ports where sea captions shuttled them back to Africa, maybe the Bahamas, to their freedom.

When Mary Spencer died around 1828, Thomas put her body in an easily transportable copper coffin. He moved back to England a few years later, taking the coffin with him. Before leaving, Thomas sold the shop to his neighbor, George Pepper, a businessman and confectioner whose brother owned a sweets shop in Boston. Pepper made a confection from blackstrap molasses and called it the Black Jack Stick. He then grew the company to include horse liniment and shoe polish and the distribution of tobacco and other goods, turning the first candy store in the nation into a thriving, multifaceted business. When George Pepper retired in the late 1800s, he sold the shop to an employee named George Burkinshaw. Now called Ye Olde Pepper Candy Companie, the Burkinshaw family still owns it today.[8]

By now, you might be wondering about *Mr.* Spencer, seeing how Mary's name was Mrs. Spencer. No Mr. Spencer, marriage certificate, or other tidbit of evidence that Mrs. Spencer was actually "Mrs." The first American candy company: run by an abolitionist, activist, and single mother. There you have it.

The Necco Wafer: From Apothecary to Candy Store Shelves

Oliver Chase, like Mary Spencer, immigrated from England to the United States in the 1840s. In 1847, he opened an apothecary in Boston. Among the medicines he made were "soft paste" lozenges . . . a little like today's aspirin. Making the lozenges was tedious, exacting work: according to *Scientific American* in 1868, the "plastic" sugar was rolled into a sheet then cut, lozenge after lozenge, like crackers from dough.[9] The batter was temperamental—it had to be just the right consistency, measured, and pressed to make close-to-exact doses, with as little handling as possible.

Chase changed all that by developing a lozenge-cutting machine where he cranked dough onto plates with lozenge-size indentations. The lozenges tumbled out in uniform sizes as quickly as his hand could turn. The ingredients in his medicines may have been peppermint or ginger for stomach problems, rhubarb for constipation, ginger for nausea, or opium for a variety of ailments. Chase then swapped out medicinal ingredients using sugar, gum arabic, a flavoring, and possibly gelatin instead. The result was a candy he called the "Chase Lozenge" or "Hub Wafer" ("Hub" referring to Boston), later called the Necco Wafer. For the first time, candymakers could quickly produce consistent pieces and medicine-makers could create predictable doses. Chase's machine was revolutionary.[10]

Legend has it Chase's candy was sent to Union soldiers, although no record can prove it. Admiral Byrd definitely *did* take two and a half tons of the lozenges on his expedition to the South Pole, and during World War II, the United States sent Necco Wafers to troops because they were "practically indestructible."[11]

In 1866, Chase's brother Daniel invented a machine that would drop little sayings on candy. That creation was called Conversation Hearts.[12]

Medicine/Candy—Candy/Medicine: The Transition That Never Was

The transition from medicine to full-fledged candy was slow for some brands. Others never fully got there. Hard candies are one of them. These favorites of old-time grandmothers and nostalgia fans of today started out as sugar boiled in water with medicinal herbs and spices mixed in. They migrated into cough drops, which are, essentially, hard candies, which are, essentially, medicines. Or are they? The lines are blurred.

One of the most enduring of the medicine-candy is Smith Brothers Cough Drops, which started when restaurateur James Smith got hold of a recipe for "cough candy," later called "cough drops." By 1852, Smith was advertising the candy/medicine widely in Poughkeepsie, New York, newspapers. By 1859, competitors were taking Smith on, the medicinal value of their products deliciously exaggerated: they could "cure" whooping cough, asthma, bronchitis, and diseases of the throat and lung, and bring relief to sufferers of consumption, a fact that is lost on modern medicine manufacturers today.

Regardless of their claims, Smith's drops endured, remaining in the Smith family until 1964. It's hard to say if their candy was superior to the others, but their marketing sure was. In 1866, after James Smith died, his sons, William and Andrew, renamed the company "Smith Brothers" and launched a steady feed of advertising so good that competitors adopted look-alike names such as "Schmitt Brothers" and "Smythe Sisters."

Ever vigilant, the brothers developed a label with their handsome, bearded faces on it, clearly distinguishing themselves from imposters. They were also among the first to use the trademark notation, which they placed directly by their bearded images—"Trade" under William and "Mark" under Andrew. Since it was new, people had no idea what "Trademark" meant, and assumed it referred to Mr. Trade and Mr. Mark, a mistake customers still make today. The company added menthol cough drops in 1922 and cherry in 1948.[14]

Smith Brothers Cough Drops are still sold today, often in the medicine aisle of grocery stores and pharmacies, if only to add to the candy-medicine confusion.

Other Candy-Medicines

Horehound drops: Considered a remedy for sore throats and upset stomachs, horehound was also a popular, albeit bitter-tasting, candy. The name comes from the word *hoary*, for the bristly hairs on the plant's stem, and *hound*, an old-fashioned name for candy. This doesn't stop people from making adolescent jokes about it.[15]

Crystallized ginger: Ginger had long been used for relief of nausea, whether from travel or pregnancy. It was also one of many ingredients in the Native Americans' healthful "root tea," later called "root beer."[16]

Rock candy: Long used to treat sore throats, rock candy was often delivered in a glass of whiskey. One advertisement in 1893 claimed the combination could also cure consumption and an array of pulmonary infections. It was also a medicine of a different kind, as an ingredient in the most popular nineteenth-century saloon drink, Rock n' Rye.

Chewing gum: Humans have always chewed tree resin to heal dental issues, cleanse the mouth, and exercise the jaw. No joke—today's science confirms that resins have antibacterial and antifungal properties, which can eliminate plaque, heal gums, and even cure peptic ulcers. Some resins contained xylitol, the sweetener in today's chewing gum, which, it turns out, fights tooth decay.

Malted milk: In 1873, malted milk was invented as a strength-building food for infants and invalids by a British pharmacist living in Wisconsin. While mothers never trusted malted milk for their kids, explorers used it on treks to such places as the North and South Poles. World War II soldiers were given a stash of malted milk tablets in their rations. In the 1930s and '40s, chocolate-covered malted milk balls became a hit, but then, as now, Americans continued to drink the "healthy" malted milk.

Licorice: The many medical uses of licorice are legendary even today, thought to relieve everything from menstrual issues to respiratory problems. In its original form of a root, licorice was chewed to clean the teeth. Eventually, that root sold as a treat in penny candy stores for over a hundred years.[17]

CANDY LOVE, PROHIBITION-STYLE

Prohibition wasn't good for spirit-makers, but it was great for candy. One memorable Prohibition success story is about none other than Lifesavers. These sweets didn't start with Prohibition. They were invented in 1912 by Clarence Crane, who started making the usual flat candies with a pharmacist's pill cutter. Then, to jazz it up, Crane put a hole in the middle. He called it a "Lifesaver," as it looked like a life preserver.

At first, Crane marketed the Lifesaver as a breath freshener, focusing on the novelty of the O shape. The first flavor was peppermint, which he called "Pep-O-Mint," with a complementary tagline, "For that Stormy Breath."[18]

In 1913, Edward Nobel, a marketer, approached Crane about making Lifesavers a star. Instead of hiring him, Crane sold him the entire business for $2,900. At that time, the temperance movement was in full swing, and alcohol was increasingly controversial. Still, people enjoyed a good drink, and nothing was going to stop them. But how could they hide the telltale smell of alcohol on their breath?

For Nobel, this situation reeked of opportunity, and he began selling the Lifesaver as a breath mint in saloons.[19] He positioned his candy next to the cash register, each roll costing a nickel. Then he arranged for the cashier to give a nickel back to customers with their change. Sales soared! The profits increased sevenfold in the first year and tripled in the one after that. Within ten years they were bringing in $11.5 million. Eventually, Edward Nobel bought out the Beechnut Gum Company.[20]

As for Clarence Crane, he started a chocolate company and died a wealthy man. His son, Hart Crane, was one of the most influential poets of his time. Unfortunately, Hart had his own troubles, alcoholism among them. He died after falling off a cruise ship at only thirty-three years old, but whether he jumped, was pushed, or fell isn't clear. Crane Senior was spared the grief of his son's death at sea and the irony of his candy being named "Lifesavers." He died just a year earlier.[21]

The Name of Prohibition

Many candymakers named their candy for illegal Prohibition-era cocktails. While funny and even creative, candymakers were also striking back at Prohibitionists. No, Prohibitionists didn't like alcohol. But they weren't too fond of candy either, which they considered hazardous to the nation's youth. Candymakers responded with predictable irreverence, which, as it happened, was great for sales. Here are some of them:

Cherry Mash: The Cherry Mash candy bar started as the "Cherry Chase," named for the company's owner, Ernest Chase. To add more sass, the candy was renamed "Cherry Chaser" and later "Cherry Mash"—both names of popular sodas, homemade punches, and more significantly, cocktails. As the anti-alcohol temperance movement morphed into full-fledged Prohibition, Cherry Mash's alcohol connection was actually a boon. People loved it.

Nik L Nip: Remember the little wax bottles with colored sugar water inside? They were called "Nik L Nip," an unlikely name that makes sense if you break it down. "Nik" for a nickel—the cost of a bag—and "Nip" because the bottles looked like a nip of whiskey.

Charleston Chew: The Charleston Chew is not named for the city of Charleston but for the *dance*, a favorite in speakeasies. It was edgy. It was daring. And it tasted great. Unlike the Prohibition-era drinks.

Chocolate boxes: The big losers during Prohibition were restaurant owners forced to stop selling cocktails and after-dinner drinks. Instead, they sold their guests candy, sumptuous chocolates among the most luxurious. After the meal, some customers split the difference and went to speakeasies for a drink.[22]

By the time Prohibition came along, chocolate was already prominent in groceries, general stores, and gift stores, often sharing shelves with fruits and nuts. Chocolate is the most popular candy today and high on the list of cakes, puddings, and pies (think chocolate cream pie) and so deserves its own reflection . . . i.e., a timeline.

CHOCOLATE—A COMPREHENSIVE TIMELINE

The story of how chocolate became an American darling *and* an international sensation starts with the ancient Olmecs and threads its way around the world.

Olmecs: What most of us know about the Olmecs is their sculptures of immense stone gods, with broad, well-defined noses, full lips, and enormous, focused eyes . . . and, possibly, their stealth in making chocolate.[23] The multistep process started with pods from the chocolate tree and ended with a paste that was formed into hard cakes.

Mayans: The Mayans cultivated the cacao tree, moving into the region now known as Guatemala. They held chocolate in great esteem—in death, the aristocrats were buried with great quantities of it for the afterlife; while living, a spicy, frothy cacao drink was their greatest culinary pleasure. As for the poor—they ate a porridge-like blend of cacao mixed with maize and spices, such as chili pepper or milder vanilla and dried flowers.[24]

Aztecs: As the cacao-loving Aztecs lived in a dry region, they were unable to grow the cacao themselves. So, they obtained it through trade or a "tribute," a tax paid in cacao bean by the provinces they had captured. For the Aztecs, the cacao was also, quite literally, money, hence the expression "money doesn't grow on trees." A large tomato was worth 1 cacao bean; a turkey egg, 3 beans; a rabbit, 100 beans; a slave, 1,000 beans; and a prostitute, a paltry 8 beans.[25]

Chocolate, Europe, and Inevitable Sex

The Spanish: In 1517, Spanish explorers led by Hernán Cortéz discovered cacao. They also discovered the great king Montezuma, made even greater through the creative talents of fellow traveler and conquistador Bernal Díaz del Castillo. From his notes about the journey, we learned the improbable truth that Montezuma drank fifty chalices of chocolate a day to get the sexual stamina necessary to satisfy his 200 wives. That story endured, igniting an unshakable, albeit debatable, belief in chocolate's aphrodisiac powers.[26]

Cacao goes to Spain: The Spanish colonists made Mexico their home, and with it they took native women as wives, concubines, or some variation of lover. Back in Spain, the Spanish kept chocolate a secret, leaving all the more for them. By the late 1500s, monks and nuns in their respective monasteries and nunneries were making a chocolate drink, adding spices such as nutmeg and sugar, which were, ironically or not, considered aphrodisiacs. They even got an idea so innovative it has lasted to this day: serve the cold drink hot. Gradually, word about chocolate spread as royal families in one nation married those in another, bringing chocolate with them.

Chocolate and the Church: Some in the Catholic Church objected to chocolate for pretty much the same reason it has panache today: they considered it an aphrodisiac from a lush pagan they knew nothing about. Pope Pius V held the drink in such low esteem, he didn't even bother to condemn it.[27]

The England-sex-chocolate link: Chocolate and coffeehouses opened in England in the mid-1600s. Chocolate's sexual persona endured, as is evident in *Chocolate, or, An Indian Drinke*, translated by Captain James Wadsworth. Here is an excerpt:

> 'Twill make Old women Young and Fresh;
> Create New-Motions of the Flesh,
> And cause them long for you know what,
> If they but Tast of Chocolate.
> Let Bawdy-Baths be us'd no more;
> Nor Smoaky-Stoves but by the whore
> Of Babilon: since Happy-Fate
> Hath Blessed us with Chocolate.[28]

Chocolate Goes to Boston

Sightings of chocolate appeared in Boston in the 1660s, when merchant John Hull announced he was trading in cocoa, and in 1670, when Dorothy Jones and Jane Barnard requested permission to "keepe a house of publique Entertainment for the selling of Coffee and Chucalettoe [*sic*]." Permission granted, licenses given. In the following years, chocolate became standard fare in public establishments.[29]

Early Bostonians had mixed views about chocolate. Some enjoyed it, but others considered it *too enjoyable* to be respectable. Then there was that unshakeable sex thing as expressed in 1676 by Benjamin Tompson, a New England poet. He lamented the passing of Puritan values, the strong character and religious piety corrupted by licentiousness and idle pleasures such as chocolate. Here's what he said in his poem "New-Englands Crisis":

> Twas ere the Islands sent their Presents in,
> Which but to use was counted next to sin.
> Twas ere a *Barge* had made so rich a fraight
> as Chocholatte, dust-gold and bitts of eight.[30]

Others appreciated chocolate, such as Samuel Whiting, a New England minister who, in 1702, received "2 balls of Chockalett and a pound of figs" from Samuel Sewall, one of the judges who sentenced women to death at the Salem witch trials.[31]

Revolutionary Chocolate

W. Baker's American, Homeopathic and French Chocolate, Prepared Cocoa, Cocoa Paste, Broma, Cocoa Shells, etc.—Ad for Baker's Chocolate, indicating various uses of chocolate over time[32]

In 1764 John Hannon, an Irish immigrant, started the first chocolate mill in Dorchester, Massachusetts, turning the cacao bean into the makings of a coveted, if not bitter, drink. Hannon was brilliant but not entirely businesslike and not at all wealthy. So, he brought in James Baker, a wealthy Harvard College graduate and businessman, for help. The colonists clearly appreciated this effort: in 1773, Hannon produced about 900 pounds of chocolate. The Hannon-Baker partnership ended for reasons unknown. The business was renamed "Baker's Chocolate," forever confusing people who thought the brand was made for bakers.

One celebrated chocolate enthusiast of the time was Benjamin Franklin. He admired the exotic bean for its health and medicinal value to the extreme. Believing it was a remedy for smallpox, he included "6 lbs. of chocolate" (plus sugar, tea, coffee, vinegar, cheese, Madeira, Jamaican spirits, and mustard) in shipments to officers in the French and Indian War. He ran ads for chocolate in his publication the *Pennsylvania Gazette*, which chocolate lovers could purchase at his Pennsylvania print shop.[33]

But chocolate was more than a health drink: at the rise of the Revolutionary War, it was an alternative to British tea. After the war, the popularity of chocolate continued to flourish. In a letter that Thomas Jefferson sent to John Adams in 1785, Jefferson said, "The superiority of chocolate, both for health and nourishment, will soon give it the preference over tea and coffee in America, which it has in Spain."[34]

> **Whatever Happened to John Hannon?**
> The man who introduced chocolate processing to the nation
> went on a trip to the West Indies in 1779. He may have gone to
> buy cacao beans or, just as likely, to escape his wife. One thing is
> certain: John Hannon never returned. After some haggling, James
> Baker bought the business from Hannon's wife.[35]

The Rise of Chocolate (but not in the United States)

In the 1800s, chocolate innovations were on the rise, but not in the United States. Europeans were ahead of the new nation, where industry was concerned anyway. Then, with the onset of the Civil War, American production halted altogether. Meanwhile, over in England, chocolatiers were approaching chocolate-making with zeal. In 1847, for example, Quaker Joseph Fry pressed cocoa powder, sugar, and cocoa into the first candy bar. Another Quaker, John Cadbury, created his own candy bar in 1849. In the following decades, the Cadburys focused on innovative packaging, creating such standards as the Valentine's Day heart box.

Over on the continent, Swiss chocolatier Daniel Peter collaborated with his neighbor, a pharmacist who had invented a version of infant formula. The mixture of chocolate and infant formula brought us milk chocolate. The pharmacist? Henri Nestlé.

Chocolate of the 1800s was gritty, not smooth and luxurious as we know it today. That changed in 1879 when Swiss chocolatier Rodolphe Lindt, the man behind Lindt Chocolate, invented a "conching" machine to massage the gritty chocolate into soft and supple consistency.

Chocolate Back in the United States

By the late 1800s, American chocolate makers were hard at work creating chocolate of their own. Then, as now, they couldn't completely separate themselves from European enterprises.

American chocolates were voluptuous, yes, but the best ones were French. By "French," the chocolates weren't necessarily from France, but were in the "French style." One, the French-style cream-filled candy, was introduced in 1851 at the Great Exhibition in London and leapt the Atlantic to appear in the United States, where they were so popular some chocolatiers devoted themselves to their existence.[36]

Others, such as the illustrious Schrafft's Confectionery of Boston, produced chocolates en masse then wholesaled them to smaller companies. Schrafft also carried chocolates in its own retail shops, complete with French-ish names such as "D'Or Elegante" and distinct, very French gold-hued packaging. Authentic French candies invented and created only in the USA.[37]

By the early 1900s, American chocolate came into its own, with thousands of small chocolate makers spanning the nation, many locally based in communities too small to make the history books. Large companies such as Hershey's Chocolate (1894) and Mars (1911 as Mar-O-Bar Co.) made their mark with tidal waves of marketing, as did Ghirardelli.

Today, chocolate is an American favorite. Among the classiest are Belgium chocolates, French chocolates, and Swiss chocolates.

SOFT STUFF—LET'S HAVE FUN!

Hard to imagine, but the ingredients in taffy are basically the same as those in candy sticks and candy canes. These entries in the candy world left their medicinal pasts and were made exclusively for fun.

Saltwater Taffy: Hold the Salt

Saltwater taffy began beachside in Atlantic City in the 1880s. In those days, shops were built right by the ocean, a bad idea given the inevitability of storms and ensuing floods. So as it happened, one dark night a storm swept up from the sea, flooding shops along the boardwalk, including a taffy shop belonging to John Ross Edminston. As he was cleaning up the next morning, a little girl stopped by asking for taffy. Looking at the water-logged mess, Edminston shook his head and said these immortal words: "I only have saltwater taffy." Yet—hold on! The name just

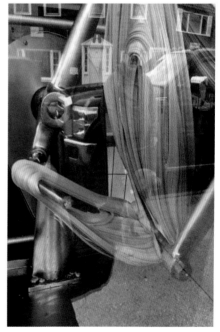

Early 1900s pull machine at storefront, Rockport, Massachusetts, *Susan Benjamin, Courtesy True Treats*

sounded right. So beach-like and fun. But saltwater? In taffy? Not so right. So Edminston kept the name but left the saltwater out.

So popular was this saltless saltwater taffy that Edminston filed for a trademark on the name. He thought of it. It should be his. In the early 1920s, the federal government agreed. Edminston went on to demand millions of dollars in back pay from all who had been using the name. His competitors fought back. The US Supreme Court took their side, making "saltwater taffy" fair game for everyone. Today, saltwater taffy is sold from the Midwest to Alaska. Still no salt.

Toffees and Taffy That Isn't

Toffee? Taffy? That depends on where you live and when you are living. The names flip-flopped in England, the treats starting as taffy, then becoming toffee, and, when cooked with extra butter, butterscotch. In the United States, the difference more or less boils down to this: (1) toffee is harder than taffy; (2) toffee is folded into neat, usually oblong shapes, while taffy is literally pulled and wrapped in chunks; and (3) Americans eat way more taffy.

In fact, many toffees have had an on-again, off-again relationship with American sweets-lovers. Mary Janes, for example, vanished and recently returned. For the record, Charles Miller invented the peanut butter and molasses treat in 1914 at his Boston home, which happened to be the former home of Paul Revere, which gives yet another reason why today's kids should appreciate history. Eventually, Cambridge-based Necco bought Mary Janes, then went under, taking Mary Janes down with it. But Mary Janes (and Neccos) are back, a little lumpier but still delicious.

Another Boston company, the Squirrel Brand, introduced Squirrel Nut Zippers in 1926. The "Zipper" part referred to an illegal Prohibition-era cocktail that was popular at the time and honored by the toff. The Squirrel Nut company eventually moved to Cambridge, close to Necco, who bought and lost the Zipper. Unlike the Mary Jane, it has yet to return.

The Chicago-based Bit-O-Honey did better. It was introduced in 1924, using honey instead of the standard corn syrup and sugar. It's been with us ever since.

Turkish Taffy: The Taffy That Isn't

Like Mary Janes, Bonomo's Turkish Taffy has been on and off and on again. And . . . just as saltwater taffy is saltless, Turkish Taffy isn't taffy. And it isn't toffee and isn't even Turkish. It was invented by Austrian immigrant Herman Herer, who was trying to create a *marshmallow* candy but added too many egg whites. One experiment led to another, and the Turkish Taffy that wasn't was born.

> Turkish Taffy's success is due, in part, to its signature tagline "Crack it up," and instructions on the packaging: "CRACK IT UP!—HOLD BAR IN PALM OF HAND—STRIKE AGAINST FLAT SURFACE—LET IT MELT IN YOUR MOUTH!"

In 1936, the Bonomo family, who had immigrated to Coney Island from—yes!—Turkey, bought Turkish Taffy. Not made *in* Turkey but made by a Turkish family. Close enough.[39]

Circus Peanuts

More than any other candy, Circus Peanuts are loved and loathed and overall perplexing. The texture is soft as a sponge, spongy as a marshmallow, flavored like a banana, and shaped like a peanut. The name is "peanut," but it is peanut-less.

This curious candy originated in the late 1800s, made for spectators at traveling circuses. The reasoning went like this: Circuses had elephants, and elephants eat peanuts. So why *not* enjoy peanut-shaped candy that doesn't contain peanuts? Logic aside, Circus Peanuts also took off in penny candy stores, general stores, and cereal bowls, where they became the prototype for Lucky Charms cereal.[40]

THE FUTURIST CANDY OF THE PAST

One of the many beauties of candy is it reflects our culture. So, you can imagine the goings-on in candy companies in the Cold War era when Americans were obsessed with UFOs, the space race, and nuclear bombs. While the variety of explosive/fizzy/neon-hued candies has hardly died down, there's nothing like the classics. Here are but a few.

Satellite Wafers

The perfect fit for the space age, Satellite Wafers, aka Flying Saucers, were created by a Communion wafer maker in Antwerp, Belgium, in the early 1950s. Sales of Communion wafers were down, so he created a pocket from two wafers, filled it with tiny sugar bits, and there you have it. Flying Saucers that even make noise and assuage guilt when you eat them.[41]

Zotz

Made in Italy, Zotz debuted in the United States in 1970. It's a hard candy shell with a blast of fizz that will shake you up even though you expect it. Zotz are still made in Italy by a family-owned company.[42]

Astro Pops

No mere lollipop, Astro Pops were invented by two rocket scientists who quit the space program in 1963 to make a three-color, rocket-shaped lollipop. The bottom of the pop is red, representing the fire when the rocket takes off. The middle is green, representing the space junk, and the top is yellow, representing, of course, the capsule that travels through space. Their timing was great! The space race was on. Kids were excited. And Astro Pops took off by the millions.[43]

Pop Rocks

Chemist William A. Mitchell was the mastermind behind quick-set Jell-O, the nondairy whipped cream Cool Whip, and Tang, the official beverage of astronauts. In 1956, Mitchell also experimented with instant "carbonated candy," using carbon dioxide. The attempt failed and he moved on. Then, twenty years later, another chemist unearthed the formula, tweaked it, and there you have it: Pop Rocks—one of the most scandal-ridden candies in history.[44]

THE GREAT POP ROCKS SCANDAL

The Pop Rocks scandal started in the 1970s when someone somewhere decided that Pop Rocks would explode in your stomach if consumed with soda. No mere cautionary tale, this tidbit escalated into near hysteria, claiming that children were dropping dead everywhere, including a TV personality who was, and likely still is, alive.

Here's how the rumor was subdued (eventually):

- Pop Rocks manufacturer General Foods took out a full-page ad in forty-five major publications nationwide promising nervous parents that Pop Rocks were completely safe.
- General Foods sent 50,000 letters to school principals, explaining why Pop Rocks were completely safe, so they could ease parental hysteria.
- The company sent Pop Rocks creator William A. Mitchell on a speaking tour to calm parents via facts. Did you know, he reassured them, that the worst that could happen if you mix Pop Rocks and soda is you burp?
- The FDA set up a hotline to ease parents' fears that their kids may have taken a lethal dose of Pop Rocks and soda.
- The company discontinued the explosive candy until everything calmed down.

In spite of the horrors circulating about Pop Rocks, kids still loved them. Maybe eating them was so daring. So rich with defiance. So deliciously *wrong*.

Pop Rocks were also profitable for General Foods, which launched a Pop Rocks spin-off of finely ground candy crystals called "Space Dust" in the late 1970s. Unfortunately, the nation was reeling from a rise in the use of powdery and legitimately lethal drugs such as cocaine, heroin, and newcomer PCP. Even worse, the street name for PCP was angel dust. In short, Space Dust, even after being renamed Cosmic Candy, was a bust.[45]

THE POP, BANG, AND NEVER-ENDING LIFE OF SODA POP

Ten Billion Nickels a Year for Soda Water! [Americans] Drink Enough to Maintain the Navy and Army Twice Over, More Than Enough to Float the Lusitania, Three Times the Value of the Yearly Automobile Output!—Knoxville Sentinel, April 30, 1910[46]

From Volcanic Springs to Soda Fountain Machines

At one time, any European aristocrat with so much as an ache went to a fashionable spa whose most salient feature was the "waters," the bubblier, the more mineral, the better. There they drank, soaked, and inhaled these waters, walked the grounds, ate greens and whole grains, then drank, soaked, and inhaled again. In the United States, the first spa to open was in Berkeley Springs, Virginia (now West Virginia), in 1776. By the mid-1800s, spas were bubbling up all over, hosted by such health enthusiasts as Harvey Kellogg.

Soda fountain with soda "jerk," *Farm and Home Magazine*, June 1924

The popularity of spas fueled many a pharmacist to investigate ways to re-create the esteemed spa bubbles in ordinary water. Yes, they could duplicate the tingling sensation of bubbles by adding sodium bicarbonate and tartaric acid to water, but the result tasted like an ultra-salty glass of Alka-Seltzer. So, they added artificial flavorings, fruit juice, and sweeteners to make it more appealing. And there, in those bubbles, conjured in apothecaries, came the modern soda pop.[47]

DRUGSTORES AND SODA FOUNTAINS: A PERFECT UNION

Soda fountains may have started as a place to get curative waters, but ended up as pharmacy counters where you could get sodas, burgers, grilled cheese, and candy, and even find a

Soda Fountain Drinks at the Start

The early soda fountain drinks weren't frilly, fizzy, or even colorful. They were hard-core medicinal, concocted to infuse pep or calm with such additions as bromides, plant extracts, cocaine, and caffeine. The reputation of soda fountains suffered, but the increasing lineup of sweet and harmless alternatives kept them from going under. The menu changed for good in 1914 when the Harrison Act banned the use of cocaine and opiates in over-the-counter products.[48]

date. As for curative waters? Those were *soda* fountains, which served a rainbow's range of flavors—coffee, sarsaparilla, pineapple, orange, grape . . . But the flavors, often accented by cherries, orange slices, or nuts of all varieties, weren't the point. The *mix* of flavors, the *creativity* of the display—that's what mattered. So, you can only imagine the tens of thousands of variations that were served in towns, urban neighborhoods, and emerging luncheonettes and department stores with soda fountains in them.

THE SODA FOUNTAIN'S SODA FOUNTAIN

The name "soda fountain" refers to the place and the actual soda dispenser. These were no Coke machines set up in fast-food joints and gas stations. The early soda fountains meant it. Soda was to be celebrated and beverages flowed freely from marble-accented affairs, with rows of ornate spigots, some as opulent and celebratory as the baths in ancient Rome.

Yet the soda fountain was born of necessity. Morphing flat water into carbonated water took some doing until John Matthews came on the scene. Matthews, who immigrated from Great Britain in 1832, created a carbonation machine, which he sold to pharmacies in New York City. The machine created the bubbles, and the pharmacists or soda jerk only needed to add the syrups, fruit juices, oils, and creams to the drinks, and voila! The soda fountain was born.

Matthews's machine was good and functional, but it took G. D. Dows, of Lowell, Massachusetts, to make them gorgeous. His fountains were equipped with measuring decanters, a soda-water tube, and eight silver-plated syrup spigots, with tiny eagles, wings spread wide, atop each, all housed in white marble from a tombstone cutter's shop. Over the decades, Dows, Matthews, and other fountain makers created ever more and more voluptuous fountains rich with carousels, tiled mosaics, embedded jewels, and musical automatons. One of over a dozen fountains featured in the Centennial Exposition of 1876 was three stories high with seventy-six spigots. It was called "Mammoth."[50]

OH NO! BABY, IT'S COLD OUTSIDE

Hot Sodas for Cold Days . . . Served as They Should Be.—Manter's Drug Store ad, 1915[51]

In the 1900s, if you owned a soda fountain, your biggest problem was winter. Who wants ice cream, cold sodas, or milkshakes in winter? Unwilling to endure a down-season that lasted for months, the soda fountain industry—vendors, industry magazines, associations, proprietors—got creative. They extended the snack-size menus to include sandwiches, salads, and other light fare. They promoted coffee and tea. But the most original option was "hot soda"—a real winter warm-me-up and tasty treat!

Granted, some hot sodas weren't exactly "sodas" but bouillons, consommés, or broths. Others were remnants of the medicinal drinks of the past, such as hot angostura tonic and hot phosphates, thought to cleanse the body of toxins.[52] Closer to the promise of "hot soda," though, were hot egg drinks, hot ginger ale, hot lemonade, hot malted milk, and a variety of

Make Your Own Hot Soda

Here are two hot soda recipes from the *Confectioners' and Bakers' Gazette* to try:

Hot Ginger Ale, 1916
Soluble ginger ale extract, 10 drops; soluble lemon extract, 10 drops; sugar, two cubes (or teaspoonfuls); fruit acid, 10 drops; hot water to fill the mug.

Hot Oyster Malt, 1917
Malted milk, oyster bullion extract, of each two tablespoons, hot water, enough to fill mug. Stir well while adding the hot water to make the mixture smooth. Season with celery salt and serve with graham wafers. If desired a teaspoon of whipped cream may be added.[53]

hot clam drinks, which fall into a category of their own.

While hot sodas were in the domain of soda fountains, they were easy to make at home just by adjusting the quantities. Of course, the purpose of soda fountains was social as well as functional, but the drinks remained the same.

THE END OF THE SODA FOUNTAIN

Soda fountains survived and thrived into the 1960s. They showed up in pharmacies, home-grown convenience stores called "spas," mid-1900s discount department stores such as Woolworth, and even restaurants so customers could eat without ordering a full meal. Ultimately, though, soda fountains couldn't keep up with bottled sodas or the slick dispensers of today. But what really did soda fountains in was the fast-food restaurants and grab-and-go culture that replaced the slower-paced soda fountain where people could relax and talk. What became of the pharmacies themselves? Walk into any Walmart or CVS for an answer.

> Hot soda ad, 1907: "There is nothing better than a good hot soda to warm you up in a hurry. Hot soda is a stimulant, the best kind of stimulant because it can only do good. It is essentially a food and stimulates like food only a good deal quicker. If you have not formed the 'hot soda habit' you have not tried the type of soda we make."[54]

Medicine to Soda Pop: The Men Who Bridged the Gap

Many of the sodas we enjoy today were invented by pharmacists and physicians. Some were trying to make curatives, others not. Here are a few of the people who were behind today's favorites.

SCHWEPPES GINGER ALE

Jacob Schweppe was born in Germany but started his professional life in Geneva, where he worked as a jeweler and watchmaker. All the while, he led another life as an amateur scientist with a keen interest in carbonation. In 1783, he launched the Schweppes Company, selling preexisting carbonation systems only on a larger, commercial scale. Some believe Schweppe's creation launched the carbonated beverage industry.

Today, though, Schweppe is best known for another invention—"ginger ale." Around the turn of the century, Schweppe moved to England, where his ginger ale caught the attention of Erasmus Darwin, the grandfather of Charles Darwin and a man of esteem. Quite possibly Darwin helped pitch ginger ale into popularity.

Anyway, Schweppe returned to Geneva and died in 1821. Ten years later, King William IV of the United Kingdom adopted the beverage, enabling Schweppe's manufacturers to use the famous "by appointment to," still on the ginger ale label.[55] Many soda manufacturers went on to manufacture their own versions of ginger ale. It went on to become a classic American soda by the mid-1900s.

At twelve years old, New Jersey native Charles Hires launched his career by apprenticing at a pharmacy. At eighteen, he became a full-fledged pharmacist, operating his own store in Philadelphia. But the salient life-changing moment occurred on his honeymoon. While visiting Niagara Falls, he sampled "root tea," a health-inspiring Native American drink that contained twenty-six roots, berries, and herbs.

Back at the pharmacy, Hires figured out a way to make root tea available to the public through a root tea powder. Unfortunately, customers had to boil the powder in water, strain it, mix it with sugar and yeast, and let it ferment. Then and only then could you drink it. The original package claimed the powder was "Made from Finest Grade Honduras Sarsaparilla, Ginger, Sassafras, Hops, and other healthful and scientifically blended roots, barks and berries," a promise that didn't quite make it worth the effort.[56]

Hires's concoction had other problems. One was the name. "Root tea" was fine but lacked pizzazz. Instead of "tea," why not call it "beer"? So, the fermented healthy tea became a fermented healthy beer. Only *another* problem. The temperance movement was gaining momentum and Hires was a Quaker. And Quakers were supporters of temperance and later, full-fledged Prohibitionists. Suffice to say the Quaker community, *his* Quaker community, was not thrilled

Hires Root Beer advertisement, 1870–1900, *American Trade Cards, Courtesy DeGolyer Library, Southern Methodist University*

Root beer float, Gloucester, Massachusetts, *Susan Benjamin, Courtesy True Treats*

about his "beer." So, how to engage the purchasing public while placating the Quakers? He branded root beer the "Great Temperance Drink" and the "Official Drink of the Temperance Movement" and other conciliatory names. One ad in the Philadelphia *Times* of 1888 put it this way: "Hires improved root beer . . . makes five gallons of the most delicious and wholesome Temperance drink in the world."[57]

Hires root beer became a hit in the 1920s with the "root beer float" and remains so today.

COCA-COLA

Coca-Cola was invented by John Stith Pemberton. Born in 1831 in Georgia, Pemberton got a medical degree when he was nineteen years old and practiced medicine and surgery early on. His career halted during the Civil War, when he fought for the South. War over, he moved to Atlanta to start a business selling patent medicines and open a laboratory where he conducted experiments.

These efforts led him to create "Pemberton's French Wine Coca," a syrup consisting of wine and cocoa extract, meant to cure nervous disorders, headaches, and other ailments. In 1885, Pemberton was forced to change the formula, as Atlanta forbid the sale of alcohol. His new recipe contained extracts of cocaine and caffeine-rich kola nuts that grow in the African rainforest. For a sweetener, he used sugar instead of wine.

After a taste test in a nearby pharmacy, Pemberton added carbonated water to turn the concoction into a soda, which he sold as a "brain tonic" and an ideal temperance drink. That drink would become Coca-Cola: "Coca" for cocaine and "Cola" for the kola nut, still used in Nigeria for festive occasions.[58]

PEPSI-COLA

As a young man, Caleb Bradham, of North Carolina, studied to be a medical doctor. His plans changed when his father declared bankruptcy and his funds for school dried up. Instead, he became a pharmacist and opened Bradham's Pharmacy, a hangout for locals who spent their nickels on a jukebox featuring the newest musical selections. And it was there Bradham invented Pepsi-Cola, a health-inspiring beverage, all-natural and, unlike other drinks, narcotic-free. One of his favorite combinations was sugar, water, vanilla, oils, and, as with Coca-Cola, kola nuts.

Coke and Pepsi, together at last, *Susan Benjamin, Courtesy True Treats*

Originally called "Brad's Drink," he renamed it Pepsi-Cola: "Pepsi" for the drink's powers to cure dys*pepsi*a, more commonly known as indigestion, and "Cola," of course, for the kola nut. The Pepsi-Cola Corporation had one of the earliest trademarks in US Patent Office history and was one of the first to distribute its drink by motor transport. Today, Pepsi is a key competitor of Coca-Cola.[59]

DR PEPPER

The year was 1885. The place, Morrison's Old Corner Drug Store in Waco, Texas. And there, Charles Alderton, a Brooklyn-born pharmacist, started experimenting with flavorful drinks at the soda fountain where he worked. One mixture in particular became a fast favorite with customers who asked Alderton to "shoot them a 'Waco.'"

The origin of the actual name is a grab bag of possibility: in honor of his friend Dr. Charles Pepper, his employer Dr. Pepper, the pepsin enzyme (think Pepsi-Cola), or the drink's ability to energize or add "pep." As with other soda makers of the time, Dr Pepper was marketed as a brain tonic and energizing pick-me-up.

For much of its history, Dr Pepper was a regional favorite. That wasn't by choice but because Coca-Cola and Pepsi-Cola stealthily locked in nationwide networks of bottlers who could turn their syrups—and no one else's—into bottled colas. So, Dr Pepper was stranded in the South and Southwest, unable to find the distribution channels it needed. Sure, the soda won notoriety and adoration, but it had limited sales. Then, in 1963 a federal court ruled that Dr Pepper was not a "cola product" that competed with Coke and Pepsi, but a unique soda with a unique taste. Therefore, bottlers could distribute Dr Pepper without infringing on their exclusive arrangements with Coke and Pepsi. By the late 1960s, Dr Pepper was available from coast to coast.[60]

Notes

BROUGHT TO YOU BY . . . SIX WOMEN AND A MOVEMENT

1. "Eliza Leslie," Cooks Info, September 8, 2005, updated November 13, 2021, https://www.cooks info.com/eliza-leslie.

2. Eliza Leslie, *Seventy-Five Recipes for Pastry, Cakes, and Sweetmeats* (Boston: Munroe & Francis, [1829?]).

3. "Eliza Leslie," Cooks Info.

4. Stephen Schmidt, "Mrs. Goodfellow and Miss Leslie, Manuscript Cookbooks Survey," September 2014, https://www.manuscriptcookbookssurvey.org/mrs-goodfellow-and-miss-leslie.

5. Eliza Leslie, *The Ladies' Guide to True Politeness and Perfect Manners; or, Miss Leslie's Behaviour Book, a Guide and Manual for Ladies* (Philadelphia: B. Peterson, 1864), 36.

6. Anne-Marie Rachman, "Farmer, Fannie Merritt, 1857–1915," MSU Libraries, Digital Repository, https://d.lib.msu.edu/msul:44.

7. Fannie Merritt Farmer, *The Boston Cooking-School Cook Book* (Boston: Little, Brown and Company, 1941 [1896]), 12.

8. Farmer, *Boston Cooking-School Cook Book*, 1–2.

9. Rachman, "Farmer, Fannie Merritt."

10. Bonnie McDowell, "History of Aunt Sammy and Her Recipes," *Quaint Cooking: For the Love of the Vintage Kitchen* (blog), January 16, 2019, https://quaintcooking.com/2019/01/16/history-of-aunt-sammy-and-her-recipes.

11. Elaine Bissell, "Cookbook Lists Uncle Sam's Favorites," *Mount Vernon Argus* (White Plains, NY), April 17, 1975, https://www.newspapers.com/image/894604629.

12. Andrew Boyd, "Aunt Sammy," *The Engines of Our Ingenuity*, episode no. 2762, first aired December 22, 2011, https://www.uh.edu/engines/epi2762.htm.

12. McDowell, "History of Aunt Sammy."

13. Bob Swift, "Aunt Sammy, Julia Child of the Thirties," *Des Moines Tribune*, May 5, 1975, 22.

14. Kathleen Collins, "Watching What We Eat: The Evolution of Television Cooking Shows," *New York Times*, May 29, 2009, https://www.nytimes.com/2009/05/31/books/chapter-watching-what-we-eat.html. "Just for Fun: Aunt Sammy's Radio Recipes," *Government Book Talk* (blog), April 19, 2010, https://govbooktalk.gpo.gov/2010/04/19/just-for-fun-aunt-sammy%e2%80%99s-radio-recipes.

15. McDowell, "History of Aunt Sammy."

16. Laura Shapiro, "'I Guarantee'": Betty Crocker and the Woman in the Kitchen," in *From Betty Crocker to Feminist Food Studies*, ed. Arlene Voski Avakian and Barbara Haber (Amherst: University of Massachusetts Press, 2005), 29–36.

17. "New Model Flour Assures Success in Baking Effort," *Chico (CA) Record*, March 19, 1930, 11, https://www.newspapers.com/image/679073904.

18. "4 Fictional Cooks Representing Food Brands," *Vintage Unscripted* (blog), April 7, 2019, https://vintageunscripted.com/2019/04/07/4-fictional-cooks-representing-food-brands.

19. Mackenzie Dawson, "This Isn't Your Mother's Betty Crocker Cookbook," *New York Post*, October 12, 2016, https://nypost.com/2016/10/12/this-isnt-your-mothers-betty-crocker-cookbook.

20. "4 Fictional Cooks," *Vintage Unscripted.*

21. Pillsbury ad, *Kansas City (MO) Times*, October 31, 1947, 16, https://www.newspapers.com/image/655661760.

22. Pillsbury ad, *Spokesman-Review* (Spokane, WA), March 21, 1948, 93, https://www.newspapers.com/image/569346598.

23. "Ration-Wise Recipes," *Macon (GA) Chronicle Herald*, July 19, 1945, 3, https://www.newspapers.com/image/81226776.

24. Carolyn Menyes, "10 Things You Didn't Know About the Pillsbury Bake-Off," The Daily Meal, October 2, 2017, https://www.thedailymeal.com/entertain/10-things-you-didnt-know-about-pillsbury-bake-slideshow.

25. Cobey Black, "Who's News with Cobey Black," *Honolulu Star-Bulletin*, January 10, 1958, 15, https://www.newspapers.com/image/269130532.

26. Dorothee Polson, "Pillsbury Bake-Off Tomorrow, Entrants Ready," *Arizona Republic* (Phoenix, AZ), February 12, 1967, 120, https://www.newspapers.com/image/118017211.

27. Dorothee Polson, "Barbara Thorton New Ann Pillsbury," *Arizona Republic* (Phoenix, AZ), August 9, 1967, 45, https://www.newspapers.com/image/117498012.

28. Robert T. Smith, "Consumer Aid Ann Pillsbury to Be Retired," *Star Tribune* (Minneapolis, MN), June 17, 1970, 13, https://www.newspapers.com/image/185341624.

29. Wikipedia contributors, "Aunt Jemima," Wikipedia, last edited October 13, 2023, https://en.wikipedia.org/wiki/Aunt_Jemima.

30. Ad for Aunt Jemima Flour, *Kansas City (MO) Star*, November 9, 1906, 15, https://www.newspapers.com/image/653582178.

31. Ad for Aunt Jemima Flour, *Carroll (IA) Daily Herald*, October 20, 1938, 4, https://www.newspapers.com/image/467589.

32. Ad for Aunt Jemima Flour, *St. Joseph (MO) News-Press*, February 12, 1976, 8, https://www.newspapers.com/image/561847868.

33. Jon Schlosberg and Deborah Roberts, "The Untold Story of the Real 'Aunt Jemima' and the Fight to Preserve her Legacy," ABC News, August 12, 2020, https://abcnews.go.com/US/untold-story-real-aunt-jemima-fight-preserve-legacy/story?id=72293603.

DINNER PARTIES: DEVILED EGGS, POACHED OYSTERS, AND PLENTY TO EAT

1. Irma Rombauer and Marion Rombauer Becker, *The Joy of Cooking* (Indianapolis, IN: Bobs-Merrill Company, 1953), 919.

2. Benito Cereno, "What It Was Really Like to Party Like an Ancient Roman," Grunge, April 14, 2021, https://www.grunge.com/306566/what-it-was-really-like-to-party-like-an-ancient-roman.

3. Carla Raimer, "Ancient Roman Recipes," Ancient Worlds, *Nova*, PBS, November 1, 2000, https://www.pbs.org/wgbh/nova/article/roman-recipes.

4. Henry Davenport Northrop, *The Household Encyclopedia* (Boston: New England Home Educational Society, [1895?]), 46–53.

5. Emily Post, "Dinner Party Menus," Good Taste Today, *Times Record News* (Wichita Falls, TX), January 20, 1933, 11, https://www.newspapers.com/image/775109158.

6. Rombauer and Becker, *Joy of Cooking*, 1.

7. Gary Regan, *Joy of Mixology* (New York: Carlston Potter Publishers, 2003), 2, 3.

8. Regan, *Joy of Mixology*, 8.

9. Mark Twain, Quotable Quotes, Good Reads, https://www.goodreads.com/quotes/54577-too-much-of-anything-is-bad-but-too-much-good.

10. Rombauer and Becker, *Joy of Cooking*, 819.

11. David Wondrich, *Oxford Companion to Spirits and Cocktails* (New York: Oxford University Press, 2022), 90–91.

12. "Glad Tiding to the Afflicted. Hampton's Vegetable Tincture," *Alexandria (VA) Gazette*, December 30, 1840, 1, https://www.newspapers.com/image/816442641.

13. Cheatham's Chill Tonic, *Indian Citizen* (Atoka, OK), November 1, 1900, 9, https://www.newspapers.com/image/611408100.

14. Row's & Cos Depot, *Buffalo Morning Express*, December 23, 1850, 2, https://www.newspapers.com/image/343480936.

15. Dan Nosowitz, "Grapefruit Is One of the Weirdest Fruits on the Planet," Gastro Explorer, Atlas Obscura, October 6, 2020, https://www.atlasobscura.com/articles/grapefruit-history-and-drug-inter actions.

16. Louis P. De Gouy, *The Gold Cookbook* (Philadelphia: Chilton, 1948), 824.

17. Julia F. Morton, "Grapefruit," in *Fruits of Warm Climates* (Miami, FL: self-published, 1987), 152–58, https://www.hort.purdue.edu/newcrop/morton/grapefruit.html.

18. Fannie Merritt Farmer, *The Boston Cooking-School Cook Book* (Boston: Little, Brown and Company, 1941 [1896]), 58.

19. "Press Daily Menu," *Pittsburgh Press*, May 19, 1912, 21, https://www.newspapers.com/image/143389853.

20. "Greatest in the World!" *Evening World* (New York), April 30, 1894, 3, https://www.newspapers.com/image/78866613.

21. Anna Thomson, "Unusual Celery Recipes," The Kitchen Cupboard, *Eagle Rock Sentinel* (Los Angeles), May 27, 1915, 3, https://www.newspapers.com/image/709987950.

22. "Greatest in the World!" *Evening World*, 3.

23. De Gouy, *Gold Cookbook*, 87, 89.

24. Jane Eddington, "The Tribune Cookbook," *Chicago Tribune*, March 18, 1917, 30, https://www.newspapers.com/image/355166894.

25. "Large Formal Dinner Party," *Los Angeles Herald*, December 27, 1898, 9, https://www.newspapers.com/image/80603433.

26. Emily Post, "Dinner Party Menus," Social Good Tastes, *Philadelphia Inquirer*, January 15, 1933, 52, https://www.newspapers.com/image/173364568.

27. "Formal Dinners," *Deuel County Herald* (Big Springs, NE), December 5, 1935, https://www.newspapers.com/image/670184050.

28. Rombauer and Becker, *Joy of Cooking*, 29.

29. Mary B. Wilson, "The Bulletin Board," *Fresno (CA) Bee*, January 31, 1925, 19, https://www.newspapers.com/image/701078254.

30. "Pig-In-A-Blanket," *Idaho Statesman* (Boise, ID), July 1, 1938, 5, https://www.newspapers.com/image/722890511.

31. "Stag at Ease? That's Hubby!" *Press of Atlantic City*, October 14, 1938, 14, https://www.newspapers.com/image/918169798.

32. "On the Home Front," *Press Democrat* (Santa Rosa, CA), February 19, 1942, 1, https://www.newspapers.com/image/265214128.

33. Pillsbury Pancake Flour ad, *Pittsburgh Sun-Telegraph*, September 20, 1945, 7, https://www.newspapers.com/image/524130622.

34. "Deviled Egg History, from Rome to Your Home," North Carolina Egg Association blog, November 2, 2018, https://ncegg.org/deviled-eggs-history-from-rome-to-your-home.

35. "The Summer Picnic," *Courier-News* (Bridgewater, NJ), August 25, 1894, 7, https://www.newspapers.com/image/218829994.

36. "Deviled Eggs Trims Calories Without Cutting Taste," *Lexington (KY) Herald Leader*, June 18, 1980, 53, https://www.newspapers.com/image/687629298.

37. Nell B. Nichols, ed., *The Country Cookbook* (New York: Doubleday & Company, 1972 [1959]), 91.

38. "The Prince of Caterers," *New York Daily Herald*, August 27, 1876, 8, https://www.newspapers.com/image/329569715.

39. "Delmonico's Restaurant, The Most Famous Restaurant in American History," Cooks Info, November 8, 2004, updated January 16, 2022, https://www.cooksinfo.com/delmonicos-restaurant.

40. "Delmonico's—the Earliest Italian-Named Restaurant in the U.S.," Grand Voyage Italy, March 5, 2019, http://www.grandvoyageitaly.com/history/delmonicos-the-earliest-italian-named-restaurant-in-the-us.

41. Paul Freedman, *Ten Restaurants That Changed America* (London and New York: Liveright Publishing, 2016), 44–45.

42. Amanda Kludt, "Remembering Delmonico's, New York's Original Restaurant," Eater NY, June 29, 2011, https://ny.eater.com/2011/6/29/6673317/remembering-delmonicos-new-yorks-original -restaurant.

JOIN US AT NOON: SALAD DAYS, SANDWICHES AND JELL-O DELIGHT

1. General Foods Corporation, *The General Foods Cookbook* (New York: Random House, 1959), 159.

2. In Woman's World, *Jersey City News*, June 4, 1900, 3, https://www.newspapers.com/image/ 856119779.

3. Fannie Merritt Farmer, *The Boston Cooking-School Cook Book* (Boston: Little, Brown and Company, 1941 [1896]), 20.

4. Mary Morton, "Household Hints," *Courier-News* (Bridgewater, NJ), August 9, 1930, 3, https:// www.newspapers.com/image/220679998.

5. Josephine Gibson, "Frozen Fruit Salad," Brides Cooking Primer, *Pittsburgh Press*, May 20, 1940, 20, https://www.newspapers.com/image/147524619.

6. Oscar Tschirky, *The Cookbook by Oscar of the Waldorf* (Chicago: Saalfield Publishing Company, 1896), 433.

7. Cicely Brownstone, "The Truth about Waldorf Salad," *Standard Speaker* (Hazelton, PA), January 23, 1972, 13, https://www.newspapers.com/image/64647391.

8. Sarah Grey, "Jell-O Salad History: The Rise and Fall of an American Icon," Serious Eats, February 7, 2023, https://www.seriouseats.com/history-of-jell-o-salad.

9. Bertha J. Roberts and G. Cox Ltd., *A Manual of Gelatine Cookery: For Use with Cox's Sparking Gelatine* (Leeds, UK: University of Leeds, 1904).

10. "Knox History," Knox, http://www.knoxgelatine.com/history.htm.

11. "The History of Gelaton, Gelatine, and JELL-O," What's Cooking America, http://whatscooking america.net/History/Jell-0-history.htm.

12. Wikipedia contributors, "Jell-O," Wikipedia, last edited September 25, 2023, https://en.wikipedia .org/wiki/Jell-O.

13. Jell-O Company, *Jell-O Brings DOZENS of Answers* (LeRoy, NY: Jell-O Company, 1928), 3.

14. "History of Gelaton, Gelatine, and JELL-O," What's Cooking America.

15. Jello-O Company, *Jell-O Brings DOZENS of Answers*, 12.

16. Jell-O Company, *Try the New Jell-O, You Make It without Boiling Water!* (LeRoy, NY: Jell-O Company, 1932), 10, 12.

17. Kendra Ackerman, "Aged Poorly: Special Effects Included Dousing the Horses in Jell-O," Screen Rant, December 5, 2020, https://screenrant.com/the-wizard-of-oz-aged-poorly-timeless.

18. Jell-O Company, *Try the New Jell-O*, 10, 12.

19. Jerry Thomas, *The Bon Vivant's Companion; or, How to Mix Drinks* (New York: A. A. Knopf, 1928), 26.

20. The Chatterer, *Portland (ME) Sunday Telegram*, July 30, 1893, 13, https://www.newspapers.com/ image/846663126.

21. Henriette Rousseau, "A Garden Party," *Gloucester County Democrat* (Woodbury, NJ), August 1, 1901, 1, https://www.newspapers.com/image/888115416.

22. Local Dashes, *Portsmouth (NH) Herald*, July 31, 1923, 10, https://www.newspapers.com/ image/56592705.

23. "Frozen Fruit Salads," Household Department, *Portsmouth (NH) Herald*, March 9, 1934, 6, https:// www.newspapers.com/image/56507794.

24. "Garden Party Menu Features Tuna Soufflé Sandwiches," *Hastings (NE) Daily Tribune*, April 26, 1951, 4, https://www.newspapers.com/image/700875735.

25. Lynne Olver, ed., "What Is an American Picnic?" Food Timeline, January 21, 2015, https://www.foodtimeline.org/foodpicnics.html.

26. Amy Vanderbilt, "Menu for Garden Party Requested by Readers," Ask Amy Vanderbilt, *El Paso Times*, August 13, 1969, 10, https://www.newspapers.com/image/429495133.

27. "Labor Will Take Its Annual Holiday Monday, a Picnic and Economic Discussion," *Lexington (KY) Herald-Leader*, September 5, 1897, 5, https://www.newspapers.com/image/682419563.

28. Jennie Ellis Burdick, *What Shall We Have to Eat?* (New York: University Society, 1922), 54–55.

29. Mrs. Mary J. Lincoln, *What to Have for Luncheon* (New York: Dodge Publishing, 1904), 41–44.

30. Good Housekeeping Institute, *The Good Housekeeping Cook Book*, 7th ed. (New York: Farrar & Rinehart, 1944), 889–90.

31. Edith Barker, *Silver Jubilee Super Market Cook Book* (New York: Super Market Publishing, 1955), 43–45.

32. James Beard, *James Beard's Treasury of Outdoor Cooking* (New York: Ridge Press, 1960), 214–26.

33. Jean Anderson and Elaine Hanna, *Doubleday Cookbook: Complete Contemporary Cooking* (Garden City, NY: Jean Doubleday & Company, 1975), 71.

34. Annabel Post, ed., *Sunset Cook Book: Food With a Gourmet Touch* (Menlo Park, CA: Lane Book Company, 1960), 155–66.

35. McCall's Food Editors, *McCall's Picnic and Patio Cook Book* (Orlando, FL: Advance Publishers, 1965), 26–28.

36. Autumn Swiers, "New Survey Reveals the Most Popular Picnic Food in the US," The Tasting Table, February 22, 2023, https://www.tastingtable.com/907126/new-survey-reveals-the-most-popular-picnic-food-in-the-us.

TEAS: HIGH, LOW, AND FLORAL

1. Micha Soto, "Little-Known History of Tea: The World's Second Most Popular Beverage after Water," Scienceinfo.net, November 5, 2021, https://scienceinfo.net/littleknown-history-of-tea-the-worlds-second-most-popular-beverage-after-water.html.

2. Ben Richmond, "The Forgotten Drink That Caffeinated North America for Centuries," Gastro Obscura, Atlas Obscura, March 28, 2018, https://www.atlasobscura.com/articles/what-is-yaupon-tea-cassina.

3. Lettice Bryan, "Tea Punch," in *The Kentucky Housewife* (Cincinnati, OH: Shepard & Stearns, 1839), 401.

4. Robert Moss, "Why 'As Southern as Sweet Tea' Isn't Very Southern at All," Serious Eats, June 15, 2020, https://www.seriouseats.com/sweet-tea-origin-story-history-south.

5. Leslie Goodwin, "An Introduction to Earl Grey Tea," The Spruce Eats, October 10, 2019, https://www.thespruceeats.com/earl-grey-tea-766432.

6. Jane Pettigrew, *A Social History of Tea* (London: National Trust Enterprises, 2001), 84–51.

7. Bess Lovejoy, "How Tea Parties Got Their Start—and How to Hold One Like a Victorian," Mental Floss, August 20, 2015, https://www.mentalfloss.com/article/67297/how-tea-parties-got-their-start-and-how-hold-one-victorian.

8. "The World's Kitchen," *Los Angeles Times*, October 21, 1936, 65, https://www.newspapers.com/image/380472886.

9. "Afternoon Tea," *Omaha Daily Bee*, October 27, 1890, 2, https://www.newspapers.com/image/201715760.

10. Anne Seymour, *A-B-C of Good Form* (New York: Harper & Brothers, 1915), 33–45.

11. Lucy G. Allen, *Table Service* (Boston: Little, Brown, 1927), 73–76.

12. Susie Root Rhodes and Grace Porter Hopkins, eds., *Economy Administration Cook Book* (Hammond, IN: W. B. Conkey Company, 1913), 630.

13. Margaret House Irwin, PhD, "Why Not Have High Tea?" *American Cookery* 37, no. 9 (April 1933): 613–14.

14. "Seven o'Clock Tea Party," *Sioux City (IA) Journal*, November 23, 1890, 9, https://www.newspapers.com/image/416340823.

15. Emily Post, "Menu of High Tea More Substantial than Formal Dinner," *Tampa Times*, December 17, 1946, 10, https://www.newspapers.com/image/332875106.

16. Dr. Annie Gray, "The History of the Biscuit: From Roman Rusk to Victorian Petite Fours," English Heritage, https://www.english-heritage.org.uk/visit/inspire-me/the-history-of-the-biscuit.

17. Russell Joseph, "Tea Tippling Femininity," *Daily Herald* (Delphos, OH), March 23, 1897, 8, https://www.newspapers.com/image/17475765.

18. Jan Whitaker, *Tea at the Blue Lantern Inn: A Social History of the Tea Room Craze in America* (New York: St. Martin's Press, 2002).

19. "Tea Story: The History of Afternoon Tea," Destination Tea, https://destinationtea.com/teastory.

20. Lewis Carroll, "A Mad Tea-Party," in *Alice's Adventures in Wonderland* (London: Macmillan, 1865), 95–111.

LET'S CELEBRATE WITH CAKE!

1. Alysa Levene, *Cake: A Slice of History* (New York: Pegasus Books, 2016), 8.

2. Levene, *Cake*, 8.

3. "Yeast, One of Humankind's Oldest Ingredients," Explore Yeast, https://www.exploreyeast.com/what-is-yeast/yeast-one-of-humankinds-oldest-ingredients.

4. Tamra Andrews, *Nectar and Ambrosia: An Encyclopedia of Food in World Mythology* (Santa Barbara, CA: ABC-CLIO, 2000), 52–54

5 Ibid.

6. Andrew F. Smith, ed., *Oxford Encyclopedia of Food and Drink in America*, vol. 2 (New York: Oxford University Press, 2004), 25.

7. Smith, *Oxford Encyclopedia of Food and Drink in America*, vol. 2, 25.

8. Smith, *Oxford Encyclopedia of Food and Drink in America*, vol. 2, 99–100.

9. Joe Pinsker, "The Strange History of Birthday Celebrations," *The Atlantic*, November 2, 2021, https://www.theatlantic.com/family/archive/2021/11/history-birthday-celebrations/620585.

10. Robert Brauneis, *Copyright and the World's Most Popular Song* (GW Law Faculty Publications & Other Works, 2010), 4, https://scholarship.law.gwu.edu/cgi/viewcontent.cgi?article=1303&context=faculty_publications.

11. Brauneis, *Copyright*, 22–55.

12. Zachary Crockett, "Who Owns the Copyright to 'Happy Birthday'?" Priceonomics, April 14, 2015, https://priceonomics.com/who-owns-the-copyright-to-happy-birthday.

13. "Birthday Cakes for Grown-ups," *Commercial Appeal* (Memphis, TN), May 22, 1927, 41, https://www.newspapers.com/image/768537057.

14. Carol Wilson, "Wedding Cake: A Slice of History," Gastronomia, May, 5, 2005, https://gastronomica.org/2005/05/05/wedding-cake-a-slice-history.

15. John May, *The Accomplisht Cook; or, The Art & Mystery of Cookery* (London: Obadiah Blagrave, 1685; repr., Devon, UK: Prospect Books, 2000).

16. "The Wedding Party," *National Tribune* (Washington, DC), October 4, 1894, 7, https://www.newspapers.com/image/46323705.

17. Martha Grey, "How to Plan and Serve the Feast Inexpensively and with Appropriate Appointments," *Chattanooga Daily Times*, August 24, 1934, 10, https://www.newspapers.com/image/604428338.

18. "Creative Confection Sharing Groom Making Comeback," Sharing the Spotlight, *Republican and Herald* (Pottsville, PA), January 15, 2015, G7, https://www.newspapers.com/image/521966042.

19. "Cut This Out for Your Receipt Book," *Star Tribune* (Minneapolis, MN), August 22, 1874, 4, https://www.newspapers.com/image/178989005.

20. "The Ratio of the Density of the Average Fruitcake to the Density of Mahogany: 1:1," *South Florida Reporter*, December 26, 2019, https://southfloridareporter.com/the-ratio-of-the-density-of-the-average-fruitcake-to-the-density-of-mahogany-11-video.

21. "The History of the Fruitcake," Culinary Agents, December 24, 2019, https://culinaryagents.com/resources/the-history-of-the-fruitcake.

22. Jan Grimes, Michael McDonald, and John Leaptrott, "The Fruitcake Capital of the World," *Journal of Business Cases and Applications* 8 (2013), https://digitalcommons.georgiasouthern.edu/cgi/viewcontent.cgi?article=1045&context=management-facpubs.

23. Bandera Library Association, *Cooking Recipes of the Pioneers* (Bandera, TX: Bandera Library Association and Frontier Times, 1936), 23.

24. "Federal Writers' Project: Slave Narrative Project, Vol. 4, Georgia, Part 3, Kendricks-Styles," Library of Congress, Manuscript Division, https://www.loc.gov/item/mesn043.

25. Herbert C. Covey and Dwight Eisnach, *What the Slaves Ate: Recollections of African American Food and Foodways from the Slave Narratives* (Santa Barbara, CA: Greenwood Publishing, 2009), 160–61.

26. Amelia Simmons, *American Cookery* (Hartford, CT: Hudson & Goodwin, 1796), 48.

27. Eliza Leslie, *Seventy-Five Receipts for Pastry, Cakes, and Sweetmeats, by a Lady of Philadelphia* (Boston: Monroe and Francis, 1828), 61.

28. Hostess ad, *Newsday* (Suffolk Edition), August 15, 1957, 65, https://www.newspapers.com/image/717230051.

29. "Vintage Hostess Snacks: Fruit Pies, Wonder Bread, Twinkies & More Retro Goodness," Click Americana, February 23, 2021, https://clickamericana.com/topics/food-drink/hostess-fruit-pies-wonder-bread-1961.

30. Alan Davidson, ed., *Oxford Companion to Food* (New York: Oxford University Press, 1999), 141.

31. Lynne Olver, ed., "Tracing the Evolution of Carrot Cake through Recipes," Food Timeline, January 23, 2015, https://foodtimeline.org/foodcakes.html.

32. Olver, "Tracing the Evolution of Carrot Cake through Recipes."

33. William Woys Weaver, *35 Receipts from "The Larder Invaded"* (Philadelphia: Library Company of Philadelphia and Historical Society of Pennsylvania, 1986), 18.

34. Daniel B. Schneider, "Say Cheesecake," *New York Times*, September 21, 1997, CY2.

35. Lynne Olver, ed., "1234 Cake," Food Timeline, January 23, 2015, https://foodtimeline.org/foodcakes.html.

36. Hazel Lim, "Favorite Recipes," *Honolulu Advertiser*, September 26, 1940, 13, https://www.newspapers.com/image/258862709.

37. Cissy Greg, "Mayonnaise Chocolate Cake," *Courier-Journal*, March 6, 1945, 8, https://www.newspapers.com/image/107254235.

38. *That Amazing Ingredient, Mayonnaise!* (Englewood Cliffs, NJ: CPC International, 1985).

39. "New Baking Recipe Puts Soap in Cake," *New York Times*, July 24, 1938, 28.

40. Wikipedia contributors, "Bird's Custard," Wikipedia, last edited June 2, 2023, https://en.wikipedia.org/wiki/Bird%27s_Custard.

41. "Couldn't Beat the Hens," *Star Ledger* (Kosciusko, MS), October 21, 1893, 3, https://www.newspapers.com/image/316639603.

42. Laura Shapiro, *Something from the Oven: Reinventing Dinner in 1950s America* (New York: Viking, 2004).

43. Melanie Fincher, "The Long and Surprising History of Boxed Cake Mix," Allrecipes, January 5, 2022, https://www.allrecipes.com/article/history-of-boxed-cake-mix.

44. Fincher, "Long and Surprising History of Boxed Cake Mix."

45. Fincher, "Long and Surprising History of Boxed Cake Mix."

46. Betty Crocker ad, *Green Bay Press*, December 14, 1950, 36, https://www.newspapers.com/image/187678578.

47. Betty Crocker ad, *Capital Journal* (Salem, OR), March 31, 1949, 15, https://www.newspapers.com/image/94702573.

48. April White, "Duncan Hines Cake Mix Maker Extraordinaire," JSTOR Daily, October 5, 2017, https://daily.jstor.org/duncan-hines-cake-mix-maker-extraordinaire.

49. Veronique Greenwood, "Why Cake Mix Lacks One Essential Ingredient," BBC Future, November 29, 2017, https://www.bbc.com/future/article/20171027-the-magic-cakes-that-come-from-a-packet.

50. Nicole Jankowski, "Duncan Hines: The Original Road Warrior Who Shaped Restaurant History," The Salt, NPR, March 26, 2017, https://www.npr.org/sections/thesalt/2017/03/26/520866833/duncan-hines-the-original-road-warrior-who-shaped-restaurant-history.

51. Statista Research Department, "U.S. Population: Usage of Dry Cake Mixes (Not Cake Flour) from 2011 to 2024," Statista, June 23, 2022, https://www.statista.com/statistics/280114/us-households-usage-of-dry-cake-mixes-not-cake-flour-trend.

PIES: APPLE, CHERRY, AND IN YOUR FACE

1. Gabriella Petrick, "Why Americans Love Their Pies," *Smithsonian Magazine*, September 2019, https://www.smithsonianmag.com/arts-culture/why-americans-love-their-apple-pie-180972852.

2. "History of Pies," What's Cooking America, https://whatscookingamerica.net/history/piehistory.htm.

3. Petrick, "Why Americans Love Their Pies."

4. John Ayto, *An A-Z of Food & Drink* (New York: Oxford University Press, 2002), 254.

5. Ayto, *A-Z of Food & Drink*, 254.

6. "History of Pies," American Pie Council, http://www.piecouncil.org/events/nationalpieday/historyofpies.

7. Jennifer Harbster, "Pie•ology: A Full Filling Story," Library of Congress Blogs, November 18, 2011, https://blogs.loc.gov/inside_adams/2011/11/pie%E2%80%A2ology-a-full-filling-story.

8. "History of Pies," What's Cooking America.

9. "History of Pies," What's Cooking America.

10. "History of Pies," What's Cooking America.

11. Andrew F. Smith, ed., *Oxford Encyclopedia of Food and Drink in America* (New York: Oxford University Press, 2004), 272.

12. Tara O'Brian, "Martha Washington's Cookbook," Historical Society of Pennsylvania, November 15, 2012, https://hsp.org/blogs/fondly-pennsylvania/martha-washingtons-cookbook.

13. "History of Pies," What's Cooking America.

14. "What Is the Matter with the American Apple Pie? *Record Union* (Sacramento, CA), July 13, 1889, 8, https://www.newspapers.com/image/78714169.

15. Smith, *Oxford Encyclopedia of Food and Drink in America*, 43.

16. Mark Twain, "Recipe for New English Pie," in *A Tramp Abroad* (London: American Publishing Company, 1880), 576.

17. Richard Holloway, "The History of Pie," HistoryNet, July 15, 2022, https://www.historynet.com/history-pies.

18. Estelle Woods Wilcox, *Buckeye Cookery and Practical Housekeeping* (Minneapolis, MN: Buckeye Publishing Company, 1877), 215.

19. Minnie Palmer, *Woman's Exchange Cook Book* (Chicago: W. B. Conkey Company, 1901), 252.

20. Annie R. Gregory, *The Blue Ribbon Cook Book* (Chicago: Monarch Book Company, 1906), 206.

21. Petrick, "Why Americans Love their Pies."

22. Young, "Meatless, Wheatless Meals of World War I America."

23. "Latest in Kitchen Camouflage," *Leaf-Chronicle*.

24. Lauren Young, "The Meatless, Wheatless Meals of World War I America," Gastro Obscura, Atlas Obscura, January 10, 2017, https://www.atlasobscura.com/articles/the-meatless-wheatless-meals-of-world-war-i-america.

25. "The Latest in Kitchen Camouflage," *Leaf-Chronicle* (Clarksville, TN), December 15, 1917, 6, https://www.newspapers.com/image/353341464.

26. Lynne Olver, ed., "Shoo Fly Pie," Food Timeline, February 21, 2015, https://www.foodtimeline.org/foodpies.html.

27. Ayto, *A-Z of Food & Drink*, 310–11.

28. "Mrs. Cole's Recipes, c. 1837," reprinted in Helen Bullock, *The Williamsburg Art of Cookery* (Williamsburg, VA: Colonial Williamsburg, 1937), 127.

29. "Letters from Readers," *Boston Globe*, April 8, 1935, 17, https://www.newspapers.com/image/431765102.

30. Betty Webster, "Hints for the Household," *Big Pasture News* (Grandfield, OK), October 8, 1931, 2, https://www.newspapers.com/image/631851065.

31. "Wesserrunsett," Grange, *Morning Sentinel* (Waterville, ME), April 14, 1932, 13, https://www.newspapers.com/image/854265728.

32. Ann Stephanie, "A Man Could Propose to This Pie," *World Turn'd Upside Down* (blog), December 8, 2017, https://www.worldturndupsidedown.com/2017/12/a-man-could-propose-to-this-pie-wwii.html.

33. Nettie Moore, "Water Pie Is the Depression Era Dessert Everyone's (Re)making These Days," *Parade Magazine*, August 2, 2022, https://parade.com/1042184/nettiemoore/great-depression-water-pie-recipe.

34. Tori Avey, "The History of Pie in America," *Tori Avey* (blog), July 4, 2011, https://toriavey.com/the-history-of-pie-in-america-2.

35. Petrick, "Why Americans Love their Pies."

36. "Two More Deaths Due to Eating Pie," *Evening Herald* (Fall River, MA), July 9, 1915, 9, https://www.newspapers.com/image/642723955.

37. Jell-O ad, "Nifty Summer Swifties," *Birmingham News*, August 12, 1951, 108, https://www.newspapers.com/image/574160055.

38. Betty Crocker ad, "From Betty Crocker's Kitchen," June 5, 1951, 8, https://www.newspapers.com/image/569866628.

39. Lynne Olver, ed., "Frozen Pie Crusts?" Food Timeline, February 21, 2015, https://www.foodtimeline.org/foodpies.html.

40. Pet-Ritz ad, "Pet-Ritz Fruit Pies, Frozen, the Work's All Done," *Nashville Banner*, January 15, 1959, 24, https://www.newspapers.com/image/603573129.

41. Contest announcement, "Valuable Prizes to be Given Winners Cake and Pie Baking Contest, in News-Review Cooking School," *News-Review* (Roseburg, OR), June 22, 1927, 3, https://www.newspapers.com/image/92428443.

42. "Young Calhoun Chefs Await Pie Baking Contests," *Battle Creek (MI) Enquirer*, January 11, 1952, 14, https://www.newspapers.com/image/204200933.

43. Pillsbury contest ad, *Buffalo News*, September 8, 1949, 16, https://www.newspapers.com/image/867970886.

44. Pillsbury Kitchens, "The Incredible True History of the Pillsbury Bake-Off," Pillsbury, August 6, 2017, https://www.pillsbury.com/bake-off-contest/history-of-the-pillsbury-bake-off-contest.

45. Debbie Vanni, "First Pillsbury Bake-Off 1949," *The Culinary Cellar* (blog), May 18, 2011, https://theculinarycellar.com/first-pillsbury-bake-off-1949.

46. American Pie Council, "History of Pies."

47. American Pie Council, "History of Pies."

48. Pillsbury Kitchens, "No-Knead Water Rising Twists," Pillsbury, July 6, 2017, https://www.pillsbury.com/recipes/no-knead-water-rising-twists/c9964bbc-64d3-43c8-84ff-0f0ae2a730f8.

49. "Pie Eating Is Sport Sublime," *San Francisco Examiner*, August 28, 1918, 9, https://www.news papers.com/image/457465350.

50. Sarah Loham, "Pie Fight," *Lapham's Quarterly*, November 22, 2016, https://www.laphams quarterly.org/roundtable/pie-fight.

51. Loham, "Pie Fight."

52. "Pie Eating Is Sport Sublime," *San Francisco Examiner*.

53. Loham, "Pie Fight."

54. *Hutchinson (KS) Gazette*, May 6, 1921, 6, https://www.newspapers.com/image/419367558.

55. Anne Ewbank, "How Pie-Throwing Became a Comedy Standard," Gastro Obscura, Atlas Obscura, July 10, 2018, https://www.atlasobscura.com/articles/why-do-people-throw-pies.

56. Ewbank, "How Pie-Throwing Became a Comedy Standard."

57. "Pie-Throwing Movies Arouse Ire of Reformer," *Buffalo News*, January 14, 1920, 11, https://www .newspapers.com/image/845367024.

58. Along the Potomac, *Chattanooga News*, September 26, 1919, 28, https://www.newspapers.com/ image/348202696.

COOKIES: HARDTACK TO SOFT AND SQUISHY

1. Time-Life Books, *Cookies and Crackers* (Alexandria, VA: Time-Life Books, 1982), 5.

2. Megan Miller, "Americans Eat About 300 Cookies a Year, or 35,000 Cookies in a Lifetime," *South Florida Reporter*, September 30, 2018, https://southfloridareporter.com/americans-eat-about-300 -cookies-a-year-or-35000-cookies-in-a-lifetime.

3. "History of Cookies," What's Cooking America, https://whatscookingamerica.net/history/cookie history.htm.

4. "Biscotti History, from the Roman Legions to Starbucks," The Nibble, https://www.thenibble .com/reviews/main/cookies/cookies2/the-origin-of-biscotti.asp.

5. "History of Cookies," What's Cooking America.

6. Amelia Simmons, *American Cookery* (Hartford, CT: Hudson & Goodwin, 1796), 5.

7. "How to Make Cookies," *Kentucky Post and Times-Star* (Covington, KY), October 23, 1912, 8, https://www.newspapers.com/image/760822514.

8. "Sis" and "Jake," in *Ma's Cookin' Mountain Recipes* (Osage Beach, MO: Ozark Maid Candies, 1966), 46.

9. Janice Jorgensen, ed., *The Encyclopedia of Consumer Brands*, vol. 1 (Detroit: St. James Press, 1994), 183–85.

10. Mary Bellis, "Fig Newton: History and Invention of the Cookies," ThoughtCo., January 13, 2019, https://www.thoughtco.com/fig-newton-history-1991793.

11. "Fig Newtons 10-Cents a Pound," *Akron (OH) Beacon Journal*, February 16, 1909, 8, https://www .newspapers.com/image/227923110.

12. "Fig Newtons," *Holton (KS) Recorder*, April 2, 1908, 3, https://www.newspapers.com/image/ 189630302.

13. Saturday Special, *Dispatch-Republican* (Clay City, KS), July 5, 1923, 4, https://www.newspapers .com/image/519781062.

14. "Fig Newtons Make Tasty Desserts," *Wisconsin State Journal* (Madison, WI), March 13, 1939, 5, https://www.newspapers.com/image/397220362.

15. Bellis, "Fig Newton."

16. Medbury Says, *Clarion-Ledger* (Jackson, MS), April 24, 1923, 2, https://www.newspapers.com/ image/202520342.

17. William Cahn, *Out of the Cracker Barrel: From Animal Crackers to ZuZus* (New York: Simon & Schuster, 1969), 106–7.

18. Medbury Says, *Clarion-Ledger*.

19. Cahn, *Out of the Cracker Barrel*, 106–7.

20. Jennifer Frey, "Circus Food," *Washington Post*, March 20, 2002.

21. Theodora FitzGibbon, *A Taste of Scotland* (New York: Avene Books, 1979), 117.

22. Ann Wallis Blencowe, *The Receipt Book of Mrs. Ann Blencowe, A.D. 1656* (facsimile repr., Cottonport, LA: Polyanthos, 1972), 14.

23. Constance Spry and Rosemary Hume, *The Constance Spry Cookery Book* (London: Pan Books, 1972 [1956]), 789–90.

24. Ernie Smith, "The Rise, Fall, and Return of Hydrox Cookies, the Proto-Oreo," Gastro Obscura, Atlas Obscura, May 17, 2017, https://www.atlasobscura.com/articles/hydrox-cookies-oreo.

25. Girl Scouts of the United States of America, *Tramping and Trailing with the Girl Scouts* (New York: Girl Scouts, 1927), 68–69.

26. Girl Scouts of the United States of America, *Girl Scout Handbook* (New York: Girl Scouts, 1947), 316.

27. Marge Canton, "Girl Scout News, Notes," *Central New Jersey Home News* (New Brunswick, NJ), February 10, 1939, 7, https://www.newspapers.com/image/320885494.

28. "Girl Scout Cookie History," Girl Scouts, https://www.girlscouts.org/en/cookies/about-girl-scout-cookies/cookie-history.html.

29. Canton, "Girl Scout News, Notes."

30. "Deliciously Different Chocolate Cookies," *Suburban List* (Essex Junction, VT), November 2, 1939, 19, https://www.newspapers.com/image/658248851.

31. "Deliciously Different Chocolate Cookies," *Suburban List*.

32. "The Story of the Toll House Cookie," *Whittemore Library Blog*, Framingham State University, April 27, 2020, https://libguides.framingham.edu/c.php?g=934037&p=6732621&t=52693.

33. "The Toll House Inn, Whitman, Massachusetts," Atlas Obscura, December 4, 2019, https://www.atlasobscura.com/places/the-toll-house-inn.

34. Irma S. Rombauer, *The Joy of Cooking* (Indianapolis, IN: Bobbs-Merrill, 1936), 543.

35. Brethren Press, *Granddaughter's Inglenook Cookbook* (Elgin, IL: Brethren Publishing House, 1942), 51.

36. Ida Migliaria, et al., *Searchlight Recipe Book* (Topeka, KS: Household Magazine, 1952), 81.

37. Betty Crocker, *Betty Crocker's Cooky Book* (facsimile repr. of 1963 ed., New York: Hungry Minds, New York, 2002), 135.

38. "Cookie Types," The Nibble, https://thenibble.com/reviews/main/cookies/cookies2/cookie-types.asp.

MEN ON COUCHES: CHIPS, DIPS, AND FOOTBALL GAMES

1. Ashley Steinberg, "The Most Popular Super Bowl Snack, According to Instacart," Mashed, February 7, 2022, https://www.mashed.com/758909/the-most-popular-super-bowl-snack-according-to-instacart.

2. "Super Bowl Foods: How Many Chicken Wings Are Consumed during the Big Game?" Marca, February 13, 2022, https://www.marca.com/en/nfl/super-bowl/2022/02/13/62092b1546163ff0868b45da.html.

3. Kristina Killgrove, "Ancient DNA Explains How Chickens Got to the Americas," *Forbes*, November 23, 2017, https://www.forbes.com/sites/kristinakillgrove/2017/11/23/ancient-dna-explains-how-chickens-got-to-the-americas/?sh=3f7eea9156db.

4. Buck, "Triolet of Gastronomic," Stars and Stripes, *Chattanooga News*, September 25, 1919, 14.

5. Swanson ad, "Flying Saucers! New Ideas Using Old Favorites, Chicken Wings and Potato Salad," *Chicago Tribune*, June 29, 1950, 37, https://www.newspapers.com/image/370873564.

6. "Mumbo Sauce, Born in Chicago, Loved Everywhere," Argia B's Mumbo BBQ Sauce, https://mumbosauce.com/about-mumbo-sauce/history.

7. Argia B. Collins Sr. obituary, *Chicago Sun-Times*, February 26, 2006, 23, https://legacy.suntimes.com/us/obituaries/chicagosuntimes/name/argia-collins-obituary?pid=788328.

8. Anchor Bar ad, *Buffalo News*, May 5, 1967, 42, https://www.newspapers.com/image/870202694.

9. Becky Little, "Who Invented Buffalo Wings?" History, May 5, 2023, https://www.history.com/news/who-invented-buffalo-wings.

10. News item, *Times Union* (Brooklyn, NY), January 30, 1936, 6, https://www.newspapers.com/image/577753576.

11. In Lighter Vein, "The Result," January 1, 1936, 4.

12. DB Kelly, "The Strange History of Potato Chips," Mashed, April 10, 2022, https://www.mashed.com/124850/the-strange-history-of-potato-chips.

13. April White, "The Story of the Invention of the Potato Chip Is a Myth," JSTOR Daily, May 4, 2017, https://daily.jstor.org/story-invention-potato-chip-myth.

14. "George Crum: Potato Chip," Lemelson-MIT, https://lemelson.mit.edu/resources/george-crum.

15. White, "Story of the Invention of the Potato Chip."

16. Lay's Potato Chips ad, *Charlotte Observer*, September, 27, 1957, 42, https://www.newspapers.com/image/619911352.

17. Charles C. Mann, "How the Potato Changed the World," *Smithsonian Magazine*, November 2011, https://www.smithsonianmag.com/history/how-the-potato-changed-the-world-108470605.

18. Kelly, "Strange History of Potato Chips."

19. Dr. Daniel R. Hodgdon, "Explains Value of Potato Chip as Food," *Harrisburg (PA) Telegraph*, December 8, 1927, 11, https://www.newspapers.com/image/41476143.

20. Kelly, "Strange History of Potato Chips."

21. Mann, "How the Potato Changed the World."

22. "Laura Scudder's," Chips & Crisps, http://www.chipsandcrisps.com/laura-scudders.html.

23. Laura Scudder's ad, *Daily News* (Los Angeles), January 10, 1936, 14, https://www.newspapers.com/image/689236675.

24. Lay's Potato Chips ad, *Charlotte Observer*, September 27, 1957, 42, https://www.newspapers.com/image/619911352.

25. "Frito-Lay Company," Company-Histories.com, https://www.company-histories.com/FritoLay-Company-Company-History.html.

26. Lay's Potato Chips ad, *Clarion-Ledger* (Jackson, MS), February 27, 1948, 13, https://www.newspapers.com/image/202705336.

27. Lay's Potato Chips ad, *Charlotte Observer*, September 27, 1957, 42, https://www.newspapers.com/image/619911352.

28. Lay's Potato Chips ad, *Courier-Journal* (Louisville, KY), October 27, 1950, 21, https://www.newspapers.com/image/108434498.

29. "Frito-Lay Company," Company-Histories.com.

30. "Atlas of Popular Culture in the Northeastern US," Central Connecticut State University, https://web.ccsu.edu/faculty/harmonj/atlas/potchips.htm.

31. "Frito-Lay Company," Company-Histories.com.

32. "Frito-Lay Company," Company-Histories.com.

33. Willa Roberts, *Woman's Home Companion Cook Book* (New York: P. F. Collier & Son, 1942), 266.

34. Amy Alden, "Have a Family Party with Dipwiches," Household Almanac, *Tampa Tribune*, March 2, 1958, 124, https://www.newspapers.com/image.

35. Mara Weinraub, "The Astronomical Success Story of Lipton Onion Soup Mix," Food52, November 15, 2019, https://food52.com/blog/24766-history-of-french-onion-dip.

36. "Tested Recipes," *Wilkes-Barre (PA) Times*, December 4, 1912, 6, https://www.newspapers.com/image/395205026.

37. "Russian Dressing," Household Department, *Boston Daily Globe*, January 23, 1914, 14, https://www.newspapers.com/image/430654395.

38. Fannie Merritt Farmer, *The Boston Cooking-School Cook Book* (Boston: Little, Brown and Company, 1941), 454.

39. Joan Whitman, ed., *Craig Claiborne's The New York Times Food Encyclopedia* (New York: Times Books, 1985), 376.

40. Michael Redmon, "Ranch Dressing Originated in Santa Barbara's Mountains," *Santa Barbara Independent*, November 25, 2015, https://www.independent.com/2015/11/25/ranch-dressing-originated-santa-barbaras-mountains.

41. Meaghan Cameron, "This Is the #1 Most Popular Super Bowl Dip in America," Eat This, Not That! February 10, 2022, https://www.eatthis.com/news-most-popular-super-bowl-dip.

42. Karen Hochman, "The History of Salsa," The Nibble, updated May 2009, http://thenibble.com/reviews/main/salsas/history-of-salsa.asp.

43. Hyatt A. Verrill, *Foods America Gave the World* (Boston: L. C. Page, 1937), 34–35, 37.

44. "Spicy Flavor of Mexican Food Due to Chili Gravy," *South Bend (IN) Tribune*, January 16, 1926, 12, https://www.newspapers.com/image/514521838.

45. "The History of Tabasco Brand," Tabasco Brand, https://www.tabasco.com/tabasco-history.

46. "Her Cooks Dishes, Receipts Tried by the Wife of a Great Novelist," *Boston Globe*, December 12, 1893, 8, https://www.newspapers.com/image/430702692.

47. Lynne Olver, ed., "Mexican and TexMex Foods," Food Timeline, March 10, 2015, https://food-timeline.org/foodmexican.html.

48. Teresa Gubbins, "Salsa Wins on Super Bowl Survey Conducted by Plano Snacks Company," Culture Map, Dallas, January 23, 2019, https://dallas.culturemap.com/news/restaurants-bars/01-23-19-frito-lay-snacks-super-bowl.

49. "U.S. Population: Usage of Salsa (Store Bought) 2016–2024," Statista, June 23, 2022, https://www.statista.com/statistics/921228/us-usage-of-salsa-store-bought.

50. Martha Lee, "Mixing Bowl: Fried Chicken, Tomato Salsa, a Perfect Team," *Oakland Tribune*, September 6, 1959, 70, https://www.newspapers.com/image/331944396.

51. "Popular Hostesses Share Their Holiday Recipes with You," *Tucson Daily Citizen*, December 10, 1960, 30, https://www.newspapers.com/image/23692358.

52. Dave DeWitt, *The Chile Pepper Encyclopedia* (New York: William Morrow, 1999), 250–60.

53. Alan Davidson, *Oxford Companion to Food*, 2nd ed. (Oxford: Oxford University Press, 2007), 171.

54. Sophie D. Coe, *America's First Cuisines* (Austin: University of Texas Press, 1994), 60–61.

55. "Chili History," Chef Lola's Kitchen, https://www.nationalchiliday.com/chili-history.html.

56. DeWitt, *Chile Pepper Encyclopedia*, 76–78.

57. Chelsea Kenyon, "7 Types of Mexican Green Chiles," The Spruce Eats, January 29, 2023, https://www.thespruceeats.com/types-of-green-or-fresh-chiles-2342638.

58. DeWitt, *Chile Pepper Encyclopedia*, 76–78.

59. DeWitt, *Chile Pepper Encyclopedia*, 78.

60. "Chili-Con-Carne," *Evening Light* (San Antonio, TX), May 27, 1882, 1, 3, https://www.newspapers.com/image/36853949.

61. "Chili Con Carne with Tomato Soup," *Moberly (MO) Monitor-Index*, December 27, 1935, 5, https://www.newspapers.com/image/34765426.

62. Gebhardt's ad, *Austin (TX) American*, April 30, 1932, 5, https://www.newspapers.com/image/385886699.

63. Alan C. Elliott, *Texas Ingenuity: Lone Star Inventions, Inventors & Innovators* (Mount Pleasant, SC: Arcadia Publishing, 2016), 117.

64. Christine Byrn, "17 Slow-Cooker Super Bowl Chili Recipes to Get You through the Big Game," Style Caster, February 3, 2019, https://stylecaster.com/lifestyle/food-and-drink/985985/slow-cooker -super-bowl-chili-recipes.

65. Byrn, "17 Slow-Cooker Super Bowl Chili Recipes."

KIDS IN THE KITCHEN: IT'S *G-R-R-R-EAT!*

1. "Sylvester Graham, Health Food Nut, Makes Butchers and Bakers Go Crackers," New England Historical Society, https://www.newenglandhistoricalsociety.com/sylvester-graham-health-food-nut -makes-butchers-bakers-crackers.

2. "Cereal as a Snack," Prepared Foods, October, 10, 2017, https://www.preparedfoods.com/articles/ 120512-cereal-as-a-snack.

3. "American Vegetarian Convention," *Portland (ME) Press Herald*, November 14, 1850, 2, https:// www.newspapers.com/image/legacy/846263748.

4. Helen Lefkowitz Horowitz, ed., *Attitudes toward Sex in Antebellum America* (Boston: Bedford/St. Martin's, 2006), 16.

5. "Sylvester Graham," New England Historical Society.

6. Hilary Greenbaum and Dana Rubinstein, "Who Made That Granola?" *New York Times Magazine*, March 23, 2012, https://www.nytimes.com/2012/03/25/magazine/who-made-that-granola.html.

7. "Death Roll," *North Adams (MA) Transcript*, July 12, 1895, 2, https://www.newspapers.com/image/ legacy/54480606.

8. Granula ad, *Los Angeles Times*, July 22, 1883, 4, https://www.newspapers.com/image/legacy/ 378340346.

9. Ransom Riggs, "The Guy Who Invented Corn Flakes Was a Strange, Strange Man," Mental Floss, February 1, 2011, https://www.mentalfloss.com/article/27016/guy-who-invented-corn-flakes-was -strange-strange-man.

10. Riggs, "Guy Who Invented Corn Flakes."

11. Knowledge at Wharton staff, "How the Feuding Kellogg Brothers Fought Their Cereal Wars," Knowledge at Wharton, University of Pennsylvania, September 26, 2017, https://knowledge.wharton .upenn.edu/podcast/knowledge-at-wharton-podcast/the-bitter-feud-behind-an-iconic-brand.

12. "Postum Cereal Company," Encyclopedia.com, https://www.encyclopedia.com/history/ encyclopedias-almanacs-transcripts-and-maps/postum-cereal-company.

13. "Corn Flake Kisses," Lucy Lincoln's Talks, *Buffalo News*, October 23, 1916, 6, https://www.news papers.com/image/352623176.

14. Austin Thompson, "How Hershey Trademarked the Word 'Kisses,'" Mental Floss, February 5, 2015, https://www.mentalfloss.com/article/61304/how-hershey-trademarked-word-kisses.

15. Mrs. Anna B. Scott, "Gems Made with Corn Flakes," Mrs. Scott's Talk About Seasonal Foods, *Philadelphia Inquirer*, June 19, 1932, 103, https://www.newspapers.com/image/legacy/173313089.

16. Kate Robbett, "Alexander Anderson and the Cereal Shot from Guns," Lemelson Center for the Study of Invention and Innovation, September, 28, 2017, https://invention.si.edu/alexander -anderson-and-cereal-shot-guns.

17. Robbett, "Alexander Anderson."

18. "Puffed Rice Brittle," The Kitchen Cupboard, *Indiana (PA) Gazette*, February 17, 1916, 4, https:// www.newspapers.com/image/532771248.

19. Harriet Cooke, "Puffed Wheat Squares," Kitchen Council, *Buffalo News*, August 2, 1930, 24, https://www.newspapers.com/image/837928934.

20. Corey Binns, "Why Rice Krispies Go Snap, Crackle, Pop!" Live Science, April 24, 2006, https:// www.livescience.com/4098-rice-krispies-snap-crackle-pop.html.

21. Marcia Steed, "Rice Krispie Treats," *AnswerLine* (blog), Iowa State University Extension and Outreach, December 17, 2018, https://blogs.extension.iastate.edu/answerline/2018/12/17/rice-krispie-treats.

22. "Try this Candy Recipe," *Los Angeles Times*, February 28, 1941, 4, https://www.newspapers.com/image/380735190.

23. Annabelle K. Smith, "The Untold Tale of Pow!, the Fourth Rice Krispies Elf," *Smithsonian Magazine*, January 16, 2014, https://www.smithsonianmag.com/arts-culture/untold-tale-pow-fourth-rice-krispies-elf-180949379.

24. "Rice Krispies through the Years," Kellogg's Rice Krispies, https://www.ricekrispies.com/en_US/our-story.html.

25. Smith, "Untold Tale of Pow!"

26. Jake Rossen, "Snap, Crackle, Keith: When the Rolling Stones Recorded a Rice Krispies Jingle," Mental Floss, December 7, 2020, https://www.mentalfloss.com/article/638179/rolling-stones-rice-krispies-jingle.

27. Smith, "Untold Tale of Pow!"

28. Nads Willow, "How Tony the Tiger Has Changed over the Years," Mashed, May 25, 2023, https://www.mashed.com/1296632/tony-the-tiger-changed-over-the-years.

29. "Parties for Pigtail Crowd," *Evansville (IN) Press*, September 23, 1957, 11, https://www.newspapers.com/image/773089284.

30. "Youngsters Will Like Their Cookies Baked Kiddie-Size," *Tampa Tribune*, August 28, 1959, 36, https://www.newspapers.com/image/329508884.

31. Joel Stice, "The Untold Truth of Trix," Mashed, April 3, 2020, https://www.mashed.com/198934/the-untold-truth-of-trix.

32. Daniel E. Slotnik, "Joe Harris, Illustrator behind Underdog and Trix Rabbit, Dies at 89," *New York Times*, April 4, 2017, https://www.nytimes.com/2017/04/04/arts/television/joe-harris-dead-created-underdog-trix-rabbit.html.

33. Jerry Beck, "The Origin of 'The Trix Rabbit,'" Cartoon Research, January 15, 2017, https://cartoonresearch.com/index.php/the-origin-of-the-trix-rabbit.

34. Stice, "Untold Truth of Trix."

35. Trix ad, *Spokesman-Review* (Spokane, WA), March 13, 1955, 152, https://www.newspapers.com/image/568466878.

36. Patricia Camerota, "The 50 Best Cereals Ranked from Worst to Best," *USA Today*, March 7, 2018, https://reviewed.usatoday.com/refrigerators/features/the-50-most-memorable-cereals-ranked.

37. "Pamela Low, 79; Created Flavored Coating for Cap'n Crunch Cereal," *Los Angeles Times*, June 6, 2007, https://www.latimes.com/archives/la-xpm-2007-jun-06-me-passings6.3-story.html.

38. Kevin Scott Collier, *Jay Ward's Animated Cereal Capers* (Create Space Independent Publishing Platform, 2017), 7–8.

39. Dr. Caroline Wood, "How Do Sound and Music Affect the Way We Eat?" Food Unfolded, March 29, 2021, https://www.foodunfolded.com/article/how-do-sound-and-music-affect-the-way-we-eat.

40. Collier, *Jay Ward's Animated Cereal Capers*, 7–8.

41. Joel Stice, "The Untold Truth of Cap'n Crunch," Mashed, February 3, 2023, https://www.mashed.com/206601/the-untold-truth-of-capn-crunch.

42. Cap'n Crunch ad, *Star Tribune* (Minneapolis, MN), November 13, 1969, 22, https://www.newspapers.com/image/184889692.

43. "The History of Lucky Charms," General Mills, March 17, 2014, https://www.generalmills.com/news/stories/the-history-of-lucky-charms.

44. Kirstie Renae, "The Real Names of These Popular Food Brand Mascots," Insider, July 18, 2019, https://www.insider.com/real-names-of-popular-food-mascots-2019-7#lucky-charms-leprechaun-mascot-is-commonly-called-lucky-the-leprechaun-but-he-also-goes-by-a-couple-of-other-names-2.

45. John Sewer, "In Candy World, Circus Peanut Is a Riddle Wrapped in Marshmallow inside Orange Shell," USA Today, October 20, 2006, http://usatoday30.usatoday.com/money/industries/food/2006-07-27-circus-peanut_x.htm.

1. Arlyn Osborne, "How Cookouts Became an American Pastime—Difference between Grilling & Barbecuing," Food52, June 28, 2021, https://food52.com/blog/26334-history-of-the-american-cookout.

2. Tammy Robinson, "Native America Survival Secrets: How They Cooked Without Metal," Off The Grid News, https://www.offthegridnews.com/extreme-survival/native-america-survival-secrets-how-they-cooked-without-metal.

3. Natasha Geiling, "The Evolution of American Barbecue," *Smithsonian Magazine*, July 3, 2023, https://www.smithsonianmag.com/arts-culture/the-evolution-of-american-barbecue-13770775.

4. Tori Avey, "The History of Barbecue and Grilling," *Tori Avey* (blog), October 18, 2019, https://toriavey.com/the-history-of-barbecue-and-grilling.

5. "Big Colored Barbeque," *St. Louis Globe-Democrat*, June 26, 1900, 14, https://www.newspapers.com/image/571354015.

6. Shannon Dawson, "'We Outside!' A Brief History of the Black People Cookout," Newsone, May, 13, 2022, https://newsone.com/4334578/history-of-the-black-people-cookouts.

7. Adrian Miller, "Barbeque on the Move: How African American Migrants Defined BBQ in the United States," Eating Well, February 8, 2021, https://www.eatingwell.com/longform/7888044/bbq-on-the-move.

8. Melanie De Proft, "Family's Weekly Guide to Outdoor Cookery," *Ogden (UT) Standard-Examiner*, May 21, 1961, 66, https://www.newspapers.com/image/600225824.

9. Osborne, "How Cookouts Became an American Pastime."

10. "The History of Grilling: How Dad Came to Love It," Hebrew National, https://www.hebrewnational.com/articles/history-grilling-how-dad-came-love-it.

11. Harris Army and Navy Store, ad for camp broilers and outdoor grills, *Press and Sun-Bulletin* (Binghamton, NY), July 1, 1937, 28, https://www.newspapers.com/image/261380490.

12. Osborne, "How Cookouts Became an American Pastime."

13. Central Hardware, ad for General Electric grills, *St. Louis Globe-Democrat*, June 14, 1960, 12.

14. De Proft, "Family's Weekly Guide to Outdoor Cookery."

15. Andrew F. Smith, ed., *Oxford Encyclopedia of Food and Drink in America* (New York: Oxford University Press, 2004), 270.

16. Tori Avey, "A Brief History of Hamburgers," *Tori Avey* (blog), October 18, 2019, https://toriavey.com/a-brief-history-of-hamburgers.

17. Avey, "Brief History of Hamburgers."

18. Hannah Glasse, *The Art of Cookery, Made Plain and Easy* (self-published, 1747), 315.

19. Mary J. Lincoln, *Mrs. Lincoln's Boston Cook Book: What to Do and What Not to Do in Cooking* (Boston: Roberts Brothers, 1884), 224.

20. Andrew F. Smith, ed., *The Oxford Companion to American Food and Drink* (New York: Oxford University Press, 2007), 216–17.

21. A. H. Jones, State Food Commissioner, "Commission Finds Much Impure Hamburger Steak," *Herald News* (Joliet, IL), March 23, 1909, 8, https://www.newspapers.com/image/548586430.

22. Upton Sinclair, *The Jungle* (New York: Doubleday, Page & Co., 1906).

23. Avey, "Brief History of Hamburgers."

24. "History of the Hot Dog," TheHotDog.org, August 5, 2022, https://www.thehotdog.org/history-of-the-hot-dog.

25. "Americans Consume About 70 Hot Dogs Per Year (+20 Other Facts)," *South Florida Reporter*, July 17, 2018, https://southfloridareporter.com/americans-consume-about-70-hot-dogs-per-year-20-other-facts.

26. "History of the Hot Dog," TheHotDog.org.

27. "Chicago-Style Hot Dog," Allrecipes, updated February 15, 2023, https://www.allrecipes.com/recipe/134483/chicago-style-hot-dog.

28. Smith, *Oxford Companion to American Food and Drink*, 303.

29. Kathryn Shelton, "Was Oscar Mayer a Real Person?" Mashed, November 12, 2021, https://www.mashed.com/659976/was-oscar-mayer-a-real-person.

30. Paul Resinkoff, "The Strange Story behind the 'Oscar Mayer Wiener Song,'" Digital Music News, September 29, 2016, https://www.digitalmusicnews.com/2016/09/29/songwriter-oscar-mayer-wiener-song-die.

31. Shelton, "Was Oscar Mayer a Real Person?"

32. "Those Forbidden Sauces," *Larned (KS) Chronoscope*, March 19, 1897, 1, https://www.newspapers.com/image/382879756.

33. Smith, *Oxford Companion to American Food and Drink*, 144.

34. "Horace Greely and Temperance," *Ebensburg (PA) Alleghenian*, November 21, 1867, 1, https://www.newspapers.com/image/71065939.

35. "Welcome Back, Condiments," *Cincinnati Enquirer*, December 15, 1918, 56, https://www.newspapers.com/image/34328565.

36. "Those Forbidden Sauces," *Larned (KS) Chronoscope*.

37. "Value of Condiments," *Tennessee Baptist* (Memphis, TN), May, 5, 1877, 9, https://www.newspapers.com/image/588969864.

38. Tim Nelson, "The History of Ketchup," Allrecipes, June 8, 2021, https://www.allrecipes.com/article/history-of-ketchup.

39. Sara Bir, "From Poison to Passion: The Secret History of the Tomato," Modern Farmer, September 2, 2014, https://modernfarmer.com/2014/09/poison-pleasure-secret-history-tomato.

40. Stephanie Butler, "The Surprisingly Ancient History of Ketchup," History, July 20, 2012, https://www.history.com/news/ketchup-surprising-ancient-history.

41. Butler, "Surprisingly Ancient History of Ketchup."

42. Butler, "Surprisingly Ancient History of Ketchup."

43. Butler, "Surprisingly Ancient History of Ketchup."

44. Ciel Adair, "Gleaning from the Home Forum," *Cincinnati Enquirer*, December 3, 1941, 7, https://www.newspapers.com/image/99724868.

45. Andrew Dalby, *Food in the Ancient World from A to Z* (London: Routledge, 2003), 225.

46. Smith, *Oxford Companion to American Food and Drink*, 398.

47. Michele Debczak, "A Brief History of Ketchup and Mustard," Mental Floss, February 19, 2021, https://www.mentalfloss.com/article/642371/ketchup-mustard-food-history.

48. "The French's Story," McCormick, https://www.mccormick.com/frenchs/story.

49. French's ad, *Baltimore Sun*, June 13, 1924, 13, https://www.newspapers.com/image/372760896.

50. French's ad, *Evening Sun* (Baltimore), November 6, 1924, 32, https://www.newspapers.com/image/369592230.

51. "How We Learned to Eat Mustard," *Tennessean* (Nashville, TN), August 20, 1916, 38, https://www.newspapers.com/image/118973686.

52. French's ad, *Kansas City (MO) Star*, October 10, 1942, 10, https://www.newspapers.com/image/655812879.

53. "The French's Story," McCormick.

54. David Merritt Johns, "Mayonnaise History: Was It Invented by the French or the Spanish?" Slate, December 27, 2013, https://slate.com/culture/2013/12/mayonnaise-history-was-it-invented-by-the-french-or-the-spanish.html.

55. Karen Hochman, "Mayonnaise History: The Evolution of a Favorite American Condiment," The Nibble, https://www.thenibble.com/reviews/main/condiments/mayonnaise/mayonnaise-history.asp.

56. *That Amazing Ingredient: Mayonnaise!* (Englewood Cliffs, NJ: CPC International, 1981 [1979]).

57. Joe Schwarcz, PhD, "The Difference between 'Mayonnaise' and 'Mayo,'" Office for Science and Society, McGill University, March 20, 2017, https://www.mcgill.ca/oss/article/food-health-quirky-science/when-mayo-isnt-mayonnaise.

58. Marion Harland, "Common Sense in the Home," *Baltimore Sun*, March 12, 1911, 25, https://www.newspapers.com/image/373279713.

59. La Salle Restaurant luncheon ad, *Chicago Tribune*, November 1, 1914, 28, https://www.newspapers.com/image/370286339.

FAIRS, FESTIVALS, AND MOVIE SCREENS

1. "A Metamorphosis," *Chicago Tribune*, July 8, 1883, 11, https://www.newspapers.com/image/349573820.

2. "Popcorn," *Boston Globe*, May 2, 1874, 10, https://www.newspapers.com/image/428215296.

3. "Popcorn: Ingrained in America's Agricultural History," USDA National Agricultural Library, https://www.nal.usda.gov/exhibits/speccoll/exhibits/show/popcorn.

4. "New Ways with Popcorn, Popcorn Sandwiches," *St. Catherines Standard* (Ontario), December 24, 1915, 5, https://www.newspapers.com/image/legacy/774676302.

5. "New Ways with Popcorn," *St. Catherines Standard*.

6. Louis P. De Gouy, *The Gold Cookbook* (Radnor, PA: Chilton, 1948), 123.

7. "A Metamorphosis," *Chicago Tribune*.

8. Andrew F. Smith, ed., *Popped Culture: A Social History of Popcorn in America* (Washington, DC: Smithsonian Institution Press, 2001), 27.

9. "Centennial Exhibition Profit," *Spirit of Kansas* (Lawrence, KS), October 12, 1876, 5, https://www.newspapers.com/image/legacy/488892095.

10. Smith, *Popped Culture*, 21.

11. "Popcorn," Encyclopedia.com, updated May 17, 2018, https://www.encyclopedia.com/sports-and-everyday-life/food-and-drink/food-and-cooking/popcorn.

12. "History of the Popcorn Popper," Pop Maize, https://popmaize.com/popcorn-popper-history.

13. Smith, *Popped Culture*, 90–91.

14. "Nickelodeon," *Encyclopedia Britannica*, updated March 21, 2022, https://www.britannica.com/art/nickelodeon-motion-picture-theatre.

15. *The Kiss*, 1896, IMBb, https://www.imdb.com/title/tt0139738.

16. Jill Hunter Pellettieri, "Make It a Large for a Quarter More?" Slate, June 26, 2017, https://slate.com/news-and-politics/2007/06/a-short-history-of-movie-theater-concession-stands-plus-a-candy-quiz.html.

17. Lauren Cahn, "This Is What Movie-Theater Foods Looked Like in the 1970s," Eat This, Not That! March 9, 2020, https://www.eatthis.com/movie-theater-foods-1970s.

18. Susan Benjamin, *Sweet as Sin: The Unwrapped Story of How Candy Became America's Favorite Pleasure* (Amherst, NY: Prometheus Books, 2016), 63–64.

19. Benjamin, *Sweet as Sin*, 63–64.

20. Christine Venzon, "How Cotton Candy Works," How Stuff Works, December 2, 2009, https://science.howstuffworks.com/innovation/edible-innovations/cotton-candy.htm.

21. Ceara Milligan, "Why the Origin of Cotton Candy Is So Surprising," Mashed, December 3, 2021, https://www.mashed.com/677125/why-the-origin-of-cotton-candy-is-so-surprising.

22. Venzon, "How Cotton Candy Works."

23. Sarah Marquart, "Cotton Candy May Be the Key to Creating Artificial Organs," Futurism, February 12, 2016, https://futurism.com/cotton-candy-may-key-creating-artificial-organs.

24. Sketches and Views, *Boston Times*, January 30, 1808, 1.

25. Andrew F. Smith, ed., *The Oxford Companion to American Food and Drink* (New York: Oxford University Press, 2007), 408.

26. Bethany Moncel, "The History of Doughnuts," The Spruce Eats, June 24, 2020, https://www.the spruceeats.com/the-history-of-doughnuts-1328766.

27. Lynne Olver, ed., "Charlotte to Millet," Food Timeline, January 25, 2015, https://www.foodtime line.org/foodfaq1.html#americandoughnutreferences.

28. "Bewitched, Be Doughnuts," *Detroit Free Press*, February 18, 1894, 16, https://www.newspapers .com/image/119514431.

29. Moncel, "History of Doughnuts."

30. Ali Miller, "Why Do We Eat Jelly Donuts on Hanukkah?" The Nosher, December 9, 2016, https:// www.myjewishlearning.com/the-nosher/why-do-we-eat-jelly-donuts-on-hanukkah.

31. Catherine Lamb, "The History of Donuts in America," Food52, June 6, 2014, https://food52.com/ blog/10133-the-history-of-donuts-in-america.

32. J.E.D., "The New England Doughnut," *Madisonian* (Washington, DC), December 22, 1838, 1, https://www.newspapers.com/image/323521013.

33. Eliza Leslie, *Seventy-Five Receipts for Pastry, Cakes, and Sweetmeats, by a Lady of Philadelphia* (Boston: Munrow and Francis, 1828), 70.

34. Estelle Woods Wilcox, *Buckeye Cookery and Practical Housekeeping* (facsimile repr. of 1877 ed., Bedford, MA: Applewood Books, [2002?]), 77.

35. George J. Frederick, *Pennsylvania Dutch Cookery* (repr. of 1935 ed., Louisville, KY: Favorite Recipes Press, 1966), 137.

36. "Corn Dog Sandwich Is Introduced Here," *Palm Beach Post*, November 24, 1940, 17, https://www .newspapers.com/image/130225247.

37. *San Angelo (TX) Evening Standard*, May 1, 1940, 3, Newspapers.com.

38. "American Hot Dog Takes on New Dress and Assumes Name of 'Corn Dog,'"*Tallahassee Democrat*, December 3, 1940, 3, https://www.newspapers.com/image/244765810.

39. "The Origin of the Corn Dog," Bar-S Food for Thought, October 2, 2017, https://www.bar-s.com/ food-for-thought/the-origin-of-the-corndog.

40. Carly Caramana, "The Untold Truth of Turkey Legs," Mashed, October 26, 2021, https://www .mashed.com/643652/the-untold-truth-of-turkey-legs.

41. Sarah Weinburg, "Nine Things You Never Knew about Disney's Giant Turkey Legs," Delish, August 15, 2018, https://www.delish.com/food/a22736394/disneys-giant-turkey-legs-facts.

42. Weinburg, "Nine Things You Never Knew."

43. Robert F. Moss, " The Fried Green Tomato Swindle," *Alforno* (blog), August, 19, 2007, https:// alforno.blogspot.com/2007/08/fried-green-tomato-swindle.html.

44. Lisa Bramen, "The Surprising Origins of Fried Green Tomatoes," *Smithsonian Magazine*, August 6, 2012, https://www.smithsonianmag.com/arts-culture/the-surprising-origins-of-fried-green-tomatoes -95832026.

45. "About Us: The Start, End and Revival of the Original, *Original* Hot Dog," Feltman's of Coney Island, https://www.feltmansofconeyisland.com/pages/about.

46. Erick Trickey, "The Origin of the Coney Island Hot Dog Is a Uniquely American Story," *Smithsonian Magazine*, June 30, 2016, https://www.smithsonianmag.com/history/origins-coney-island-hot-dog -uniquely-american-story-180959659.

47. "About Us," Feltman's of Coney Island.

ICE CREAM: POP, BOWL, AND SANDWICH

1. Seale-Lilly Ice Cream ad, *Brandon (MS) News*, June 28, 1923, 2, https://www.newspapers.com/ image/854372352.

2. Robin Weir, "Legend Has It . . .," Ice Cream Alliance, https://ice-cream.org/about-the-ice -cream-alliance/history-of-ice-cream.

3. Weir, "Legend Has It . . ."

4. "A Brief History of Gelato," *Botolino Blog*, June, 2, 2017, https://botolino.com/blog/post/a-brief-history-of-gelato.

5. Philip Lenzi, Confectioner, ad, *New-York Gazette* and *Weekly Mercury*, May 12, 1777, 3.

6. Allison Aubrey, "George Washington's Ice Cream Recipe: First, Cut Ice from River," The Salt, NPR, February 20, 2012, https://www.npr.org/sections/thesalt/2012/02/20/147054700/george-washingtons-ice-cream-recipe-first-cut-ice-from-river.

7. Hannah Glasse, *The Art of Cookery Made Plain and Easy* (facsimile repr. of 1st [1747] ed., Devon, UK: Prospect Books, 1995), 168.

8. Hilarie M. Hicks, "Dolley Madison & Ice Cream: The Real Scoop," Montpelier's Digital Doorway, July 8, 2019, https://digitaldoorway.montpelier.org/2019/07/08/dolley-madison-ice-cream.

9. Elizabeth Yuka, "The World of Ice Cream: One of the World's Oldest Desserts," *Reader's Digest*, February 13, 2023, https://www.rd.com/article/who-invented-ice-cream.

10. Lester A. Walton, "Philly Citizen Was First Maker of Ice Cream," *Pittsburgh Courier*, May 19, 1928, 12.

11. "Ice Cream," Baker's Helper, *New York Times*, March 11, 1894, 18.

12. Anne Cooper Funderbird, "The Inside Scoop," *Invention & Technology* 11, no. 3 (Winter 1996), https://www.inventionandtech.com/content/inside-scoop-1.

13. Funderbird, "Inside Scoop."

14. "Ice Cream" lyrics, International Lyrics Playground, https://lyricsplayground.com/alpha/songs/i/icecream.html.

15. "Dr. Mitchill's Letters From Washington: 1801–1813," *Harper's New Monthly Magazine*, April 1879, 744.

16. Soda Fountain Manufacturers Association, comp., *The Dispenser's Formulary*, 4th ed. (New York: Soda Fountain Publications, 1925), 26.

17. Lynne Olver, ed., "Ice Cream Sandwiches," Food Timeline, February 8, 2015, https://www.foodtimeline.org/foodicecream.html.

18. Lynne Olver, ed., "Sherbet & Sorbet," Food Timeline, February 8, 2015, https://www.foodtimeline.org/foodicecream.html.

19. Lynne Olver, ed., "Why Call It 'Sundae?'" Food Timeline, February 8, 2015, https://www.foodtimeline.org/foodicecream .

20. W. O. Rigby, *Rigby's Reliable Candy Teacher* (Topeka, KS: W. O. Rigby, 1916), 239–41.

21. Alan Davidson, *Oxford Companion to Food* (Oxford: Oxford University Press, 1999), 163.

22. Listing of maraschino cherries, *Miltonian* (Milton, PA), July 12, 1907, 3, https://www.newspapers.com/image/363566555.

23. "Pure Food Ban on Sundaes," *Fort Wayne (IN) Sentinel*, June 26, 1912, 4, https://www.newspapers.com/image/29145929.

24. Colleen Graham, "What Are Maraschino Cherries?" The Spruce Eats, January 19, 2023, https://www.thespruceeats.com/the-truth-about-maraschino-cherries-759977.

25. "Charlottes and Floats" *Chicago Tribune*, December 26, 1902, 7, https://www.newspapers.com/image/350274202.

26. "Is There Formaldehyde in Maraschino Cherries?" Reference, updated April 4, 2020, https://www.reference.com/world-view/formaldehyde-maraschino-cherries.

27. "Sandwiches of Ice Cream, Quick Dessert for Guests," *Philadelphia Inquirer*, August, 27, 1948, 16, https://www.newspapers.com/image/174472020.

28. Josephine Gibson, "Serve Ice Cream in Fancy Dress," *Pittsburgh Press* , February 4, 1947, 6, https://www.newspapers.com/image/143407992.

29. "Ice Cream Sandwiches Make Money," *Daily Republican* (Monongahela, PA), January, 27, 1906, 2, https://www.newspapers.com/image/55260666.

30. "The Average Number of Ice Cream Sandwiches Eaten per Second Is 48," *South Florida Reporter*, August 1, 2020, https://southfloridareporter.com/the-average-number-of-ice-cream-sandwiches-eaten-per-second-is-48.

31. "Soft Drinks That Are Hard to Eat," *Idaho Statesman* (Boise, ID), August 4, 1912, 4, https://www.newspapers.com/image/722575563.

32. "Banana al la Crème," Woman's from Mirror, *Times-Picayune* (New Orleans, LA), July 16, 1897, 3, https://www.newspapers.com/image/28299348.

33. "Banana Split," Tried Recipes, *Williamsport (PA) Sun-Gazette*, July 10, 1015, 10, https://www.newspapers.com/image/37071235.

34. Verifine Banana Split Ice Cream ad, *Green Bay Press Gazette*, March 15, 1962, 20, https://www.newspapers.com/image/189329892.

35. James Trager, *The Food Chronology* (New York: Henry Holt, 1995), 380.

36. Chase Chustack, "The Surprising Controversy behind the History of the Banana Split," Mashed, June 17, 2022, https://www.mashed.com/899559/the-surprising-controversy-behind-the-history-of-the-banana-split.

37. Tracy Corris, "The Banana Split: A Rich History," Pennsylvania Center for the Book, Spring 2010, https://pabook.libraries.psu.edu/literary-cultural-heritage-map-pa/feature-articles/banana-split-rich-history.

38. "Brooklyn's 1922 Ice Cream Bill," *Standard Union* (Brooklyn, NY), May 21, 1922, 5, https://www.newspapers.com/image/544436992.

39. "Frozen Suckers to be Real Innovation," *Pawhuska (OK) Daily Journal*, December 18, 1924, 1, https://www.newspapers.com/image/666394468.

40. Van's Lunch Room ad, *Olney (IL) Times*, July 9, 1925, 4, https://www.newspapers.com/image/601568423.

41. Layfette Ice Cream Company ad, *Journal and Courier* (Lafayette, IN), July 18, 1925, 18, https://www.newspapers.com/image/261708509.

42. Shelby Pope, "How an 11-Year-Old Boy Invented the Popsicle," The Salt, NPR, July 22, 2015, https://www.npr.org/sections/thesalt/2015/07/22/425294957/how-an-11-year-old-boy-invented-the-popsicle.

43. Creamsicles ad, "Creamsicles. A Frozen Treat. 5-Cents," *Montana Standard* (Butte, MT), June 17, 1938, 13, https://www.newspapers.com/image/354690642.

44. Polar's Velvet Ice Cream ad, *Tampa Tribune*, June 23, 1939, 18, https://www.newspapers.com/image/332782831.

45. Popsicle, Creamsicle, Fudgsicle ad, *Valley Morning Star* (Harlington, TX), June 9, 1950, 18, https://www.newspapers.com/image/42436693.

46. "Company History," Hugh Moore Dixie Cup Company Collection, 1905–2008, Lafayette College, https://sites.lafayette.edu/dixiecollection/company-history.

47. "History of the Burt Confectionery & Creation of the 'Good Humor' Bar," Mahoning Valley Historical Society, https://mahoninghistory.org/tyler-history-center/the-good-humor-story.

48. Susan Benjamin, *Sweet as Sin: The Unwrapped Story of How Candy Became America's Favorite Pleasure* (Amherst, NY: Prometheus Books, 2016), 299–300.

49. Benjamin, *Sweet as Sin*, 299–300.

50. Colin Dickey, "How the Ice Cream Truck Made Summer Cool," *Smithsonian Magazine*, July 2020, https://www.smithsonianmag.com/innovation/ice-cream-truck-innovation-history-180975199.

51. Chris Shott, "The Unstoppable Allure of Soft Serve Ice Cream," Food Republic, August 3, 2016, https://www.foodrepublic.com/2016/08/03/the-unstoppable-allure-of-soft-serve-ice-cream.

52. Funderbird, "Inside Scoop."

53. "Howard Johnson's Ice Cream Shops & Restaurants: Good Old Days Goodness from the '50s & '60s," Click Americana, last updated April 22, 2020, https://clickamericana.com/topics/food-drink/howard-johnsons-ice-cream-shops-restaurants-1950s.

54. Howard Johnson's ad, *Miami Herald*, February 18, 1939, 20, https://www.newspapers.com/image/617170339.

55. Kate Kelly, "Howard Johnson: Host of the Highway," America Comes Alive! https://americacomesalive.com/howard-johnsons-host-of-the-highway.

56. Dana Hanson, "20 Things You Didn't Know about Baskin Robbins," Money, Inc., January 25, 2020, https://moneyinc.com/baskin-robbins.

57. Tori Avey, "Banking on the Butterfat—The History of Haagen-Dazs, *Tori Avey* (blog), July 28, 2023, https://toriavey.com/banking-on-butterfat-the-history-of-haagen-dazs.

58. Gary Hoover, "The First Giant Restaurant Chain: Howard Johnson's: Rise and Fall," American Business History Center," August 26, 2021, https://americanbusinesshistory.org/the-first-giant-restaurant-chain-howard-johnson-rise-and-fall.

59. Jessica A. Scott, "The Untold Truth of Baskin-Robbins," Mashed, December 19, 2019, https://www.mashed.com/177683/the-untold-truth-of-baskin-robbins.

60. Avery, "Banking on the Butterfat."

MORE THAN A SPOONFUL: SODA AND CANDY

1. Darra Goldstein, ed., *Oxford Companion to Sugars and Sweets* (New York: Oxford University Press, 2015), 671.

2. Susan Benjamin, *Sweet as Sin: The Unwrapped Story of How Candy Became America's Favorite Pleasure* (Amherst, NY: Prometheus Books, 2016), 248–49.

3. Laura Mason, *Sugar-Plums and Sherbet: The Prehistory of Sweets* (Devon, UK: Prospect Books, 2004), 122.

4. Ivan Day, "Syllabub Revisited and Sugar Plumb Theories," *Food History Jottings* (blog), February 8, 2012, http://foodhistorjottings.blogspot.com/search/label/Sugar%20Plums.

5. Benjamin, *Sweet as Sin*, 248–49.

6. Author's interview with Brenda Sandoval, August 12, 2023.

7. Mason, *Sugar-Plums and Sherbet*, 89–91.

8. Benjamin, *Sweet as Sin*, 192.

9. "Confectionery—How It Is Made and What It Is Made Of," *Scientific American*, December 2, 1868, 358.

10. Wendy Woloson, *Refined Tastes: Sugar, Confectionery, and Consumers in Nineteenth-Century America* (Baltimore: John Hopkins University Press, 2002), 146–48.

11. "New England Confectionary Company (NECCO)," Local Legacies, Library of Congress, http://lcweb2.loc.gov/diglib/legacies/loc.afc.afc-legacies.200003102/default.html.

12. Benjamin, *Sweet as Sin*, 210–11.

13. NECCO ad, *Evening News* (Harrisburg, PA), January 28, 1943, 9, https://www.newspapers.com/image/58356452.

14. Benjamin, *Sweet as Sin*, 191.

15. "Horehound," Encyclopedia.com, updated May 23, 2018, https://www.encyclopedia.com/plants-and-animals/plants/plants/horehound.

16. "Charles E. Hires, Seeing Opportunities," *American Druggist and Pharmaceutical Record* 61 (October 1913): 27–28.

17. Benjamin, *Sweet as Sin*, 63–64.

18. "Clarence A. Crane," Ohio History Connection, http://www.ohiohistorycentral.org/w/Clarence_A._Crane.

19. Joan Monahan, "Lifesavers: A 'Summer Candy' Celebrates a Hole Lot of History," *Ledger*, June 26, 2007, https://www.theledger.com/story/news/2007/06/26/life-savers-a-summer-candy-celebrates-a-hole-lot-of-history/25929435007.

20. "The Life Saver Candy Sweet Book Story," *Historically Speaking* (blog), Greenwich Library, May 2012, http://www.greenwichlibrary.org/blog/historically_speaking/2012/05/the-life-saver-candy-story.html.

21. Benjamin, *Sweet as Sin*, 257–59.

22. Benjamin, *Sweet as Sin*, 257–59.

23. Mort Rosenblum, *Chocolate: A Bittersweet Saga of Dark and Light* (New York: North Point Press, 2005), 10.

24. Deborah Cadbury, *The Chocolate Wars* (New York: Perseus Books, 2010), 26–27.

25. Benjamin, *Sweet as Sin*, 164.

26. Rosenblum, *Chocolate*, 10.

27. Tim Richardson, *Sweets: A History of Candy* (London: Bloomsbury, 2002), 220.

28. Antonio Colmenero de Ledesma, *Chocolate; or, An Indian Drinke*, trans. James Wadsworth (London: printed by J.G. for John Dakins, 1652).

29. Gerald Ward, "Silver Chocolate Pots of Colonial Boston," in *Chocolate: History, Culture, and Heritage*, ed. Louis E. Grivetti and Howard-Yana Shapiro (Hoboken, NJ: Wiley, 2009), 143.

30. Benjamin Tompson, "New-Englands Crisis," Poetry.com, https://www.poetry.com/poem/4253/new-englands-crisis.

31. "Samuel Sewall," Celebrate Boston, www.celebrateboston.com/biography/samuel-sewall.htm.

32. *Bangor (ME) Daily Whig & Courier*, May 6, 1847, 3.

33. James F. Gay, "Chocolate Production and Uses in 17th and 18th Century North America," in *Chocolate: History, Culture, and Heritage*, 289

34. "Thomas Jefferson Letter to John Adams, November 27, 1785," in *The Papers of Thomas Jefferson*, vol. 9 (Princeton, NJ: Princeton University Press, 1954), 63.

35. Benjamin, *Sweet as Sin*, 144–46.

36. John F. Mariani, *Encyclopedia of American Food and Drink* (New York: Lebhar-Friedman, 1999), 54–55.

37. Schrafft's Elegante Chocolates ad, *New-York Tribune*, December 13, 1922, 6, https://www.newspapers.com/image/466286070.

38. Dani Zoeller, "The History of the Ghirardelli Chocolate Company," The Tasting Table, March 3, 2023, https://www.tastingtable.com/1217288/the-history-of-the-ghirardelli-chocolate-company.

39. "Museum/History," Bonomo Turkish Taffy, http://www.bonomoturkishtaffy.com/MuseumHistory_ep_40.html.

40. Benjamin, *Sweet as Sin*, 290.

41. Briana York, "Satellite Wafers—UFO Candy," Snack History, https://www.snackhistory.com/satellite-wafers-ufo-candy.

42. Zotz Fizz Power Candy, https://zotzpower.com.

43. "Astro Pop History," Astro Pop Original, https://web.archive.org/web/20140413123600/http://www.astropopcandy.com/articles/view/history-4d111b46-25a0-4bee-b106-7409ac101063.

44. Brent Furdyk, "The Untold Truth of Pop Rocks," Mashed, April 20, 2022, https://www.mashed.com/193454/the-untold-truth-of-pop-rocks.

45. Furdyk, "Untold Truth of Pop Rocks."

46. "Ten Billion Nickels a Year for Soda Water," *Knoxville (TN) Sentinel*, April 30, 1910, 18, https://www.newspapers.com/image/586520341.

47. "History of the Soda Fountain," Soderlund Drug Store Museum, https://www.drugstoremuseum.com/soda-fountain/soda-fountain-history.

48. "History of the Soda Fountain," Soderlund Drug Store Museum.

49. *Confectioners' and Bakers' Gazette*, vol. 38 (1916), 19.

50. Cara Giaimo, "Victorians Drank Soda Out of Monstrous Gilded Machines" Atlas Obscura, July 15, 2016, https://www.atlasobscura.com/articles/victorians-drank-soda-out-of-monstrous-gilded-machines.

51. Manter's Drug Store ad, "Hot Sodas for Cold Days," *Burlington (VT) Free Press*, November 11, 1915, 12, https://www.newspapers.com/newspage/197315733.

52. "Begin Hot Water Drinking if You Don't Feel Right," *Niobrara (NE) Tribune*, February 10, 1916, 2, https://www.newspapers.com/image/728484633.

53. *Confectioners' and Bakers' Gazette*, vol. 39 (1917), 23; vol. 38 (1916), 22.

54. Hot soda ad, *Elwood (IN) Daily Record*, November 23, 1907, 5, https://www.newspapers.com/image/86602508.

55. Jeffrey Morgenthaler, *Bar Book: Elements of Cocktail Technique* (San Francisco: Chronicle Books, 2014), 54.

56. Ibid.

57. Benjamin, *Sweet as Sin*, 41–44.

58. "John Pemberton: Coca-Cola," Lemelson-MIT, https://lemelson.mit.edu/resources/john-pemberton.

59. Dr. Troy Kickler, "Caleb Bradham (1867–1934)," North Carolina History Project, https://northcarolinahistory.org/encyclopedia/caleb-bradham-1867-1934.

60. Mary Bellis, "The Early History of Dr Pepper," ThoughtCo., updated July 7, 2019, https://www.thoughtco.com/history-of-dr-pepper-4070939.